THE
BEST
SHORT
PLAYS 1987

edited and introduced by
RAMON DELGADO

Best Short Plays Series

NOTE: All plays contained in this volume are fully protected under the Copyright Laws of the United States of America, the British Empire, including the Dominion of Canada, and all other countries of the International Copyright Union and the Universal Copyright Convention. Permission to reproduce, wholly or in part, by any method, must be obtained from the copyright owners or their agents. (See CAUTION notices at the beginning of each play.)

Copyright © 1987 by Ramon Delgado
All Rights Reserved
Published in New York, by Applause Theatre Book Publishers
Library of Congress Catalog Card No. 38–8006
ISBN 0–936839–94–5 (paper) 0–936839–95–3 (cloth)
ISSN 0067–6284
Manufactured in the United States of America

APPLAUSE THEATRE BOOK PUBLISHERS
211 W. 71st Street, New York, NY 10023
(212) 595–4735
All rights reserved. Printed in the U.S.A.
First Applause Printing, 1987

Contents

for Don Sobolik

BOOKS AND PLAYS BY RAMON DELGADO

The Best Short Plays 1981 (with Stanley Richards)
The Best Short Plays 1982
The Best Short Plays 1983
The Best Short Plays 1984
The Best Short Plays 1985
The Best Short Plays 1986
Acting With Both Sides of Your Brain

The Youngest Child of Pablo Peco
Waiting for the Bus
The Little Toy Dog
Once Below A Lighthouse
Sparrows of the Field
The Knight-Mare's Nest
Omega's Ninth
Listen, My Children
A Little Holy Water
The Fabulous Jeromes
The Jerusalem Thorn
Stones

INTRODUCTION

Even as producers lamented 1985-86 as one of the thinnest seasons on Broadway, the one-act play was a robust survivor in many Off Broadway and Off Off Broadway theatres. During the months of April and May of 1986, New York theatregoers could have enjoyed *Orchards*, seven one-act plays adapted from stories by Anton Chekhov, ten short plays by Tennessee Williams, twelve in the Ensemble Studio Theatre's Marathon of one-act plays, nine short plays presented by the Working Theater at the INTAR Theater, and two produced by Playwrights Preview Productions at the Hartley House Theater. These productions followed on the heels of ten short plays presented the previous December by the Manhattan Punch Line. The One Act Theatre Company of San Francisco and the Philadelphia Festival Theatre for New Plays continued their focus on the short play form with seasons of one-act plays. A notable loss from the roster in 1986 was the Actors Theatre of Louisville's SHORTS Festival which sang its swan song in 1985, though artistic director Jon Jory assures us he will include one-act plays in A.T.L.'s Humana Festival each spring.

Acknowledging that no one makes a living writing one-act plays, screenplay Oscar winner Horton Foote, whose short plays have appeared in two recent E.S.T. Marathons, praises the form for the opportunities, challenges and satisfactions it affords the playwright: "The form allows me to flesh out and explore facets of what has become for me an attempt to create a moral and social history of a particular idea over a period of time . . . There is, of course, a great challenge in fitting a complex character or situation into one act. It demands concentration, great clarity and economy."

Selecting the best representatives of the form has been a stimulating challenge as well for this editor, now in his seventh volume of the series, and working on the eighth. During these years the emphasis has been on finding quality plays that are interesting in both the reading and the viewing. The vast majority of the plays selected have already passed the test of production or are in production at the time of selection. And I have made an effort to include a number of plays in each volume that have not been published elsewhere. Meeting these qualifications has not been an easy task, but few reviewers of past volumes have agreed on which plays they liked the best and which they liked the least—a fair barometer that a broad representation for a variety of tastes has been achieved.

The quality of the selections for the *Best Short Plays* series was affirmed during the past year when The Fireside Theatre Book Club selected the combined 1984 and 1985 editions for its major selection in August of 1986 with a combined 1982-1983 volume as the first alternate selection. Knowing that these distinguished plays now have an expanded reading audience is a source of pride, and it encourages the search among the hundreds of one-act plays produced each year for the best representatives of the short play form.

This year's selections run the gamut of styles from the sophisticated comedy of manners of Richard Greenberg's *Life Under Water* to Lanford Wilson's wistful romance on iris breeders in *A Betrothal* through Amlin Gray's brooding character study reminiscent of August Strindberg in *Wormwood* to Grace McKeaney's folksy comedy on battered women, *How It Hangs*. There is also Louis Phillips's slant on the media through the cartoon *Goin' West;* Shannon Keith Kelley's gently humorous and poignant search for meaningful rituals in *Practical Magic;* Martin Epstein's absurdist venture of a liberated woman into the bastion of an all-male club in *How Gertrude Stormed the Philosophers' Club.* Romulus Linney makes his fourth appearance in *Best Short Plays,* weaving a charming mountain tale in *Why the Lord Come to Sand Mountain;* Stephen Metcalfe examines the depths of human loneliness in the aftermath of the Viet Nam War in *Spittin' Image;* and Doug Wright probes the explosive combination of repressive religion and adolescent sexuality in *The Stonewater Rapture.*

But such collections cannot exist without the cooperation and generosity of the playwrights and their agents who make these plays available for our reading and viewing pleasure. Once again our thanks.

RAMON DELGADO
Montclair, New Jersey

Richard Greenberg

LIFE UNDER WATER

Richard Greenberg

Richard Greenberg's *Life Under Water* takes us to the Hamptons, Long Island, where the restless waves of summer batter the fragile love affairs of two generations. Here the playwright has etched a portrait of the idle, upper middle-class Long Islanders, who by the end of the summer flounder as helplessly as if their lives were spent under water. When the play premiered in Ensemble Studio Theatre's (E.S.T.) Marathon '85, Frank Rich, reviewing the play for the *New York Times,* showered the play with praise: "*Life Under Water* . . . is no mere gem. It is a full-bodied 45-minute work that marks the arrival of a young playwright with a big future. . . . It is Mr. Greenberg's own arresting sensibility that informs every pungent line and bristling scene." Even the redoubtable John Simon of *New York* magazine was impressed: "Greenberg, like a champion fencer, hits—with the fewest, fastest, most economical strokes—right to the heart. And with what witty disenchantment, what heartbreaking humor!"

Mr. Greenberg grew up in East Meadow, New York, the son of second-generation, ex-urban, Jewish parents. The first professional production of his work was in the fall of 1984, when the E.S.T. presented his play, *Bloodletters,* a family comedy laced with biting wit. *Bloodletters* brought Mr. Greenberg the *Newsday* award for "Best New Playwright" in 1985. E.S.T. also produced his short play, *Vanishing Act,* in Marathon '86.

While an undergraduate at Princeton, where he received his B.A. magna cum laude in English in 1980, Mr. Greenberg wrote a novel for his senior thesis. The work was graded by novelist Joyce Carol Oates, who dubbed Greenberg, ". . . a young novelist of genuine promise." Also at Princeton Mr. Greenberg received the Ward Mathis Prize in short fiction in 1980. After a year of graduate work in literature at Harvard, Mr. Greenberg entered the M.F.A. playwrighting program at Yale School of Drama where he was awarded the coveted Molly Kazan Playwrighting Award in 1984. Among his current writing projects are *Gangway,* a screenplay for 20th Century Fox, and two plays, *Satin Century,* and *The Maderati,* produced at Manhattan's Playwrights Horizons in the 1986-87 season.

[*AUTHOR'S NOTE ON STAGING:* Blackouts and fades between scenes are only occasionally noted in the text. The rest may be left to the discretion of the director, but, in general, cross-fading is the most effective technique for the scene shifts. Except when otherwise indicated, scenes should begin quickly, as though in midstream; dialogue might even anticipate the light change by a beat. The greatest possible fluidity is desired.

If a restrictive playing area makes scene changes difficult, musical bridges might be desirable. Among the musical selections used in the Ensemble Studio Theatre's production were: Cyndi Lauper's "Girls Just Want to Have Fun" right before Scene One, fading into a disk jockey announcement and then a Madonna tune which played under Scene One, supposedly coming from an onstage radio; a jazz violin version of "Satin Doll" leading into and underscoring the beginning of Scene Six; the Beach Boys' "Fun, Fun, Fun" after Scene Ten and into Scene Eleven (the opening business of that scene had Amy-Joy attempting to read Amy-Beth's Colette collection while Amy-Beth returned happily from swimming and raised the volume of the radio; Amy-Joy vindictively slammed it off); "What's Love Got to Do With It?" by Tina Turner between Scenes Eleven and Twelve; and—incredibly effective—The Police's "Every Move You Make" coming on with the blackout of Scene Thirteen, playing at low volume all the way through Scene Fourteen, rising in volume at the end of that scene and continuing virtually until Kip's entrance in Scene Fifteen.*]

---

*See Special Note on copyright page.

AMY-JOY, *early twenties*
AMY-BETH, *early twenties*
KIP, *twenty-one or twenty-two*
JINX, *forty-five*
HANK, *forty-eight*

Setting:

Various locations on Long Island's Southern Fork. Summer.
The sound of the ocean is heard low throughout the play,
gaining emphasis at specific moments, most especially in Scene
Nine.

Scene One:

The beach. Amy-Beth and Amy-Joy.

BETH: So tell me.
JOY: You'll die. I'm bad, I'm so bad.
BETH: What did you do?
JOY: You will just die.
BETH: And what if I don't?
JOY: I'll be very disappointed. But it's not gonna happen, it's just not gon— . . .
BETH: So you went out to allay her fears . . .
JOY: I went out because the little one, the girl . . .
BETH: Yes, I know who you mean.
JOY: *Isolde?* Shit, what kind of people name the kids Tristan and Isolde and the dogs Brian and Susan? I mean . . .
BETH: Your uncle.
JOY: Uncle *Andre,* wouldja believe? Andre Vinegrad as in Abe Weingarten. I mean, the whole family.
BETH: And you went out to allay her fears.
JOY: 'Cause she thinks she sees a sea monster. I find out. I go there, I find it out. The other kid . . .

BETH: Tristan,this is.

JOY: Tristan—you believe that? A name like that he's gonna have serious trouble dating.

BETH: And then what happened?

JOY: And then what happened is like the other kid's a one-of-those-kids-he swims-like-a-fish . . . water baby! Like this article in *People Magazine* and he's in it naked. So he's cool about the whole deal, he's working on her, saying there is no such thing as a sea monster, you know?

BETH: Mm-hm.

JOY: And he's got her just about I would say *half* convinced. And I'm watching and I'm thinking, well, nothing for me to do, a child is more likely to respond to a sibling anyway—I took this Family Planning course . . .

BETH: Things are going smoothly.

JOY: Things are going smoothly. And I think—I don't know what came over me—I see this little child, five years old—I see this kid, she looks so goddamn innocent, and I think—wouldn't it be kind of neat to scare her shitless?

BETH: You didn't.

JOY: I did.

BETH: Of course you did.

JOY: Who knows why?

BETH: Sea monsters exist.

JOY: In a big way.

BETH: Amy-Joy . . .

JOY: Shame on me, I know, I know. But you should see this kid. Too dumb for life. Her eyes look like . . .

BETH: A simile?

JOY: . . . Big. Very big. The eyes are very big. 'Cause I tell her these sea monsters in the sea—and they eat anybody's ever been in the sea so too late now—and they especially eat little girls who someday intend to have expensive nose jobs—'cause already they're planning it, you can tell. And they especially *especially* eat little girls with stupid names. And they got these big, humongous —this is the best part—these big, humongous . . .

BETH: Jaws.

JOY: Jaws, you said it. 'Cause like she's got the lunch box? with the shark? with the mouth? with the kid? with the blood?

BETH: So right now she's . . .

JOY: Right now she's shitting her pants. But the beauty part is even if she never goes back in the water again, I fixed it so she's terrified. I traumatized her.

BETH: Why?

JOY: Why? Because. It was something to do. I was bored. Because her father's a fairy antiques dealer.

BETH: I wonder what she saw actually . . .

JOY: Probably Tristan's little zorch.

BETH: Would that have scared her?

JOY: It scares you, doesn't it?

BETH: I'm another story.

JOY: You're telling me . . . Hey.

BETH: *(Pause)* Yes?

JOY: You're all right, aren't you? I mean . . you're all right.

BETH: I'm all right.

JOY: Good. Let's do something tonight.

Scene Two:

Kip alone in his room, lying on his bed. His mother's voice offstage.

JINX: Kip? . . . Kip! Telephone! . . . It's your father. He's calling from Indianapolis . . . It's long distance so take your time. Bleed him dry . . . Kip! . . . *(She enters, putting on her earrings, perhaps barefoot—she's getting ready for the evening)* Are you or aren't you? *(He doesn't respond)* Do you want to talk about it?

KIP: There's a call from Indianapolis. Shouldn't you be on the line?

JINX: You're more important.

KIP: You just want to frustrate my father. You want him to lose his patience and his money.

JINX: He can afford it. The man is not a pauper.

KIP: Why don't you talk?

JINX: Do you know what he netted last year? *Netted?*

KIP: I'm not interested.

JINX: Of course if he's got any of it left, it's a miracle, with that blushing young bride of his.

KIP: I don't care.

JINX: Twenty-three years old, well, I don't want to talk about it, it's too sickening . . .

KIP: What time is it in Indianapolis, anyway?

JINX: And have you heard the latest? Did I tell you? In deference to the new Barbie doll, he's having—it's *too* funny—plastic surgery. Could you . . . ? *(She might exit here to get her shoes, deliver her next line offstage, re-enter, sit, put on shoes, etc. The scene should have that kind of activity, that slight distractedness on Jinx's part)*

KIP: I think they're central time, aren't they? Isn't that the time they go by . . . ?

JINX: The middle-aged man's recipe for rejuvenation—a nip and a tuck and a youngish fuck.

KIP: Mother!

JINX: Oh, I'm sorry. I've forgotten your sensibility. An entire generation and I'm stuck with the one member who has a *sensibility*. In any case, he's dead to me now. Talk to him. Get it over with.

KIP: No.

JINX: Why not?

KIP: He's a phony.

JINX: I should never have let you read *Catcher in the Rye*. Phony. Your concerns are hopeless.

KIP: *(Sitting up, readying himself for the evening)* I need fifty.

JINX: I don't think so.

KIP: For tonight. Look, I'll pay you back. I'll mow a lawn or something.

JINX: It won't be necessary.

KIP: It's a gift then?

JINX: The fifty won't be necessary.

KIP: Oh? How do you figure?

JINX: You're staying in tonight.

KIP: I don't think so.

JINX: I'm going out so you're staying in.

KIP: You're going out so I'm staying in? What is that, physics?

JINX: Common sense. I don't want the house to be left alone.

KIP: It's a big house, Mother. It can take care of itself. What's the matter? Don't you trust me?

JINX: Not since you were sixteen and had that affair with that rock singer . . .

KIP: Folk singer.

JINX: Whatever. She had gonorrhea.

KIP: Pyorrhea! Pyorrhea! When will you learn? Her gums were infected not her sex organs. She was a virgin.

JINX: Many times over. Listen, I don't want to argue. Your father's on the phone. Sound prosperous and well-adjusted and happy that he's gone. There's money in it for you. And merchandise. Maybe a Porsche.

KIP: I don't want to talk to him.

JINX: That's the spirit. Try to convey that during the conversation if you can. I hate that shirt.

KIP: It's tailor-made from England.

JINX: Don't lie to me. I know where it's from. And it's all frowsy around the elbows.

KIP: Overseas shipping.

JINX: Why do you lie the way you do? I mean, I can understand lying in the abstract. For a purpose. But you tell people you summer in Newport instead of the Hamptons. That your father is in steel instead of oil. That's lateral mobility, what does it get you?

KIP: It feels more real.

JINX: *(Fed up)* You're such a *problem child!* Change the shirt.

KIP: Have I offended you? Did I say something to offend you? What? Tell me.

JINX: Kip, please.

KIP: I didn't mean to offend you. I never do. It just happens. If you'd just make a list—just make a list—of acceptable things to say and unacceptable things to say, I'd be grateful, I would. I'd study it.

JINX: Now, Kip . . .

KIP: Because, Mother, I really *don't* mean to offend. I just say what's on my mind sometimes.

JINX: I'm leaving. Do what you want about the phone.

KIP: Where are you going?

JINX: Out.

KIP: Who with?

JINX: Is that a *significant* question?

KIP: Only if it leads to a significant answer.

JINX: Hank Renshaw.

KIP: It's a significant question.

JINX: You over-interpret.

KIP: He's *married*.

JINX: Drinks, that's all. Maybe a late supper.

KIP: Maybe an early breakfast. I can't stand it. It's disgusting to me.

JINX: Kip!

KIP: Did I do it again? I'm sorry. I didn't mean to offend you.

JINX: Don't wait up.

KIP: Mother, I'm too old for this. I can't have curfews any more. I can't have my life run by you. What will I do with my night?

JINX: I leave you to your own devices.

KIP: No you don't. You strip me of my devices. I need human society.

JINX: I don't know why. You're not very good in it.

KIP: I'm improving.

JINX: Read something. Drink something. *(She kisses his forehead)* Good night.

KIP: You make me so lonely.

JINX: Good night. *(She exits)*

Scene Three:

Amy-Joy and Amy-Beth toss around a beach ball intermittently through the scene, Amy-Beth dispiritedly.

JOY: You're not being very helpful.

BETH: Sorry.

JOY: It's fun. Don't you know what fun is?

BETH: Yes. Fun is a repetition-compulsion centered on tossing a piece of inflated rubber.

JOY: I remember another one.

BETH: Who?

JOY: The guy I met on Third Avenue.

BETH: The *guy?* Singular?

JOY: No, I mean the sort of classy guy. With the profession. He was a—you know, security analyst! Which I still don't know what it means.

BETH: Security analyst. Someone who analyses security. Sort of the opposite of a psychiatrist.

JOY: He was a pretty neat guy. Some of them ...

BETH: You're telling me?

JOY: It got pretty bad. You just don't know with the guys you meet. You gotta be so careful.

BETH: You do.

JOY: In the modern world. Like who knows what's gonna happen? You gotta live as if nothing's gonna happen. You can't go around being careful. You can't be *timid*. 'Cause who knows? You can be hit by a truck any day of the week, am I right?

BETH: Of course you're right.

JOY: You just gotta be so careful.

BETH: Mm-hm.

JOY: Caveat emptor.

BETH: Impressive.

JOY: Of course. I've thought about this.

BETH: The effort shows. Maybe you should lie down.

JOY: 'Cause life is already wearing me out, you know?

BETH: Drying you up?

JOY: Sort of. I'm hardly ever horny any more. It's a routine; that why I want to get married.

BETH: That's a terrible idea.

JOY: Yeah, but I want to marry someone boring so I don't ever have to think about it.

BETH: You lead a ridiculous life.

JOY: Some people would think so.

BETH: Meaning?

JOY: Don't get tight-ass.

BETH: I'm not getting tight-ass*ed*.

JOY: Give me a back rub.

BETH: Forget it.

JOY: Some friend.

BETH: Fuck you.

JOY: Hey, I'll make dinner later. I got lobster and mussels. I got crabs.

BETH: I don't doubt it.

JOY: I mean, *shellfish*. You. I'll make a salad. I got sprouts, mushrooms, radishes, cauliflower, snow pods. Then we can do something later. *(A beat)* Is there something we can do later? *(Throws her the ball. Beat. Beth throws down the ball)*

BETH: I hate this game.

JOY: What's to hate?

BETH: It feels like recreational therapy.

JOY: Well . . . I don't know from recreational therapy.

BETH: Meaning?

JOY: Meaning my personal history does not include basket weaving.

BETH: Meaning mine does?

JOY: Meaning nothing. Meaning I said words and forget about it.

BETH: In other words, I'm a neurotic bitch.

JOY: Did I say that? Did you hear me say that?

BETH: We didn't weave baskets. We made lanyards. And we attached whistles to the end of them. There were sixteen people per class. Our instructor was named Sunny. She was the most depressing person I ever met. Are you satisfied?

JOY: They gave whistles to sixteen crazy people? *(Beth turns sharply away)* Oh, Christ! I'm sick of you being sick.

BETH: It's your own fault for hooking up with a convalescent.

JOY: Why don't you go back to school?

BETH: It started at school. If I go back it will start again. School. People. Masses of people. I need quiet. I need solitude.

JOY: *(Sympathetically)* You had all that and you freaked again.

BETH: Environments reject me.

JOY: Get a job.

BETH: I had a job. I lost it. I was a receptionist. I was afraid of the telephone. People would drop off packages. They ticked.

JOY: Jesus.

BETH: When I was away, I almost had an affair. With a short-order cook.

JOY: Who couldn't cope with life.

BETH: Well, you see, that was a *tall* order. But what I mean is, shall we compare notes? Would that be a pleasant diversion?

JOY: *(Gently)* The thing we gotta do is, we gotta find an activity. *(Commotion off)*

BETH: *(Looks up)* What's that?

JOY: Oh my God! Isolde is burying Tristan!

(Quick blackout)

Scene Four:

Lights up on Kip's room. It is empty. After a moment, we see Jinx through Kip's window overlooking a deck.

JINX: Kip! Kip! I'm back. Where are you? Are you in your room? Kip, I'm sorry I made you stay in last night—where are you? I apologize. Humbly. You can come out now. Are you hung over, is that it? Is that why you're not answering me? I'll make you a Prairie Oyster. Kip? Kip? I've got to tell you. Something wonderful happened last night. Mr. Renshaw—Hank—do you know what she said? He said my hair was the color of tea roses. I'll give you the fifty now, Kip! Are you sulking? Are you *sleeping?* At this hour, my God! But I don't care. Sleep the day through, vomit all over the percale. Get rid of the poisons. I'll clean you up. And I'll give you money. And I'll hold your head. Tea roses. Imagine.

(Lights fade on an empty room)

Scene Five:

The two girls on the beach. Kip comes on, faint, swaying, having walked and drunk all night. He has just arrived. The girls look up from their reading.

JOY: Looking for somebody? *(He collapses)* God!
BETH: Who is that?
JOY: How do I know?
BETH: What are you doing, going to him? He could be dangerous.
JOY: I think I can handle myself. *(She kneels beside him, starts shaking him mildly, slapping his face)* Hey. Hey! Are you all right? Hey! Wake up. Come on, wake up! Jesus, you must have had a night. Do you think he's cute?
BETH: Please.
JOY: Wake up. *(Kip begins groggily to awaken)*
KIP: What's happening?
JOY: Who are you?
KIP: What . . . ?
JOY: Your name.
KIP: Kip.
JOY: That's perfect . . . Are you sick?
KIP: I've been walking.
JOY: Walking where . . . ?
KIP: All over. All night. I'm looking for . . .
JOY: What . . . ?

KIP: Work.

JOY: Looking for work? All night? Very few people hire at 4:00 A.M.

KIP: No . . . I was . . .

JOY: What?

KIP: Running away.

JOY: Are you a fugitive?

KIP: In a manner of speaking.

JOY: What did you do?

KIP: Had a mother.

JOY: What? You're running away from home?

KIP: I guess so, yes.

JOY: Did you bring your skate key and a twinkie?

KIP: It may sound juvenile, but it's not.

JOY: No, I'm sure.

KIP: God, I must have walked twenty miles. I kept looking for a refuge. I recognized every house. Everybody in every house. They were all members of the club.

JOY: Which club?

KIP: Whichever. I don't know you.

JOY: I'm visiting.

KIP: Good. Nice . . . Oh God! I'm in no condition to face what I have to face.

JOY: What's that?

KIP: Poverty. I'm penniless. And I'm trying to make my way to the city. Do you have work?

JOY: . . . That depends.

KIP: I'll do anything. I'll mow your lawn.

JOY: There's no lawn. Why can't you just go home and get money?

KIP: Never. I can't even go in the vicinity of that place again. I'm not very resourceful. This was a whim and I've got to stick to it or I'm dead. Dead. Finished. I just want to get to New York.

BETH: He's lying.

JOY: Hitch.

KIP: That's dangerous.

JOY: What about a ride from a friend?

KIP: I have no friends.

JOY: Oh.

KIP: Are you sure there's not something I can do?

JOY: . . . You can . . . hang out . . .

KIP: Excuse me?

JOY: Here.

BETH: Amy-Joy!

JOY: There are all these rooms and no people. Like you can stay here until you find a lawn to mow. You know? I mean—we got these two kids we gotta take care of—my cousins . . . You can help, we'll pay for that, I mean *I* will.

KIP: Is it legitimate work?

JOY: Wait till you meet them. They were raised by wolves.

KIP: I like children.

JOY: *Now* you say that.

BETH: Amy-Joy, this is ridiculous!

KIP: I don't know your name.

JOY: *(When Amy-Beth says nothing)* Amy-Beth. She'll like you once she gets to know you.

BETH: That's never going to happen.

KIP: You really will, though. I'm very nice. I'm . . . harmless. I promise, I won't wear out my welcome.

BETH: You'll have to leave retroactively.

JOY: She doesn't mean it.

KIP: Look—I'm sorry—it's just that I can't go back there. Not if I want to be human. And I do. My mother's life is depraved. I like you two. Automatically. Instantaneously. You're not like the people I know. This gives me a lot of hope.

JOY: Why don't you go up to the house . . .

BETH: No!

JOY: . . . To the house where people are allowed to stay only because I say so . . . and why don't you clean up? I'll be up in a minute and get you something for your hangover. Be careful of Tristan and Isolde. They're playing Apache.

KIP: Which house is it?

JOY: The big glass one at the edge of the hill.

KIP: Thank you. *(To Amy-Beth)* We'll get along well. You'll see.

(He exits. Amy-Joy smiles. Amy-Beth glares at her, then looks away. They sit, not looking at each other)

BETH: Shit.

JOY: He'll give us something to do.

Scene Six:

Hank and Jinx are seated at a restaurant table drinking a summer drink.

JINX: *(Broaching a sensitive topic)* Hank . . .

HANK: Something rather odd happened the other day. Would you like to hear about it?

JINX: Of course.

HANK: It was at the Princeton Club. I'd had my racquet ball and my steam and was drinking a vodka gibson at the bar when who should tap me on the shoulder but Prescott Fowler?

JINX: Oh, yes.

HANK: Well, you know Press and I are old chums, dating back to Exeter, but I hadn't seen him much lately—only once or twice in the past few years, in fact. Anyway, we got to talking about old times and new times and whatever—and then suddenly—it was the liquor loosening him up, I suppose—he told me the most startling thing.

JINX: What was that?

HANK: Well, let me set it up for you. You know, Press is only a year or two younger than I and he has a daughter at Smith and a son at Princeton. And it seems that over the past few years he's found himself a bit straitened financially. Not critically, of course, just enough to feel the pinch. But Press, I find, is quite resourceful.

JINX: How do you mean?

HANK: I don't know if you've seen him lately, but he's in as good a shape as I am. Lean, hard as a rock. We did tennis together at Exeter. And it seems that Press has turned his fitness to economic advantage.

JINX: How is that?

HANK: Apparently—I never knew this before, did you?—there's a woman named Honoria. A very elegant woman named Honoria who operates a most discreet business out of a brownstone on East 64th Street.

JINX: Honoria what?

HANK: No last names. Ever.

JINX: My God.

HANK: Not rough trade, of course. Women. Dowagers, even. Lonely and . . . stimulated.

JINX: Press? Really?

HANK: Yes. And not only Press—and this is what cast a whole new light over things. As I said, we did tennis together at Exeter —that was a great bunch of guys. There was a real solidarity among us. And an innocence. Young men, you know.

JINX: And?

HANK: Well, Press whipped out our old tennis photo. At first I thought it was a nostalgic gesture. But there was something strange about this photograph, something dreamlike. My dream. Because in it we had all aged somehow. Gracefully, to be sure, but nevertheless . . . aged. Thickened. Grown tired. And strangest of all, I was missing. From the picture. I was—quite literally—no longer in the picture. As it might well have happened in a dream. And those who *were* . . . in the picture . . . some six or seven of them in all . . . wore unnatural expressions. Gross, somehow. Lurid. Unseemly.

JINX: Well, of course it was . . .

HANK: Yes. A picture of Madame Honoria's stable. My old class at Exeter. My teammates. It seems they had all suffered reversals of one kind or another and one-by-one Press had . . . offered them this solution. You see, Honoria only takes bona fide Social Register types. She caters to the sort of woman who will not condescend. Even when all she wants is a good screw.

JINX: Doesn't that cause uncomfortable moments? People knowing people, I mean.

HANK: Oh, to be sure. But the embarrassment is strictly mutual, making disclosure . . . unlikely.

JINX: My God. I just realized. These people you're talking about, they're . . . they must be . . . my friends.

HANK: The friends we have in common. I'm not so casual at cocktail parties any more. And East 64th Street has absolutely transformed itself for me.

JINX: I'd imagine.

HANK: But here's the other extraordinary thing. One of Press's . . . clients . . . the other week—and I think this is the only reason he told me the whole story to begin with—a client he met with just a few days ago . . .

JINX: Yes?

HANK: Well. They met in a room at the Hotel Carlyle—which I think is dangerous—but never mind. Press and the woman went through the usual protocol. No names. Discreet undressing in separate rooms. Lights out. He took her in his arms. Began. The woman was a wreck. Emaciated. Ravaged face. Nervous eczemous rashes. Press, of course, was tender, sensitive, aware, careful not to show the revulsion he felt for the woman. For her ruined body. And her grief. And he made love to her. Like a gentleman and a scholar. Midway through . . . it . . . she began to sigh in a distinctive way. A kind of little chihuahua yelp. Well, it was like Proust's *madeleine:* a flood of memories. He pulled back, too quickly, and looked at her face, the face of this woman he had been hired to service, and in utter, absolute, blinding shock, he cried out: "Claudia du Plessix!" She closed her eyes then and asked, "Is that you, Press? I thought it might be, but I was afraid to say anything!"

JINX: All of which means?

HANK: Well, some thirty years ago when he was at Exeter and she at Concord Academy, Claudia du Plessix and Press Fowler lost their virginities to each other. One weekend at a mixer. He was a tennis champion and she was the prettiest girl at Concord and after that weekend they never met again.

JINX: What did they do when they realized?

HANK: They clung to each other for dear life.

JINX: And I suppose he declined any fee for his . . . services.

HANK: To the contrary. He charged double. *(Pause)* What I mean is, don't you sometimes think that we're the last moral people on earth? The last people with a sense of the common decencies? Who know about the fitness of things. Who adhere to a standard. *(Pause)*

JINX: Does your wife know about us? Is that what you're saying?

HANK: All right, then, yes.

JINX: What should we do?

HANK: Have I ever told you that your hair is the color of tea roses?

JINX: Incessantly.

HANK: Does it make you happy?

JINX: Yes.

HANK: Then what's the problem? *(A beat)* I mean, I'm not being obtuse. I really don't see the problem. *(They look at each other)*

Scene Seven:

Amy-Beth in chaise lounge, reading. Kip enters, twirling a beach ball on his finger.

BETH: I thought you were supposed to be working. I haven't seen it.

KIP: I've been bathing the kids, feeding them, washing the dishes, windexing the glass . . . which in this house is a chore, believe me. What kind of people build a glass house on the edge of a hill in front of an ocean?

BETH: Facetious people.

KIP: Why are you playing with that string?

BETH: Why not?

KIP: Whenever I see you, you've got something . . . string, marbles, a daiquiri glass. Your hands are never unoccupied, why is that?

BETH: Do you have money for train fare yet? It can't be more than ten dollars to the city from here.

KIP: I've decided to stick around for a while. Until I've got enough to get started. It's not the best idea to arrive in Manhattan empty-handed. Lots of people on the street waiting for you if you do that. Terrible types on the streets of Manhattan. Muggers. Rapists. Mimes. *(Amy-Beth laughs)* Ah-hah!

BETH: That was a spasm.

KIP: No, it wasn't.

BETH: I promise you it was.

KIP: I don't believe you.

BETH: I don't care. *(Pause)*

KIP: Amy-Joy tells me you went to Radcliffe for a while. I got kicked out of a lot of schools, too.

BETH: I did not get kicked out. I left.

KIP: Really? Why?

BETH: Reasons. Amy-Joy never understood why I went in the first place. She said, "Once you get in, why bother?"

KIP: *(Laughs)* I like her.

BETH: Of course. Everybody does.

KIP: I like you, too.

BETH: That's a less common reaction.

KIP: Why don't you ever talk to me?

BETH: Kip, listen. You're here because Amy-Joy wants you here. You're her boy, not mine.

KIP: I like you better. I like her a lot, but I like you better. *(Pause)* What did I say? Did I offend you? I didn't mean to offend you.

BETH: I want you to leave soon.

KIP: Look—I'm sincere. Utterly. I think we have a lot in common. I have trouble with people too. I look as if I don't, but I do. *(A beat)* Do you know before I came here I used to gaze up at this house? I used to wonder about it. There's a green light that burns all night at the end of your dock . . .

BETH: That's the goddamn "Great Gatsby." I can read! Oh, you sensitive boys with your quotations—I don't trust you as far as I can throw you.

KIP: You should. I only tell nice lies. The past five days here I've been looking for a method to approach you. I think unapproachable people like us have a responsibility to seek each other out. The only thing I've come up with is to tell you exactly how I feel. But it's hard to express something like this. You must know how hard it is.

BETH: Meaning?

KIP: I'd like to get you between the sheets.

BETH: I'd like to get you between the eyes.

(Blackout)

Scene Eight:

Kip's room. Kip is stuffing clothes into a bag. Jinx enters in a bathrobe.

JINX: The prodigal son returns.

KIP: I've come to collect my things.

JINX: I'm not giving you money to walk out of here again.

KIP: I'm not taking your money.

JINX: Sit down and talk.

KIP: Why are you wearing your robe in the afternoon? . . . My God . . .

JINX: Oh leave it alone . . .

KIP: You're disgusting.

JINX: There's no one here, why not drop it? *(Kip drops it)* I've missed you. Everyone talks slowly and in long sentences. Where have you been?

KIP: I've been living down the shore. With two girls.

JINX: Two girls. Does that mean . . . ?

KIP: Orgies every night.

JINX: What are you living on?

KIP: I'm a sort of . . . caretaker at their place.

JINX: Gigolo, you mean?

KIP: You have a sleazy mind. I'll get my things and go.

JINX: Don't be silly. Let's talk. The best part is talking.

KIP: I don't have much time.

JINX: We should get together regularly. I like it. We can be like those people in Henry James who do things so they have something to talk about after.

KIP: I've never read Henry James. *(Hank enters in bathrobe)* Now that's just . . . great . . .

HANK: Hello, Kip. How are you? *(No answer)* Huh, Kipper? You doing all right? *(Pause)* Not talking to me? Okay. Your mom's been frantic.

KIP: Don't come near me.

JINX: Kip . . .

KIP: This . . . is not my idea of a romantic relationship.

JINX: If you'd just listen . . .

KIP: Forget it. *(He leaves)*

JINX: What was the point of that?

HANK: My son knows, why shouldn't yours?

JINX: Skip knows?

HANK: Yes. He saw us someplace.

JINX: What do we do now?

HANK: That question is rapidly becoming monotonous. Come here. *(She goes to him. They kiss. Fade)*

Scene Nine:

Darkness. The sound of the ocean, continuous through the play, more prominent here. After a moment a flashlight, carried by Amy-Joy, switches on, beamed towards the audience.

JOY: Tristan! Isolde! Where are you, you little bastards? *(Another flashlight comes on—Kip's)*

KIP: Tristan! Tristan! Come on out now! Isolde!

BETH: *(Also with a flashlight)* Tristan! Isolde! Where are you?

JOY: The little sons-of-bitches, I hope they're dead.

KIP: We should separate.

JOY: Form teams or something, Kip?

KIP: Why don't you take the area around the house?

JOY: Come with me.

KIP: No. It'll be better if we spread out.

JOY: Shit. Those bastards.

BETH: I'll look by the dock.

JOY: Okay. See you later.

KIP: Good luck.

JOY: Does that mean find them or not?

KIP: Find them. *(She exits. Kip shines the flashlight on Amy-Beth)*

BETH: We should go.

KIP: Wait. *(Amy-Beth shines the light on his face)*

BETH: Why?

KIP: I want to look at you.

BETH: You're hurting my eyes.

KIP: It's been two weeks. We've talked. We've *failed* to talk. I've told you how I feel about you, but you won't believe me. I've told you everything there is to know about me. That didn't take very long. What can I say? Can I make up a story, is there some lie, is there an anecdote I can tell you that will break through?

BETH: I'm squinting in that light.

KIP: You look beautiful.

BETH: Don't say that.

KIP: I mean it. *(Amy-Beth shines the light on his face)* See?

BETH: It's a weak light.

KIP: I love you.

BETH: "Why did you climb that mountain?" "Because she was there."

KIP: No.

BETH: Why don't you love Amy-Joy?

KIP: That would be ordinary. And very easy.

BETH: Oh.

KIP: She wants me.

BETH: I know.

KIP: She doesn't need me, though.

BETH: And I do?

KIP: Don't you?

BETH: The Salvation Army mentality—save anything that needs it. *(Pause)*

KIP: It's a beautiful night.

BETH: We should be looking for the children.

KIP: Talk to me. *(Pause)*

BETH: Turn off the light.

KIP: Why?

BETH: It's hurting my eyes. *(He turns off the light. All we see is Kip's face)* It didn't happen. It didn't happen anywhere. It didn't happen at school. It didn't happen at home when I escaped from school. It didn't happen when I moved in with Amy-Joy—not even in Manhattan.

KIP: What? What didn't?

BETH: I don't know. Do you? I think Amy-Joy does. Sometimes I think if I could study her like Latin, drilling the way she is, everything would be all right. Her life works somehow. Other people seem to have figured this problem out.

KIP: What problem?

BETH: Don't you know? *(A beat)* How could you? *(A beat)* Every gesture it took to live out a day was like some kind of absurd gymnastic event I was too clumsy to perform. You can't imagine what it's like to feel ridiculous all the time. All I could do was watch people. I'd get stomach cramps. I couldn't sleep. Something wanted to jump out of me, but my body contained it. Trapped it. Then one night, when it wouldn't stop raining and I couldn't sleep no matter what I did, I started tearing off my skin. It seemed very hopeful at the time but I didn't stop until there were deep bloody grooves in my face as if I'd been slashed at with a knife. It's amazing what a little effort can do. I had doctors. A plastic surgeon. He did good work, didn't he? Sealing me up again. *(Kip turns the light on her)* No, turn that off! *(Kip quickly turns the flashlight off. After a moment, Beth turns the light off him, too. They are in darkness. We hear the water)*

KIP: I love you.

BETH: On an island with no money, you love me. But what about under less desperate circumstances?

KIP: In Manhattan with millions. *(Beth turns the flashlight on his face. He is kneeling now before her, beaming up at her)*

BETH: What is that, a smile? *(He rises and kisses her. Their faces are ringed in light. She turns the flashlight off)*

Scene Ten:

Hank and Jinx in semi-dishabille. Post-coital. Hank cradles a drink in his hand.

HANK: I don't relish the idea . . . !

JINX: What?

HANK: I don't relish the idea of working out my anxieties as a stud on you. And I don't relish the idea of you using me to scratch your itch.

JINX: We're not doing that.

HANK: Love is supposed to make you feel innocent. I don't feel innocent. I feel . . . *un*innocent. All the people we're hurting. *(A beat)* Hello, Jinx.

JINX: Hello, Hank.

HANK: Jinx. Jinx and Hank. And Dot. My wife, Dot. And your son Kip and my son Skip. Jinx and Hank and Dot and Kip and Skip. We sound like elves.

JINX: Let's go to bed.

HANK: I'm not happy in this house.

JINX: No. It's your wife's house you're not happy in.

HANK: Unhappiness is portable. That's one of its chief characteristics.

JINX: Let's go to bed.

HANK: Did I ever tell you . . . ?

JINX: What?

HANK: Did I ever tell you . . . that I *detest* tea roses?

(Fade out)

Scene Eleven:

The two Amys on the beach.

JOY: Why are you so happy all of a sudden?

BETH: I just am.

JOY: That really stinks.

BETH: Sorry. Did you visit Tristan?

JOY: Yes.

BETH: How is he?

JOY: Fine. Hardly singed.

BETH: You got there in time.

JOY: No help from you, thank you very much.

BETH: I told you . . .

JOY: Right, right, deep talk, deep talk. *(A beat)* Shit.

BETH: How's Isolde?

JOY: I don't know, the shrink's an asshole. He says, like, maybe she's a pyromaniac, like that helps to know or something.

BETH: Do you think she's a pyromaniac?

JOY: Anybody named Isolde, she could be anything. You were no help at all.

BETH: I'm not the one who told her the sea monster story.

JOY: Yeah, well who taught her how to build a fire?

BETH: That she must have picked up on her own.

JOY: Shit. I see this kid sleeping with all those sticks around him, these flames lapping at his feet, the little bitch screaming. "Burn! Burn! Burn!" I almost lost it—I tell you. Meanwhile you're off getting laid. Well, what the hell, you were hard up.

BETH: When are the Vinegrads coming home?

JOY: Oh this is good, get this. Since everything's all right and nobody was hurt, they're gonna stay in Paris two more days until he closes the deal. A sense of responsibility? He's importing antique andirons or whatever-the-fuck, meanwhile his children are setting each other on fire. They're such Protestants, I swear.

BETH: It gives us a couple of more days here, at least.

JOY: That's a thrill.

BETH: We can go out now. Wherever you want.

JOY: I got news. At the best of times, the Hamptons are not a hotbed of activity.

BETH: Clubs. Movies.

JOY: Jesus.

BETH: Are you angry at me?

JOY: Disappointed. I am extremely disappointed. That's all. You come here a sick person, and you hop into bed with the first man you meet. That's not a solution. I gave you credit for more intelligence than that. I'm just disappointed. But no skin off my nose—you should excuse the expression.

BETH: I'm sorry.

JOY: Look, that's life.
BETH: I guess so.
JOY: Everybody's a shit.

Scene Twelve:

Hank is doing calisthenics. Jinx watches.

JINX: That's fascinating but what's it for? *(A beat)* Are you in training? *(A beat)* You're forty-eight years old and you look sixteen. I'm forty-five and look twelve. When we were thirty we both looked thirty. Do you think we're receding? *(A beat)* What do you do with your afternoons? *(A beat)* Because you're not in your office, I know. I call. *(A beat)* That was a confession. You can hit me for it. Punch, pummel, strike. Any form of physical contact will be gratefully received. *(A beat)* You know, that's a kind of onanism. *(A beat)* The way you're treating me, if I didn't trust you, I'd . . . be much wiser. *(A beat)* What's going on?

Scene Thirteen:

Amy-Beth and Kip on the beach.

BETH: What happens next?
KIP: I've got some money.
BETH: You have fifty dollars.
KIP: It's something.
BETH: Not enough.
KIP: You're going back to your parents' house.
BETH: For a little while.
KIP: I don't suppose that . . .
BETH: No.
KIP: No. I didn't think so. *(Pause)*
BETH: You're going home.
KIP: No, I won't. I'll do something. I'll mow a lawn.
BETH: Lucrative.
KIP: Not so far. *(A beat)* I want to be a responsible person. *(A beat)* Is there a place where they teach you that? *(A beat)* I don't know what the hell I'm doing.

BETH: That's fine.

KIP: I have no money. I don't properly exist.

BETH: You're enough.

KIP: No. I'm not. *(Pause)*

BETH: After you go home and get money, come to me. I'm leaving home and getting a job. Then I'm going back to school. I'll get an apartment in the city. You can come live with me. There are lots of things you can be.

KIP: Like what?

BETH: You can be a ... steward! *(A beat)*

KIP: Maybe I can go back to school, too. I think I'm a high school graduate. I think my father bought me a diploma somewhere.

BETH: Good.

KIP: It doesn't sound very likely, does it?

BETH: Sure it does.

KIP: I'll take care of you.

BETH: I know. *(Pause)*

KIP: Is there stuff to drink? A lot?

BETH: Stop looking as if you've committed a crime.

KIP: The thing is ...

BETH: What? *(A beat)*

KIP: The thing is ...

BETH: What?

(He looks at her. Fade)

Scene Fourteen:

The porch. A wicker loveseat. Kip is drinking. Amy-Joy is with him.

JOY: So tell me. *(Pause)* Amy-Beth is giving Isolde a bath. I told her to use a blowtorch. That girl is like "Most Likely to Succeed" in a snakepit.

KIP: She should be under psychiatric care.

JOY: Amy-Beth?

KIP: Isolde.

JOY: Yeah, her too.

KIP: Why are you two friends?

JOY: Are you kidding? Amy-Beth couldn't live without me. She's my responsibility. You've gotta take care of your friends. We've been bests since forever. First grade.

KIP: Oh.

JOY: She needs somebody like me for protection.

KIP: You don't seem very compatible.

JOY: That's what I mean. Amy-Beth ever met somebody compatible within the hour they'd be dragging the river for the bodies. Why are you depressed?

KIP: Don't know.

JOY: I mean, finish the wine by all means 'cause I want Uncle Andre to have a "connipsh," but what's the problem?

KIP: I made a mistake.

JOY: Yeah, I know.

KIP: I don't know what to do about it.

JOY: That's easy.

KIP: Yeah?

JOY: Go home to mommy. Some guys are always gonna end up going home to mommy, no shame in that. What else can you do?

KIP: Nothing.

JOY: At least you got a mother who'll take you. Big maternal instinct, I guess.

KIP: No. Not the way my mother wants things. She really shouldn't have children, she should have a puppy.

JOY: She's got one.

KIP: I guess so.

JOY: Look, so you're bored, you're guilty, you're evil—is that a reason not to be happy?

KIP: What do you mean?

JOY: You make things so goddamn complicated. *(She touches his face)* I can help. I really can.

Scene Fifteen:

Night. Amy-Beth alone in a chair, partially in a shadow. A long moment. Muffled voices off: "Go through the patio ..." "The what?" "The patio ..." "But ..." "On tiptoe ..." "But just give me the ..." "Just go ..." Kip enters, naked. He does not see Amy-Beth at first. She says nothing. He notices her. They stare. He walks over to her, kneels beside her, touches her face.

BETH: *(Quietly)* Put something on. The children might see you.
(Fade)

Scene Sixteen:

The next morning. Amy-Beth alone, suitcase at her side. Amy-Joy enters, gathering stuff from floor, stashing it into a bag.

BETH: So how did it go off?

JOY: Please. They're slobbering over the little girl like she did something so *clever,* like it was so *clever* you knew how to set your brother on fire like that, it's to vomit. They're all so fucked up. You think of all the nice people in the world who die in freak accidents . . . You only brought out the one suitcase?

BETH: I left the others on the porch, is that okay?

JOY: Sure. Maybe Uncle Fartface'll bring 'em down, though I seriously doubt it. Is Kip still here?

BETH: No. He left with his mother.

JOY: Oh. *(A beat)* Typical. God, it's a beautiful day, isn't it? I can't wait to get back to New York. You looking forward to Merrick?

BETH: Yes.

JOY: You're kidding. Hey, you know what I was thinking last night? I was thinking that at the end of the summer I'd either look for a job or go back to school. I think my father's getting a little sick of paying my rent. Or else I'll get married. I'll probably end up getting married.

BETH: Oh? Who to?

JOY: Who knows? I may draw straws.

BETH: That's as good a way as any. *(Pause)*

JOY: So.

BETH: So. *(Pause)*

JOY: What time does the train leave, do you remember?

BETH: No.

JOY: No problem. The schedule's in the house.

BETH: Your uncle will drive us to the station.

JOY: Sure. Maybe we can eat lunch before, you know? We can get a salad. Seafood.

BETH: I don't think so.

JOY: Something.

BETH: No.

JOY: Okay.

BETH: Look, do you think your uncle would mind if I took a later train? After you? I'd just like to stay here for a while.

JOY: No . . . I guess that'll be all right.

BETH: Good. *(A beat)*

JOY: I better get my other suitcases. Old Fartface never will.

BETH: Sure.

JOY: It's been fun. Call me tonight, okay?

BETH: If I'm home.

JOY: Great. *(She exits. Amy-Beth remains)*

Scene Seventeen:

Lights remain on Amy-Beth sitting. Lights rise on the other side of the stage: Kip and Jinx together. Evening. Later in the summer.

KIP: *(Looking at photograph)* I'm glad he doesn't come around any more.

JINX: So, I guess, am I.

KIP: Did it just stop? I mean, or what?

JINX: More or less.

KIP: I don't understand. Why would he send you a picture of all these middle-aged men?

JINX: It's a reunion photograph. Of a tennis team. Exeter, Class of Fifty-something.

KIP: God. Hank looks awful.

JINX: Doesn't he? *(Pause)* Kip . . . ?

KIP: What?

JINX: When you were living down the shore . . . Those two girls you spoke about . . .

KIP: Yes, mother?

JINX: Did you become . . . involved . . . with one of them?

KIP: In a way.

JINX: . . . I caught a glimpse from the bottom of the hill when I picked you up. One looked very pretty.

KIP: No. It was the other one.

JINX: Oh.

KIP: Are you cold?

JINX: What were their names?

KIP: You'd laugh if I told you.

JINX: Oh. Cold, no. I don't think so.

KIP: Cooler, though.

JINX: Well. Fall, soon.

(They sit together. Amy-Beth's hand goes up to her face. Slow fade on Kip and Jinx. Slightly slower on Amy-Beth)

The End

Lanford Wilson

A BETROTHAL

Lanford Wilson

"Lanford Wilson is probably our greatest functioning American playwright." Thus wrote Rob Baker of the New York *Daily News* in reviewing the Circle Repertory Company's production of Mr. Wilson's *Brontosaurus* (which appeared in *Best Short Plays 1979*).

Since that assessment in 1977, Mr. Wilson has written his most ambitious project to date—three plays depicting the Talley family of Lebanon, Missouri. In 1979 New York's Circle Repertory Company produced *Talley's Folly,* a two character romance between Sally Talley and Matt Friedman set on July 4, 1944. Walter Kerr in the *New York Times* raved about the subsequent production on Broadway: "a charmer, filled to the brim with hope, humor and chutzpah." The play won the 1980 Pulitzer Prize for Drama, the Theatre Club Inc. Award for Best American Play and the New York Drama Critics' Circle Award. The second play in the series, *5th of July,* set in 1977, depicts the next generation of Talleys attempting to piece together their lives after a disruptive decade of social change. The third Talley play, *A Tale Told*—Wilson's 29th production directed by Marshall W. Mason—again takes place on July 4, 1944, showing the family that Sally Talley wanted to escape. Julius Novick in the *Village Voice* responded to *A Tale Told*: "What an old-fashioned play Lanford Wilson has written; and what a good one!" . . . Mr. Wilson writes in his "customary Chekhovian fashion, bringing very specific selves and viewpoints and relationships with them . . . The people of his trilogy go on living when they are offstage." A revised version of the play entitled *Talley & Son* was presented by the Circle Repertory Company in 1985. It is reported that there may be as many as five more plays forthcoming in the Talley saga.

Lanford Wilson was born in Lebanon, Missouri, in 1937, and was educated at San Diego State College and the University of Chicago, where he started writing plays. His professional career began at the now-defunct Caffe Chino in Greenwich Village. After having had ten productions at this pioneer Off Off Broadway cafe-theatre and six at the Cafe La Mama, he moved to Off Broadway in 1965 with the presentation of *Home Free!* at the Cherry Lane Theatre. In 1966, Mr. Wilson again was represented Off Broadway, this time with a double bill, *The Madness of Lady Bright* and *Ludlow Fair,* at the uptown Theatre East. *This is the Rill Speaking,* another of his short plays, was seen during that same season at the Martinique Theatre in a series of six works originally presented at the Cafe La Mama.

In 1967, Mr. Wilson won a Drama Desk-Vernon Rice Award for his play, *The Rimers of Eldritch,* a lyrical study of life in a small town in the Middle West. This was followed by another full-length play, *The Gingham Dog,* which opened in 1968 at the Washington Theatre Club, Washington, D.C., and was presented on Broadway the following year. The author returned to Broadway in 1970 with *Lemon Sky,* which drew the following comment from reviewer Clive Barnes: "Mr. Wilson can write; his characters spring alive on stage; he holds our attention, he engages our heart." A New York revival of *Lemon Sky* in December of 1985 presented by the Second Stage Company won plaudits from critics and audiences.

In 1972 Mr. Wilson received considerable praise for his libretto for the operatic version of Tennessee Williams' *Summer and Smoke.* The opera, with music by Lee Hoiby, was performed by the New York City Opera at Lincoln Center.

Mr. Wilson's highly acclaimed play, *The Hot L Baltimore,* written under a Guggenheim Fellowship, originally was presented by the Circle Repertory Company in January, 1973, then transferred in March to Off Broadway's Circle in the Square Downtown for a commercial engagement; it ran for 1,166 performances, and won the New York Drama Critics' Circle Award for Best American Play of the 1972-73 season; the Outer Critics' Circle Award; and an Obie award for Best Play.

Among the author's other works for the theatre are *Balm in Gilead,* presented in a highly acclaimed revival in New York in 1985; *Wandering; So Long at the Fair; No Trespassing; Serenading Louie; The Mound Builders; The Great Nebula in Orion,* introduced in *Best Short Plays 1972; The Sand Castle* in *Best Short Plays 1975;* and *Thymus Vulgaris,* commissioned by Edward Albee for New York's Lincoln Center One-Act Festival at the Mitzi E. Newhouse Theatre and published in the *Best Short Plays 1982.* Another play, *Angel's Fall,* presented by Circle Rep in 1982, joined *Talley's Folly* and *5th of July* in receiving a nomination for the Tony Award. A new translation of Chekhov's *The Three Sisters* was commissioned and produced by the Hartford Stage Company in 1984. Mr. Wilson's most recent play, *Burn This,* starring John Malkovich, opened at the Mark Taper Forum theatre in Los Angeles in 1987.

Mr. Wilson has been the recipient of Rockefeller, Yale, and Guggenheim Fellowships, as well as an award from The American Academy of Arts and Letters for "the body of his work as a playwright." In the fall of 1981 the University of Missouri at Kansas City awarded Mr. Wilson the honorary degree Doctor of Humane Letters.

A Betrothal, a charming romantic tale of two lonely flower enthusiasts, joins Mr. Wilson's four other short plays appearing in this series. Mr. Wilson dedicates this play: "For Uta Hagen and Herbert Berghof."

Characters:

MS. J. H. JOSLYN
MR. KERMIT WASSERMAN

Time:

An afternoon in mid-May.

Setting:

The corner of a large tent. A flap door nearby. Folding card
table, a large coffee urn, paper cups, milk cartons, folding
chairs, programs on some chairs. Drizzle outside.
Ms. J. H. Joslyn enters, miffed. She is perhaps fifty, attractive but doesn't care, maybe a little heavy and doesn't care about
that either. She has got herself up in a neat suit and is annoyed
that she bothered. She throws off a makeshift plastic bag or
some such rain protection.

JOSLYN: But then, what did I expect? What could I possibly
have expected? (Pours coffee from the urn. Without skipping a
beat she shakes three milk cartons; they are empty, pours the dribble
from two into the one, pours a bit of coffee in the one, sloshes it
about, pours milk into cup) I expected nothing. (Sits, sips) I had no
expectations. The bastards. It's the way of the world; it's the lay of
the land. Well, if they have not eyes in their heads! If they're blind
to progress. Pearls before swine. What did I expect? (Looking
off) Haven't got sense enough to come in out of the rain. Pouring
on them; ruining the whole show. Good. Fogging up their
bifocals. Not that they could see anyway: (Mimicking) "Oh, my,
isn't that quaint. Oh, how cunning; fetching color, delightful
rhythm; amusing play of the various parts. A bit coarse, of course."
What faggots. Well, what did I expect? I said there was no hope. I
had no hope. It was a hopeless situation. What did I expect? (Mr.
Wasserman enters. Dejected. Sighs. He is perhaps sixty, neat, and
though he is a large man he is decidedly soft, almost delicate.
Looks around, seeing nothing. Shakes water from his umbrella,
stands it somewhere. Murmurs: "Oh, my . . ." Pours coffee.
Sits on the other side of the table) There's no milk.

WASSERMAN: No, fine, thank you, nothing serious . . .

JOSLYN: I took the last.

WASSERMAN: I'm sorry?

JOSLYN: Of the milk.

WASSERMAN: Oh. No, no, I . . . just needed to hold something. I'll be fine. *(Pause)* Oh, dear . . .

JOSLYN: They're getting soaked.

WASSERMAN: Yes, they'll like that. That's something.

JOSLYN: The people. Haven't got the sense to come in out of the rain.

WASSERMAN: No, it's stopped. Nearly. Nearly stopped. They're all but finished, anyway. They finished the Tall Beardeds before it started, so no damage done . . . They're on the Arils, now.

JOSLYN: Damn the Arils. Shouldn't even be in the show.

WASSERMAN: No, not my thing, though interesting, I suppose . . . to those who . . . find them interesting.

JOSLYN: Too damn particular.

WASSERMAN: Yes, very fussy I'm told.

JOSLYN: Ship'em back to Persia or wherever the hell they came from. Don't belong here.

WASSERMAN: I've had no first hand experience with them, I'm sure they're very rewarding . . . to those who . . . find them very rewarding.

JOSLYN: Waste of energy.

WASSERMAN: Oh, I'm sure.

JOSLYN: Look like shit, anyway.

WASSERMAN: They are terribly muddy, some of them, for my taste.

JOSLYN: Fuck 'em.

WASSERMAN: *(Starts)* Ah, when I was leaving the house, and of course, it was so early, I had this terrible feeling that I was missing something—couldn't for the life of me—that's always so annoying—then, of course, half-way here, in the middle of the parkway, i realized I'd forgotten my galoshes. I had to pull over, I can't think and drive; it certainly looked like rain. I'd remembered my raincoat, my . . . of course I was so nervous because this is my first time.

JOSLYN: *(A beat)* What are you talking about?

WASSERMAN: To show. So I didn't want to be late. So of course it did. Rain. I mean, I didn't go back so of course

... it ... I don't mind ruining my shoes so much, but I hope I don't come down with something. Of course it's probably just nerves. It did rain very hard there for a moment.

JOSLYN: I hope it ruins everything.

WASSERMAN: I come every year, but this is the first time I've had the nerve to show. Actually the first time I thought I had something really very special. Vanity. Oh, dear, dear ...

JOSLYN: You're a breeder.

WASSERMAN: Yes, and you?

JOSLYN: Ummm. Pearls before swine. I thought you were a judge. You have that judgy look.

WASSERMAN: Oh, no, no, I wouldn't presume.

JOSLYN: Your first?

WASSERMAN: Uh, yes, and, uh, never again. At least not for years. I haven't the strength. I should have known. Hubris. Ah, well. Oh, dear ... poor little darling. Such a sweetheart. Never should have exposed her to the harsh ... light ... of reality ... in the world ... of the real. And me. Oh, dear.

JOSLYN: You might as well know I have no use for you or any of your kind.

WASSERMAN: I'm sorry?

JOSLYN: Vulgar, disgusting, tasteless, showy and useless in a garden. So expect no sympathy.

WASSERMAN: Then, what are you doing here?

JOSLYN: *(She keeps her cards very close to her chest)* I have my own pursuits, thank you, I've been scoffed at before. I'm quite immune. Slings and arrows; roll right off my back.

WASSERMAN: I understood you were a breeder, too.

JOSLYN: I have my pursuits. Nothing you would understand. For your information I was tickled pink when it started to rain. The spectacle of that huge, vulgar mess of a Tall Bearded that they had just awarded Best of Show, falling right over flat in the mud the moment they turned their backs! Ha! Everyone running to stake it up. In five minutes the whole damn lot of them were leaning and staggering like drunken sailors. No wind, mind you, just a spring shower. And my baby was standing up at attention like a little soldier.

WASSERMAN: Which one is your Little Soldier?

JOSLYN: I have my pursuits.

WASSERMAN: I really must say. *(Looking around)* I have no love for the Tall Beardeds. I'm an Intermediate Breeder. May I take it you're an Intermediate Breeder, too?

JOSLYN: I have my pursuits.

WASSERMAN: I'm so glad, I never really go to any of the meetings, I couldn't possibly. I get the Quarterly, I pore over the Quarterly . . . uh . . . which one is your Little Soldier?

JOSLYN: Never you mind, never you mind. Slings and arrows. I came back to the tent because I thought no one would be here. Everyone was acres away down at the other end, I expected to be alone here.

WASSERMAN: Yes, it did look very deserted.

JOSLYN: It was, then you came.

WASSERMAN: Yes, yes, I simply couldn't any longer. I was trying to be brave, but I came all over with the feeling I was going to faint. I simply had to sit down. Little Tanya stood up to the rain at first, she just sparkled like dew, but I'm certain she was beginning to feel it. I gave her a little shake, I don't think anyone saw. As soon as I looked around I realized I'd been wrong to enter Big Judy, I told her I was sorry, but for Little Tanya—to be overlooked—I know, of course, she's frail. Part of her charm for me. Oh, such vanity. Never again.

JOSLYN: I have no idea whom you're talking about.

WASSERMAN: Oh, I'm sorry. I thought . . .

JOSLYN: Who are these women? Why are you telling me about them? I don't know them. I don't know anyone. I wouldn't like them. I want to be alone here.

WASSERMAN: Oh, no, they're my babies, of course. They're in the trial garden of the Intermediate Iris Bed. I thought Little Tanya had a very good chance of attracting attention.

JOSLYN: You named your iris Big Judy and Little Tanya?

WASSERMAN: Maybe you at least noticed Tanya. Many people seemed attracted to her—but, alas . . . not . . . oh, dear . . .

JOSLYN: I noticed nothing. I don't parade about ooing and ahing, thank you. I guarded my entry. I wouldn't put it past some of these—I saw their jealous eyes, their itchy fingers. I stood my ground.

WASSERMAN: Over your Little Soldier? I saw everything. I must say I thought some were very inferior. Others, frankly, I know what you mean, made me not jealous at all, but simply burn with envy. I do think the Intermediates are just developing in leaps and . . . such strong branching, what texture.

JOSLYN: Branching. You know nothing of branching; nothing of texture.

WASSERMAN: It's just that it's something I've neglected horribly. Something I must take the time to work on.

JOSLYN: Time, oh, time. Try thirty years.

WASSERMAN: I'm sorry?

JOSLYN: Of no other thought. Day and night. Try perfection.

WASSERMAN: That's remarkable.

JOSLYN: Ha. Tell it to the judge.

WASSERMAN: Oh, dear. Oh, your Little Soldier wasn't overlooked?

JOSLYN: I expected nothing.

WASSERMAN: Oh, I must say I was foolish enough to expect Best of Show.

JOSLYN: I had no expectations.

WASSERMAN: Oh, I so hoped.

JOSLYN: I had no hope. What did I expect? Another story of the unsung hero. Slaving in their labs; Marie Curie in that godawful unheated barn, day and night. All the nameless laborers of the field. Who knows their plight? Who their hopes and dreams? Who celebrates their tiny joys? The doubling of chromosomes, the increase of bud-count. The miracle of texture. Perfectly round falls that stand out utterly horizontally in a hurricane! Triple branching, and at ninety degrees not a hundred eighty, who's ever seen it before? Who will ever know who changed the course of history? Who will care? Lost in the shuffle. Taken for granted. The builder of the Trojan Horse, the inventor of the wheel, the discoverer of Pluto, the principle of pi . . . What in the hell are you doing? *(He has been searching through a pocket notebook)*

WASSERMAN: I have it here—"Good blue," no, "Bad yellow," branching, branching, texture . . . somewhere . . . "Lovely white," no . . AH! You are *(Reading)* J.H. Joslyn, Carmel, New York. And your Little Soldier is entry number 3a-I-916.

JOSLYN: What have you got there?

WASSERMAN: I take copious notes. "Most outstanding falls, utterly round, perfectly horizontal, astonishing branching, holding flowers quite apart, remarkable texture of fall and standard, terribly unfortunate muddiness in—" and so on, and so on. I must say, Ms., er, ah, Joslyn, I'm very pleased to meet the breeder of that

Little Soldier. I made special note of Carmel, as I'm from Mahopac, which is a hop, skip, and a jump down the road.

JOSLYN: Were I from Carmel, I'd certainly know the where-abouts of a town so nearby and visibly disagreeable as Mahopac.

WASSERMAN: I must say I can't believe your Little Soldier didn't at least receive a citation for extraordinary branching and texture. Why, the branches are at angles to one another instead of directly across from—I must say, what dimension it gives the whole stalk. Like a candelabra; I've never seen it before.

JOSLYN: Neither has anyone. Nor do they care, apparently. The builder of the Great Wall of China, the . . .

WASSERMAN: And texture! Like carved ivory. I actually reached to feel the thickness—quite inadvertently, I didn't even realize I'd done it—the way one instinctively smells a rose.

JOSLYN: I know nothing of smelling roses. I have no use for them. Or for what you call instinct, which of course is thoughtlessness.

WASSERMAN: I didn't feel it, however. Someone barked at me so fiercely I just moved on, but I certainly took note. You're starred in my book, and there are only four or five entries that are starred.

JOSLYN: Humf!

WASSERMAN: I'm sorry?

JOSLYN: What care I? Slings and arrows. One among four, one among five, right off my back.

WASSERMAN: I'm sorry?

JOSLYN: *(Looking at him levelly)* Oh, yes. Humf! Oh, sure . . . I've seen you.

WASSERMAN: Oh, well, there you have the advantage, I'm afraid . . . I . . . maybe it's unsocial, but I . . . at a flower show, at least . . . I don't think I see people. I'm taking notes, moving on, admiring, getting so many ideas, that I think perhaps I don't look . . . uh . . . up. And then, of course, I find it so confusing to look at people. What if I should catch their eye? A perfect stranger? What would they think? And maybe it would be a judge, thinking I was trying to influence him . . . or . . . her . . . in some influential way.

JOSLYN: At the Grand Union. On Route Six.

WASSERMAN: I'm sorry?

JOSLYN: Pawing the lettuce and teasing the kiwi fruit. It's only a bad habit, you know, neglectful mother, probably. Father away at sea a good deal, or some such. It could be corrected with a little self-discipline.

WASSERMAN: I'm sorry?

JOSLYN: Pinching, testing, squeezing, pawing. Some people think they're the only man on God's earth. Mauling everything, trying to make it their own. How would you feel if you were the iris? How would you feel if you were the fruit?

WASSERMAN: I'm sorry?

JOSLYN: It can be corrected.

WASSERMAN: What's that?

JOSLYN: A word to the wise . . .

WASSERMAN: *(Reaching out his hand)* You must admit the texture of your Little Soldier's falls invites the touch. It looks like it would feel of . . . oooo, I don't know, of velvet or chamois or ivory or oooo, something extraordinary.

JOSLYN: *(Slapping his hand)* Just never you mind, sir. Never you worry about it. You're not the only one, remember.

WASSERMAN: I'm sorry?

JOSLYN: Reaching out their grubby paws to cop a feel. There was fifty if there was one. Two judges, if you believe it. With their judgy little thumb and finger. I put them in their places, don't think I didn't. Inadequate guidance at school probably. All this permissive behavior.

WASSERMAN: Thirty years . . . my goodness. I've been working that long of course, but I would never presume, I wouldn't know where to begin. I breed for color, so I wouldn't know . . .

JOSLYN: Color, oh, my goodness! Yappidy-yap, yappidy-yap, it's all I hear. Blue this and puce that. Ruby Glow and Pink Reward.

WASSERMAN: Oh, when I first saw my first Lillipinkput, I began to work the very next week.

JOSLYN: Sing me no first Lillipinkputs, read me no rhymes, thank you. It's all I hear. One has enough to contend with without your Lillipinkputs.

WASSERMAN: I was quite inspired by her. I saw a whole clump blooming in Presby Gardens, before she won the Sass Award, and I must say I was bowled over by her.

JOSLYN: Sing me no Sass Awards, read me no bowled overs, I've no use for it at all.

WASSERMAN: Your world, of course, is of quite a different order.

JOSLYN: I have my pursuits.

WASSERMAN: You wouldn't see it, I quite realize.

JOSLYN: I'm not blind. I could be impressed. I can see, and what I see is as far as any of them have gone. There's one today, hardly to be overlooked, tangerine, maybe, orange maybe, I have eyes. Striking color, but then what? I went over to it, one could hardly fail to see it, but on close inspection—the hypocrisy! Flimsy wouldn't begin. Insubstantial, wilting falls lying practically flat against the sheathing spathe, crest styles of crepe paper, standards so tissue thin I'm surprised the first drop of rain didn't go straight through them. One branch, mind you, and it hardly held up even this anemic, cobwebby . . .

WASSERMAN: *(Hardly audible)* Madam.

JOSLYN: —pissant of a—and God knows the bud count. Probably not even two. Nothing so wispy could . . .

WASSERMAN: Madam.

JOSLYN: —support more. And a crowd around it ooing and ahing! Over this feeble . . .

WASSERMAN: Madam.

JOSLYN: —debilitated, sapless, pithless, impotent . . .

WASSERMAN: *(A little louder)* Madam.

JOSLYN: —lustless, flaccid, feckless, limp . . .

WASSERMAN: Madam!

JOSLYN: Wishy-washy, insipid . . . !

WASSERMAN: *(quite huge)* MADAM, YOU ARE SPEAKING OF MY CHILD!

JOSLYN: *(A beat)* I beg your pardon?

WASSERMAN: *(Still outraged)* You are speaking of Little Tanya! Though she may not be to your liking, many people were very admiring. Several times when I drew close enough to hear their remarks, several people were wondering if the breeder was at the show. Many were struck. *(His hand on his throat)* I think I've injured my voice. I'm terribly sorry. I don't know what I can be thinking. I've never spoken like that before to anyone. Once to a very, *very,* truculent raspberry, never to a person. Certainly not a lady. It's the strain of the occasion. I've not been myself all day. I shouldn't be around people, they make me terribly . . . and the agony of competition, it isn't human. Oh, dear . . .

JOSLYN: *(After a beat)* That *vapidity* is Little Tanya?

WASSERMAN: *(Eyes closed, a strangled admission)* Yes . . .

JOSLYN: That *whisper?*

WASSERMAN: Please. I know she isn't to your taste.

JOSLYN: I say nothing of my taste.

WASSERMAN: I realize you're working in quite a different field.

JOSLYN: Fields abound, I say nothing of fields.

WASSERMAN: You have your pursuits.

JOSLYN: Just never you mind.

WASSERMAN: But you must understand another choosing to endeavor in an endeavor of . . . another choosing.

JOSLYN: I say nothing of my understanding.

WASSERMAN: That orange has been the achievement of thirty years. And I can't help the vanity of being somewhat . . . vain . . . about . . . achieving it. You understand, failings apart, it is a remarkable orange.

JOSLYN: It's a very good color, as colors come and go.

WASSERMAN: No rose has an orange like it.

JOSLYN: I know nothing of roses.

WASSERMAN: Well, I can tell you any orange rose is impossible to use with anything. Little Tanya is the only orange I've seen, and many people remarked on it, that mixes. She's a mixer! She looks charming with other oranges, with lemons, with peaches, with red. Red! With lavender and blue. She blends! People would want her. Many said so. They can use her. She's a blender!

JOSLYN: I care nothing about what people can use.

WASSERMAN: Well, you should. Many people were remarking about your Little Soldier, you surely heard them . . .

JOSLYN: Yammerings of the crowd.

WASSERMAN: But it can't be used in a . . . what I mean to say is . . . it's absolutely . . . nothing could . . . well, exactly what color would you call it? I mean it isn't a light yellow, it isn't buff. It isn't green, it's muddy, sure, but what? mustard? Bluish maybe, but I was at a loss to make out what . . . .

JOSLYN: *(She has been collecting her things and rises)* I see it's quite impossible to hope that you'll ever leave here. Some people are like that. It's a lack of respect for another's privacy. It's a bad habit, of course, it could be worked on, but in your case I doubt any serious improvement. The rain has let up, I'll remove myself and allow you, doubtless, to find another victim.

WASSERMAN: *(Looking at her with amazement)* I know you. How extraordinary. I don't know anyone. I've seen you.

JOSLYN: Sing me none of your seens.

WASSERMAN: You're a teacher.

JOSLYN: I beg your pardon, I am not.

WASSERMAN: You most certainly are.

JOSLYN: I am not, I know what I am.

WASSERMAN: You teach.

JOSLYN: I do not.

WASSERMAN: You did, you must have.

JOSLYN: *(A beat)* I have my pursuits, thank you. What I do and what I've done are not for the ears of idle strangers.

WASSERMAN: Last year you taught!

JOSLYN: I did not!

WASSERMAN: You came to the gate!

JOSLYN: I came to no gate of yours, you can be sure. I peer through no gates, thank you.

WASSERMAN: You came just inside, and there you stood. Looking just as you do now.

JOSLYN: I did not. I come in gates only when I'm invited in, and I'm invited in only where I ask to be and I did not ask, thank you.

WASSERMAN: You came to Castle Crampton. I saw you at the gate. Believe me, I certainly didn't intend to see you, I don't see any of them, they sometimes see me, it can't be helped, they ask their questions, they talk on and on, some of them, it's all very . . . and the children pour in on their field trips, the musicians, you know they have hundreds of them for the chamber orchestras, the quartets, and they're so talky, I'm afraid. You were a chaperone to one of the children's classes.

JOSLYN: I beg your pardon, I have no class.

WASSERMAN: And in they poured and there you stood. Just inside the gate.

JOSLYN: In the line of one's employment one is sometimes called upon, quite against one's will, to fulfill the place of those who are irresponsible enough to become ill.

WASSERMAN: I would never insist, of course, you know where you did and didn't go. I must say I don't at all feel comfortable around children. They don't seem to watch where they're going, they tend to step on me. But if you're the principal and went along in place of one of the . . .

JOSLYN: I am certainly not a principal.

WASSERMAN: Or an assistant principal with the duty of replacing some . . .

JOSLYN: I am certainly no assistant principal.

WASSERMAN: Or the librarian and were asked to fill in for . . .

JOSLYN: I am not a librarian for any of your . . .

WASSERMAN: Or the assistant librarian.

JOSLYN: I have my pursuits.   You, of course, might be interested in the likes of Castle Crampton Gardens, I assure you I would not be.

WASSERMAN: Oh, my goodness, no.

JOSLYN: I disdained to step one foot into such a place. One look was all I needed to understand the whole of Castle Crampton completely. Tacky little bedded-out beds, looking as though they belonged in front of a gas station.

WASSERMAN: *(Loving it)* Oh, my goodness!

JOSLYN: Municipal gardening, indeed. Worse here than abroad if you can believe it, and Crampton worst of all.

WASSERMAN: Oh, yes!

JOSLYN: I know the philosophy. Rows of wax begonias, never was a plant so aptly named. Your cup of tea, well, you can have it. No doubt little Tanya would blend in well . . .

WASSERMAN: Oh, dear, no. I'm afraid even Tanya couldn't save the place.

JOSLYN: All your geometrical beds, squares and circles and triangles. Yellow marigolds, surrounded by a cunning little ring of blue *Ageratum houstonianum,* surrounded by a nice contrasting lip-stick red of, maybe, *Salvia splendens* "Harbinger." "Castle Crampton" spelled out in petunias and lobelia. They might as well use spray paint. A Spanish castle, a Venetian court, a ballroom lawn, no doubt, with German statuary.

WASSERMAN: Yes, yes, yes . . . all of it.

JOSLYN: Tulips by the hundreds, I'm sure, in the spring.

WASSERMAN: By the thousands! I plant them, they buy them by the truckloads, ripped out the day they're shot and replaced by marigolds, not even stock.

JOSLYN: You plant them? You? Not just an innocent tourist, but responsible for that mess?

WASSERMAN: Oh, Lord no, responsible, never, I wouldn't presume. I wouldn't make a decision myself, what if someone saw it? Oh, I'm terribly sorry, I know you and you don't know me, what am I thinking . . . I'm not in the habit of meeting . . . allow me to introduce . . . uh, Ms. J. H. Joslyn, this is Mr.

Kermit Wasserman; Mr. Wasserman, Ms. Joslyn. How do you do? It is my misfortune to be one of the assistant gardeners at Crampton.

JOSLYN: How do you do? I was just going.

WASSERMAN: Oh, my yes, I'm afraid you'd better, because if you're going to be wicked about Crampton, I couldn't tear myself away and I shouldn't hear it. My own garden, of course, very small, is a cottagy, Englishy sort of thing, very modest, but enough for me and my iris. And yours?

JOSLYN: Sing me no yourses, my garden's my garden. Certainly not Englishy cottage. I farm, I don't decorate. I breed. I grow eggplant and squash, kale and kohlrabi. And I breed intermediate iris for strength and substance. I'm none of your watercolorists.

WASSERMAN: You're not, by any chance, colorblind?

JOSLYN: I beg your pardon?

WASSERMAN: I'm terribly sorry, I don't know what came over me. It's just that one who has created such a lovely texture and, as you say, substance, and neglected so completely . . .

JOSLYN: Rolls right off my back. There's no reason for me to stay, what did I expect? I don't know how some people call themselves scientists.

WASSERMAN: Ms. Joslyn, I may be vain, I may have expected too much, but you cannot . . .

JOSLYN: How could you have overlooked so basic a thing as stalk?

WASSERMAN: I could say the same for you, you know, were I the sort who . . .

JOSLYN: The color may be striking but there's nothing under it!

WASSERMAN: You have created a castle without a flag!

JOSLYN: I care for more than flashy headgear, thank you!

WASSERMAN: And you might as well be breeding galoshes!

JOSLYN: I am a great breeder, sir!

WASSERMAN: And, madam, so am I!

JOSLYN: I've toiled in the fields, sir, for thirty years!

WASSERMAN: And so have I!

JOSLYN: And you've nothing to show for it.

WASSERMAN: No one wants your Little Soldier!

JOSLYN: No one needs your Tanya!

WASSERMAN: If my Tanya had the texture of your Little Soldier!

JOSLYN: If my Soldier had the color of Tanya . . . !

(There is a dead pause. It extends. Their words hang in the air. They think for a moment. They consider, each with their own thoughts. They picture it. She sits)

WASSERMAN: *(Imagining it)* Oh, my . . .

JOSLYN: Hummm . . .

WASSERMAN: Oh, my, that would be something . . .

JOSLYN: Hummmmm . . .

WASSERMAN: In four years . . . maybe five. Six at the outside . . . Can you see it?

JOSLYN: *(Musing)* Just never mind, I see what I see . . .

WASSERMAN: I've never seen anything like it.

JOSLYN: There's never been anything like it.

WASSERMAN: Not to push, and I don't think it's vanity, but Best of Show would be in the bag.

JOSLYN: In a jerkwater show like this? I wouldn't waste our time.

WASSERMAN: One might easily interest the nurseries in such a . . . uh . . .

JOSLYN: Oh, my good man, beating them away with our umbrellas.

WASSERMAN: The Sass Award is not at all out of the question.

JOSLYN: Sing me no Sass Awards, we're talking the cover of the Royal Horticultural Society's Garden Magazine.

WASSERMAN: Perhaps you had better be listed as breeder, I wouldn't be able to tolerate the limelight. Fame has always . . .

JOSLYN: *(Musing)* Sing me no limelight, read me no fame; we're talking fortune.

WASSERMAN: Indeed. Not to be crass, but . . . ?

JOSLYN: Thousands. Tens of thousands.

WASSERMAN: A better income, I would think, than assisting at a school library.

JOSLYN: Fuck the school library.

WASSERMAN: Indeed.

JOSLYN: Fuck Castle Crampton.

WASSERMAN: Oh, indeed. *(A long pause, they dream. Then delicately turn to particulars. She clears her throat)*

JOSLYN: *(Inquiring lightly)* Ah . . . how are . . . her . . . uh . . . rhizomes?

WASSERMAN: Well, actually, now that you ask, very strong indeed, really quite remarkable.

JOSLYN: Are they?

WASSERMAN: And . . . uh . . . his?

JOSLYN: Well, uh . . . adequate certainly . . . uh . . . perhaps not absolutely . . . the . . . uh . . .

WASSERMAN: Only that?

JOSLYN: I've probably seen better increase.

WASSERMAN: Tanya increases like a weed.

JOSLYN: *Does* she? The little devil.

WASSERMAN: And, uh, his . . . seed pod?

JOSLYN: Oh, marvelous, of course, with all that upper strength. Unfailing.

WASSERMAN: I thought so. I must tell you, Tanya has been known to disappoint me there.

JOSLYN: Well, she's terribly delicate, it would be uncaring to expect . . .

WASSERMAN: I'm afraid, though, we'd much better have your Little Soldier as the seed parent.

JOSLYN: Absolutely. He won't mind playing the girl. Not for Little Tanya. Of the Golden Hair! I assume the bud-count, actually . . . ?

WASSERMAN: Oh, yes, two. And she has been known to have two branches.

JOSLYN: Oh, I'm glad to hear it. That might make it much easier. Though we have to get some starch in her. Strengthen those limbs. Not stout—just strong. He'll do wonders for that.

WASSERMAN: And as for color, I'm glad to say, there, Tanya is very dominant.

JOSLYN: The little vixen! He's not very sure of himself there, I'm glad to say.

WASSERMAN: Oh, she'll take care of him nicely.

JOSLYN: My, my, my . . .

WASSERMAN: I must say . . .

JOSLYN: So convenient that you live so close.

WASSERMAN: Isn't it?

JOSLYN: Lovely Mahopac. *(Pause)* You understand, I think this should be exclusive. I don't want to see her red hair pussy-footing around with . . .

WASSERMAN: Madam! You overreach yourself. Tanya's fidelity, I assure you is irreproachable. You had much better be concerned about your Little Soldier.

JOSLYN: You have his word.

WASSERMAN: Well . . . one hears stories . . .

JOSLYN: Would you agree to begin with my seed bed? I make all my own soil, pure compost. A good grade of builders sand.

WASSERMAN: That's quite fine by me ... You won't mind if I visit the site first, just to ...

JOSLYN: Oh, by all means. I think we should begin first thing in the morning. I'll drive over to your place ...

WASSERMAN: Oh, excellent, excellent ... We can collect her lovely pollen at the crack of dawn ...

JOSLYN: I have a divine set of sable brushes—never been touched. So exorbitant, but I couldn't help myself.

WASSERMAN: How impulsive!

JOSLYN: Oh, I know. I've been waiting for the right occasion ... I knew it'd come.

WASSERMAN: Intuition ... I don't expect to sleep a wink.

JOSLYN: Nor I.

WASSERMAN: Well. I must say. *(He gets up, walks a few steps, a new dignity)* They're all drifting back, the judging must be over. Ha! If they only knew.

JOSLYN: Look at them. Do you watch the presentation of the ribbons? And all their giggling little squeals when they win?

WASSERMAN: Not usually, I'm afraid. Crowds, you know, with nothing to look at ... except people, of course ... but perhaps this year ... just to see how it's done. Just to get into practice.

JOSLYN: Might as well get in the habit of being notable. I must say, Mr. Wasserman, you're looking like a championship breeder.

WASSERMAN: And you, Ms. Joslyn.

JOSLYN: Ah! The sun's come out. And look whose golden hair is flashing in the light. She must be a hundred yards away.

WASSERMAN: She has reason to be excited tonight.

JOSLYN: I'm as nervous as a schoolgirl.

WASSERMAN: I think you're blushing.

JOSLYN: So are you.

WASSERMAN: Well, let us sit here, then, and wait for the onslaught of the unsuspecting crowd. *(They sit)*

JOSLYN: I must say it has been a very good show this year.

(They open their programs and begin to study them)

The End

Amlin Gray

WORMWOOD

Amlin Gray

When *Wormwood* and its companion piece *Outlanders* opened in Manhattan under the collective title *Zones of the Spirit,* they were greeted warmly by Alisa Solomon in the *Village Voice:* "The language and construction of these two plays . . . add to Gray's reputation as an inventive and thoughtful playwright." Mel Gussow, writing in the *New York Times,* highlights *Wormwood* as "a tale of the purgative depths of art and of a man who is haunted by specters who inhabit his autobiographical archives. . . . The play deals not only with crosscurrents of malice and domination but also with the abuses of truth in the name of art. . . . The play has a deadly fascination."

First presented by the Milwaukee Repertory Theatre in March of 1984 under artistic director John Dillon, the two plays were directed by Eric Hill. A New York production at the Theatre for the New City (with artistic directors George Bartenieff and Crystal Field) followed a month later, directed by Sharon Ott. Though not written explicitly as a biographical play about August Strindberg, *Wormwood* summons memories of that disturbed, obsessed, 19th century playwright. Mr. Gray reports that parts of the play "incorporate images from Strindberg's memoir-novels called collectively *The Son of a Servant*" and that Strindberg, like Ossian Borg in the play, did "briefly frequent a Berlin tavern called 'At the Black Pig' and, at a later period, wrote with a feather from the hat of his third wife, Harriet Bosse."

Born in New York City in 1946, Amlin Gray trained as an actor at the American Musical and Dramatic Academy and in England at the Royal Academy of Dramatic Art. Later turning his talents to playwriting, he received productions of his many plays at major resident theatres around the country, including the Milwaukee Repertory Theatre, Theatre Three in Dallas, Trinity Square Repertory in Providence, the Actors Theatre of St. Paul, and the Los Angeles Public Theatre.

Mr. Gray's published plays include: *How I Got That Story, The Fantod, Villainous Company, Kingdom Come,* and *Zones of the Spirit.* Works not yet published include: *Founding Father* and *Pirates,* both presented as workshop productions at the O'Neill Center in Waterford, Connecticut; and *Captain Williams, Bindle Stiff,* and *Six Toes.*

Numerous awards and grants have recognized Mr. Gray's work, including an Off Off Broadway Obie Award for Distinguished Playwrighting in 1981, the Best Play Award given by the

Society of Midland Authors in 1979, and an American Theatre Critics Association citation in 1980 for *The Fantod.* He has received grants from the Wisconsin Arts Board, the Rockefeller Foundation, the New York State Council for the Arts, the Guggenheim Foundation, and the National Endowment for the Arts.

Additionally, Mr. Gray is a member of the Dramatists Guild and New Dramatists organizations. He also has served as a consultant on theatre panels for the Ohio Arts Council, the Playwrights Center in Minneapolis, and the National Endowment for the Arts.

Characters:

MARIKA BORG, 25, *blond and fair-skinned with incongruously dark eyes; a reformed painter in danger of recidivism.*

JOHAN EKDAHL, 25, *a somewhat feckless young former fellow student of Marika's, now a waiter at The Snout.*

MALACHI, *a malicious old man in his 70's; proprietor of The Snout; the muse and evil angel of Ossian Borg.*

OSSIAN BORG, 29, *but looking older; Marika's husband; has a broad, high forehead and a great mane of hair he can never quite tame; himself a former artist—not a painter but a writer—and also insecurely reformed.*

Setting:

The setting, very dimly visible at first, is a windowless store-room off the main room of The Snout, *a low tavern in Stockholm. The tavern might be imagined as a cut or two below the one depicted in Munch's "Christiania Bohemians" etchings. Much of the room is occupied by a long table littered with crates, broken furniture and assorted junk. A good deal of the floor is similarly taken up. Over all lies a thick layer of dust. On the walls, somewhat incongruously, hang a couple of undistinguished expressionistic paintings—dim, muddy landscapes and one murky study of the room itself. A door to stage right is the room's only exit and entrance.*

A key is heard in the lock. The door is opened. Marika Borg steps into the doorway. We can hardly see her yet, but her voice is full and musical.

MARIKA: This is it?

JOHAN: *(Behind her, not yet visible at all; a fresh, direct voice)* That's it.

MARIKA: I can't see a thing.

JOHAN: Go on in.

MARIKA: Can't you go in first and light a lamp?

JOHAN: *(Squeezing past her)* I'll go ahead of you, but we'll have to shut the door before we can have any light. The old spider's still in his quarters upstairs, but there'll be customers for supper soon. It's as good as my job if he catches us. *(He shuts the door behind them. The room is once again in almost total darkness)*

MARIKA: This room smells like the inside of an old shoe.

JOHAN: I'm not allowed in here myself unless he sends me to fetch liquor for behind the bar. Excuse me once more—the gas-lamp is there where you're standing.

(He strikes a match on the wall and lights a lamp to the upstage side of the door. We see now that he is a pleasant-looking man of twenty-five. His threadbare suit would just pass muster, given a few points for effort, at a fairly formal afternoon occasion. Marika, the same age, is a fair-haired woman of fine bearing. Of her superbly clear features, the most notable are her incongruously dark eyes, set deep in her face. Her clothes are as formal as Johan's but less worn and more imaginative. She surveys the room with great interest)

MARIKA: So this is the famous Back Room.

JOHAN: It's just a storeroom now.

MARIKA: When Ossian was living here, it can't have been this dark. Ah, there's another lamp. Let's light that one too.

JOHAN: We don't want too much light in case it shows under the door. You don't know Malachi. He's got the eyes of a snake.

MARIKA: I thought he was a spider.

JOHAN: He's the worst of both combined.

MARIKA: If he does come in, then, I'll want to be able to see him. May I have the matches, Johan? *(Reluctantly, he allows her to take them)* Thank you. *(Moving to the lamp on the center of the back wall and lighting it)* The odor is less overwhelming with light in the room. Still it's enough to turn your lungs to mummy.

JOHAN: No one's lived here since your husband left, and that's almost four years ago.

MARIKA: Where did Ossian sleep?

JOHAN: *(Pointing to a pile of boxes, rungless chairs, etc., to the left)* There's a roll of blankets there under the cobwebs. They say he laid those on the table for a mattress.

MARIKA: *(Trying to picture it)* And he slept here every night, a whole year?

JOHAN: Not at night. He just slept in the daytime. He loved the night.

MARIKA: My husband hates the night.

JOHAN: He didn't always.

MARIKA: Is that something else that "they" say?

JOHAN: He said that. *(Quoting)* "The nighttime, even in a closed room like the prison where I die away my life, is as fertile as the mucky soil where worms nest. The day is as barren as glass."

MARIKA: Do you know his books by heart?

JOHAN: Just sections.

MARIKA: Which book is that from?

JOHAN: *The Snout.*

MARIKA: I've read *The Snout.* I've never read the other book.

JOHAN: You've never read *The Orphan?*

MARIKA: Ossian asked me not to. I'd read *The Snout* already, back when you and I were students at the Institute. All the budding artists had to read about the scandalous writer's bohemian life.

JOHAN: They're both extraordinary books. They're not like anything else ever written.

MARIKA: And a good thing—that's what Ossian would say.

JOHAN: I read them all the time. It's like nibbling on food that's so rich you can hardly keep it down. I sometimes come in here to read *The Snout.* Your husband wrote it at this table. This is where he sat. These blue stains might be spills from his pen. In the preface to *The Snout,* he says he wrote the book in ink instead of blood because he really should have written it in . . . *(Quickly editing)* . . . in matter.

MARIKA: "Matter"?

JOHAN: Well, the word he used was "pus."

MARIKA: That sounds like what a tenant of this room would write with.

JOHAN: I'd move in here and paint in . . . matter if I thought that it would help me paint the way he wrote.

MARIKA: You're still painting, then?

JOHAN: Oh, I'm still painting, absolutely.

MARIKA: Then why do you wipe tables for this Malachi?

JOHAN: I have to make a living.

MARIKA: But don't people buy your work?

JOHAN: I don't try to sell it.

MARIKA: Why not?

JOHAN: It isn't very good.

MARIKA: Well, but it must have gotten better since the Institute.

JOHAN: It can't have gotten worse, you mean?

MARIKA: I suppose it could have stayed the same . . .

JOHAN: I'm afraid it has.

MARIKA: Are your figures still out of proportion?

JOHAN: I don't try figures anymore. Trouble with figures is, you have to use a model. When you're done, the model wants to look.

MARIKA: What do you paint then? Still lifes?

JOHAN: Painting indoors is depressing. You begin with a perfect white canvas, then you mark it and it's ruined forever. Of course you do the same outdoors, but there are more distractions. So what I paint is mostly landscapes. Painting landscapes is like fishing. You don't really go to catch fish. The line in the water is just an excuse to let you sit out in the scenery. I do enjoy my painting. I just don't need to bother other people with it.

MARIKA: What did you think of Gustav's exhibition today?

JOHAN: What a surprise to meet you there! I go to all the openings, but this was the first time I'd seen you at one.

MARIKA: I don't go to the galleries. But with all the hoopla in the papers about Gustav—I *thought* that that was why I went, but now I'm here I wonder . . .

JOHAN: Gustav's made a lot of progress, don't you think?

MARIKA: His career is right on schedule. He had it all mapped out while we were still at school. He'd start off doing portraits of the wives of senior clerks. Their husbands would give dinners to unveil the portraits and he'd work up new commissions there. He's progressed to the middle-range bureaucrats. With this current exhibition, he'll soon be painting presidents and chairmen. In five years he'll have painted the King and then the world will be his oyster.

JOHAN: Do you envy him?

MARIKA: His work's not worth a whistle, but I am fond of oysters. And of sour grapes, you're thinking?

JOHAN: I'm not thinking.

MARIKA: No woman who had any kind of station to protect could ever work up a career like Gustav's. She wouldn't have the freedom of the private homes, or of the public places either. *(With a gesture, she has cited* The Snout *as an example of the last)*

JOHAN: I have the freedom. I could never do what he's done, though. The Countess of Wherever would take one look at her left eye halfway down her cheek and have her butler throw me out. But I'm really quite content with what I'm doing now. Maybe when I'm old and looking back I'll think I should have been dissatisfied, but

I'm perfectly fine for the present. In fact, if I'm to keep my job we'd better go now.

MARIKA: *(Is still looking around the room. She's never really stopped since she arrived here)* I still can't see it.

JOHAN: See what?

MARIKA: Ossian here, in this room. I can't picture it. But then, I can't imagine him writing those books. Who's still here that knew him?

JOHAN: There's just Malachi.

MARIKA: Would your snake-eyed spider talk to me?

JOHAN: He loves to talk about your husband. He's been trying to get him back here since he left.

MARIKA: Oh, has he? How?

JOHAN: When I started at The Snout, I was the errand boy. One of my jobs was to run messages from Malachi to Mr. Borg, inviting him to come and have a drink.

MARIKA: You could have saved your shoes. Ossian made a vow. He swore he'd never set foot in The Snout again. If he ever came back here, he told me, he'd stay for the rest of his life.

JOHAN: Oh, Malachi would like that even better. Your husband's reputation brought in tourists. If he were living here again . . .

MARIKA: This place was a tourist attraction?

JOHAN: Yes. That's pretty much dropped off by now. They used to come, though. Swedes, Norwegians, Germans, even French and English. They'd sit down, muss their hair and tear their shirtfronts open, and order an "Ossian Borg."

MARIKA: Is that something you drink?

JOHAN: Straight absinthe, like he drank when he was here. The funny thing is, we can't serve that to the tourists. It's been outlawed.

MARIKA: Outlawed? People still drink absinthe.

JOHAN: Not the real stuff, though. The distillers still make something they call absinthe, but it doesn't have the principal ingredient.

MARIKA: What was that?

JOHAN: Wormwood. The government found out that it was poison. It caused fever and myopia and persecution mania. What we sell now is just anisette.

MARIKA: And your employer thought that, if he lured my husband here, he wouldn't notice that the offered drink was counterfeit?

JOHAN: The difference in flavor is subtle, they say.

MARIKA: Ossian has a subtle palate, such as only men whom food and drink almost disgust can have. An almost squeamish sensitivity. If your Malachi believes that he could fool my husband with a substitute, he doesn't know him.

JOHAN: He likes to say he knows him very well.

MARIKA: These notes he sends—they never come to Ossian at home. They must go to his office.

JOHAN: Yes.

MARIKA: Does Ossian accept them?

JOHAN: Not in person, but his secretary takes them.

MARIKA: Does Ossian send back answers?

JOHAN: He never did while I was running them.

MARIKA: Who runs them now?

JOHAN: Axel's the new errand boy.

MARIKA: Is Axel here?

JOHAN: He should be here by now.

MARIKA: Let's have him in.

JOHAN: He'd tell on us. He's terrified of Malachi.

MARIKA: Then let's have Malachi himself. It's time that we two met.

JOHAN: You mean call Malachi in here? I've told you . . .

MARIKA: I can't talk to him out front. There are windows. Very small ones and with filthy glass, but still the world outside is passing by. *(Starting for the door)* Let's see if Malachi's come down yet.

JOHAN: Marika, this isn't fair. You wanted to see the Back Room so I smuggled you in. You can't let me lose my job for it.

MARIKA: I don't see why you want this job. If waiting tables is your goal in life, you're even-tempered and presentable, any cafe in Stockholm would hire you.

JOHAN: I like it here.

MARIKA: Why?

JOHAN: It has a history. People gathered in the front room to argue ideas. They started trends and they formed schools and movements. Your husband was the catalyst. He wouldn't let the others back here very often. They'd knock and knock and, most times, he'd just sit here with the door locked. But then other times he'd throw it open and have everybody in. Painters, sculptors, novelists, poets and playwrights, philosophers and students on a spree all rubbing shoulders with the routine drunkards.

MARIKA: *(Pointing to the painting of the* Back Room *on the wall)* Was one of them responsible for this?

JOHAN: All the paintings are by men who drank here.

MARIKA: *(Examining the painting)* This must be a version of the Chamber of Debauchery itself. It's signed "Jansen."

JOHAN: Karl Jansen, yes.

MARIKA: Should I have heard of him?

JOHAN: I don't suppose so. He died two years ago out in the front room, in a fit of delirium tremens.

MARIKA: *(Dismissing the painting)* No loss to his movement. How would *you* paint this room?

JOHAN: Who, I? No particular way. *(Swimming)* In browns and grays with—I don't know, perspective so it looked like three dimensions . . . how would you?

MARIKA: I wouldn't.

JOHAN: I mean if you hadn't stopped painting.

MARIKA: I *have* stopped painting.

JOHAN: So you told me at the gallery. You didn't tell me why. Was it because a woman couldn't build up a career—what you said before?

MARIKA: That might have stopped me if I hadn't had another reason.

JOHAN: What?

MARIKA: The night that Ossian proposed to me, he said we'd have to make a bargain. I'd stop painting and he wouldn't start writing again.

JOHAN: Did you want him to stop writing?

MARIKA: He'd already stopped before we met.

JOHAN: What kind of bargain was he offering, then?

MARIKA: One I found acceptable.

JOHAN: But, Marika, your work was brilliant.

MARIKA: You all thought so at the Institute.

JOHAN: No one was even close to you. You knew how good you were.

MARIKA: I had a strong suspicion. I didn't really know until Ossian asked me to stop. He only saw my paintings once. He'd been working for my father for a year. One night he came to supper and we met. After that he called quite often. He was gracious and polite and very charming. One evening he came back to my studio next to my room. He looked at my self-portraits and the series I'd done of the storms on the skerries.

JOHAN: I remember those.

MARIKA: Ossian stared at the self-portraits. A look came on his face I'd never seen before. He was terrified. Two days later he proposed to me and asked me if I'd give up painting. At first I thought that he was testing me to see how much I cared for him. He wasn't testing. I'd really have to stop, as he'd stopped writing. If his books hadn't had their terrible corrosive power, he could have peacefully continued writing, just as you've continued painting. But he'd had to stop and so would I. That's when I knew that my painting was good.

JOHAN: And that's when you renounced it.

MARIKA: Yes.

JOHAN: Marika—excuse me if I make a little speech. You've probably guessed that I spend more time in the museums and the galleries than standing at my easel.

MARIKA: *(Picking up a small mauve vase that is lying on the table)* Was this Ossian's, do you suppose?

JOHAN: I don't know. What I'm saying is, I love to look at paintings that I couldn't do myself. I'm glad they're in the world. I feel it as a loss—I feel it as a loss to me—that you're not painting anymore. That's all.

MARIKA: That's a very generous sentiment. But it's really not my problem, is it?

JOHAN: Don't you miss painting?

MARIKA: I don't actually know. I might be here to find out some part of the answer. *(Still examining the vase)* Ossian likes to gather mountain violets for our parlor. I wouldn't think that flowers could survive in here.

JOHAN: Have you found out the answer?

MARIKA: Not yet. *(Deliberately, she drops the vase, which smashes loudly)*

JOHAN: Marika!

MARIKA: Butterfingers.

JOHAN: You did that on purpose!

MARIKA: *(Not condescending to dissemble)* Oh, dear. The famous Malachi won't come, I hope.

JOHAN: Of course he'll come. There goes my job, right out the window!

MARIKA: You've done nothing wrong.

JOHAN: Tell him that!

MARIKA: I will. He can't be such an ogre as you say he is.

JOHAN: He's such an ogre as you can't imagine.

MARIKA: I can't imagine how I'd paint this room. I can't imagine how Ossian lived here. All right, then, now I'll meet a man I can't imagine.

MALACHI: *(Bursts through the door)* What's going on in here? *(He is a bristling old man in his seventies, twisted with malice, without a drop of moisture in his scaly skin from head to foot. He wears black trousers and shoes and a cutaway coat; their formality combined with their filthy condition is a calculated insult to his customers)*

JOHAN: It's just me, Malachi.

MALACHI: *(Eyeballing Marika)* It's just you, is it? What's this, then? Your left foot, perhaps? Or your left testicle?

JOHAN: She's no one you should talk that way in front of.

MALACHI: Should I talk that way on top of her?

JOHAN: You shouldn't talk that way at all.

MALACHI: Why shouldn't I?

JOHAN: This lady is—a lady.

MALACHI: Oh, a *lady*.

MARIKA: Yes, a lady. What's more, she isn't deaf, so you can speak to her directly.

MALACHI: May I really take that liberty?

MARIKA: You may, till I revoke it.

MALACHI: Well, then. *May* I see your papers?

JOHAN: Oh, no, Malachi . . .

MARIKA: Be quiet, Johan. *(To Malachi)* I don't know what papers you can mean.

MALACHI: I'm sure you're registered.

MARIKA: Registered where?

MALACHI: It *is* the law, you know.

MARIKA: The law, that I be registered? I've never heard of such a thing.

MALACHI: It really works to your advantage. You get free treatment when you need it. In the course of your profession you must need it fairly often.

JOHAN: You don't know who you're talking to!

MALACHI: I don't care who I'm talking to. What is she doing in the Back Room?

JOHAN: This is Mrs. Ossian Borg! *(To Marika)* Tell him!

MARIKA: That's right. Ossian Borg is my husband.

MALACHI: *(Despite himself is taken aback)* You're Ossian's wife?

MARIKA: Since he's my husband, that's right, I'm his wife. The two things go together.

MALACHI: Well, well, well. That's not an answer to my question. What I asked was what you're doing here. But still— Ossian's wife. That's really very interesting. I *can* have you arrested, though.

MARIKA: Can you? I'm not arguing the point, I'm only curious. On what charge?

MALACHI: Even if you weren't back here, if you'd just come into the tavern with no escort . . .

JOHAN: I'm her escort.

MALACHI: You're not anybody's escort. You're my waiter.

JOHAN: I conducted Mrs. Borg here.

MALACHI: Well, I can't deny that's interesting as well. If I pressed charges, would you say that in a court of law? Would the lady want you to? Excuse me for thinking out loud. I'm just considering the options that you've handed me. I always like to think what I could do if I decided to. It gives me many happy hours.

MARIKA: I'm sure it does. Consider all the things that you could do. For example, you could die. I'm sure you're old enough.

MALACHI: I'm too old. If I'd ever planned on dying, I'd have done so long ago.

MARIKA: I'm perfectly willing to fight with you. It would help me to know why we're fighting, however. It can't be because I've stirred up the vermin in your storeroom.

MALACHI: Why have you come here?

MARIKA: I'm not sure I know myself.

MALACHI: Let's have no evasive answers.

MARIKA: I don't give evasive answers. If I don't want to answer a question, I don't answer it. I'll say more, though, if you wish to hear it.

MALACHI: Be so kind.

MARIKA: I know I've come here looking for my husband. I'm beginning to suspect I'm also looking for myself, or for a self I've put aside. Is that direct enough?

MALACHI: I can tell you about *Ossian.* There is a price.

MARIKA: I don't take charity. What is it?

MALACHI: That you stoop to taste a sample of my stocks. Perhaps some wine, or something stronger.

JOHAN: *(Eagerly, to Malachi)* Can I get the lady something?

MARIKA: Your employer has stopped using the third person in my presence. I'd prefer it if you'd stop as well.

MALACHI: *(To Johan, as he checks his watch)* You're not on duty for ten minutes. And besides—*(To Marika)* third person, please excuse me—*(To Johan)* Mrs. Borg might not be comfortable alone with me.

MARIKA: I'm comfortable with either of you, thank you very much.

MALACHI: I insist on serving you myself. What can I offer you?

MARIKA: Why not an "Ossian Borg"?

MALACHI: *(With a glance toward Johan)* You've heard about our tourist trade? It's pretty well played out now, I'm afraid. You understand our so-called absinthe . . .

MARIKA: Isn't absinthe, yes, I know. That's quite all right.

MALACHI: And, Johan, what for you?

JOHAN: For me. . . ?

MALACHI: Don't inhale your tongue. I can't have you strangling before you start your shift.

JOHAN: Well . . . I'll have an "Ossian Borg" myself.

MALACHI: Two "Ossian Borgs" coming up. *(To Johan)* Clear Mrs. Borg a place, you noodle! Do you mean to keep her standing up all evening? *(Tossing him a white cloth from his belt)* Dust down the table and give her a chair! She's our particular guest! *(He exits)*

MARIKA: There, you see? You didn't lose your job. In fact, he's pleased with you for bringing me. Have you discussed me with him?

JOHAN: I've told him that we went to school together, and I've said how well you paint . . .

MARIKA: How well I used to paint.

JOHAN: I've only just found out you'd stopped . . .

MARIKA: Shouldn't you clear off the table before he comes back?

JOHAN: *(Going into action)* Oh, yes, I'd better, thanks. *(He kicks a piece of the vase and stoops to pick it up)*

MARIKA: I broke the vase. I'll clean it up.

JOHAN: No, that's all right.

MARIKA: I'll do it. Clear the table.

JOHAN: *(Lifting broken chairs, stools, and small tables off the big table)* Malachi should put all this out back for the dustman to carry away. Instead he dumps it here.

MARIKA: He's right to dump it here. It suits the room. *(Examining a shard of the smashed vase)* Violet is Ossian's favorite color. I'm sure this vase was his. I'm going to keep a piece. What shall I do with the rest?

JOHAN: *(Indicating a pile of refuse left)* Throw it there. All right now, hold your breath. I'm going to dust the table. *(Marika takes out a handkerchief and covers her mouth and nose. Johan pelts the table with the white cloth, raising suffocating clouds of ancient dust. Coughing, he completes his task, wiping the surface as clean as he can)* The front room is almost as filthy as this one. Most tavern keepers put out salted biscuits so their customers stay thirsty. Malachi leaves layers of dust for his. *(Malachi has come in and heard the last of this. An uncomfortable moment for Johan. Malachi is carrying a small tray with two drinks on it—liqueur glasses filled with a crystal-clear liquor)*

MALACHI: Here we are, then. Have you made our guest comfortable, Johan? Seat her where her husband used to sit. *(Johan places a chair for Marika as indicated; dusts it off and holds it as Marika sits. Malachi serves her drink, which she will scarcely touch. To Johan, setting down his drink)* You can sit opposite. *(To Marika)* If I may sit with you, I'll set a chair right here. *(He does so, as Johan seats himself. Malachi has a second cloth with which he dusts down his own chair before sitting)* Ossian always locked the door whenever he was in here. I had a key, however, and the privilege of entering at will. I didn't even have to knock. There were no secrets between Ossian and me. You don't mind if I call him Ossian, incidentally?

MARIKA: If he allowed you to, it's not for me to quarrel.

MALACHI: No, it's not.

MARIKA: You think you knew my husband.

MALACHI: I knew Ossian. I know him still.

MARIKA: Tell me how he first came here.

MALACHI: He came alone, one midnight. He told me he'd been drinking for ten hours and I said he was a liar. Men with blue skin on their necks can't hold more liquor than a squirrel. I told him, "If you've come here to get drunk, show me your money and we'll get to work." He'd been drinking wine. I guessed that brandy ought to be his drink. Not right, but near enough for starters. Before too long, he'd shown me why he wanted to be drunk, or to believe that he was drunk. He had some things to say no sober man could listen to, not even from himself.

MARIKA: You listened, though.

MALACHI: Of course I listened. I'm a barkeep.

MARIKA: What did Ossian say?

MALACHI: He talked about his father—or the man he swore was *not* his father. You know what he said. It's in his first book.

JOHAN: She's never read his first book.

MARIKA: Tell me *how* he talked.

MALACHI: In every slanderous sentence he uttered, you could taste how he depended on the old professor, both financially and otherwise. Does he need you very badly? If he does, take care. That puts him in a very weak position. He'll exact revenge.

MARIKA: Is that a friendly warning or a threat?

MALACHI: There's no reason I should threaten you, but I'm not friendly either, so I'd say it's neither one.

MARIKA: Get back to Ossian.

MALACHI: In my young years, when I was working at the Grand Hotel, I served men who, just with words, could change how people saw the world. Ossian had that power, or the spark of it. I saw that right away. That first night it was very faint, though. By the time he'd drunk enough to free his feelings, his tongue had turned to muck. I'd gotten the prescription wrong. The next night, when he came back, I'd figured out his drink.

JOHAN: Absinthe.

MALACHI: Not this sugar-water, though. The real poison.

JOHAN: *(Of his anisette)* I'm enjoying this.

MALACHI: I wouldn't serve it to a *woman*. *(Graciously, to Marika)* Except, of course, at her request.

MARIKA: What did the wormwood do for Ossian?

MALACHI: It helped him see the good professor's kindness as the folly of a doting cuckold. Ossian's mother had died—as Ossian saw it—just to spite them both. From that time on, the widower forwent his every comfort to cram Ossian with learning. Half the languages of Europe were dunned into him. Old Borg set back his own career to take a puny post in Germany, then one in France, to help the boy master those languages. However cramped and insect-ridden Ossian's room was, the professor's was always filthier and smaller. Now they'd come back to Sweden. At the age of twenty-three, Ossian was about to reap the harvest of the old man's years of sacrifice: a triple doctorate from the University of Stockholm. In all that time, the man had asked for nothing. But Ossian knew what he owed, and he knew he didn't have it.

MARIKA: That was . . .?

MALACHI: Gratitude. No man feels a debt like a man who can never repay it. Every night, out in the front room, Ossian labored at his libels, going over them and over them—revising them, I came to see, like chapters in a novel. At last his picture of the old man grew so rank that Ossian couldn't live with him. I offered Ossian the Back Room. I'd give him food. I'd give him absinthe. When his mind was racing faster than his hand could write, I'd take dictation for him. My one condition was that what he spoke here, what he wrote here, was my property, lock stock and barrel. I could profit by it any way I saw the chance.

MARIKA: Did he know you meant to have it published?

MALACHI: Of course he knew. How else would he take revenge on everyone—most cruelly on himself? I only stole what Ossian threw away. I'm as honest a man as you'll find in this world.

MARIKA: You've gotten rich off his writings, while old Mr. Borg has been shamed into exile. He's back teaching at that miserable school in Bonn.

MALACHI: Ossian's second book was just as hard on me.

MARIKA: You get the royalties, however, and the tourist trade.

MALACHI: They don't amount to much, now that the flurry's died down. But I somehow feel, this evening, that things could pick up very quickly. In the meantime, I'm not destitute. If you'll empty your glass I can fill it again.

MARIKA: I find that I don't care for anisette.

JOHAN: *(Rising)* I can fetch you something else.

MARIKA: What time is it?

JOHAN: Twenty-five minutes to six.

MARIKA: Ossian's nearly due home from the office. I like to be there when he comes.

MALACHI: Johan! You call yourself an escort. Ask your friend to stay awhile longer.

JOHAN: I'd love it if she stayed, but if she has to go . . .

MARIKA: Third person again. That's a truly irksome habit that you both should break.

MALACHI: I shouldn't scold you, Johan, when I've been remiss myself. Mrs. Borg has asked for something and I've brought her a poor substitute.

MARIKA: You brought me what I asked for.

MALACHI: You asked for an "Ossian Borg," and you deserve the real thing. We were ordered to destroy our stocks, but I held onto mine.

JOHAN: You've kept real absinthe here?

MALACHI: *(Takes a key from his pocket and tosses it to Johan)* I thought it might prove useful. Open that box there. The one with iron bands around it.

JOHAN: *(Finding a small, sturdy wooden crate among the rubble to the left)* This one?

MALACHI: That one. *(Johan puts the key into the crate's large padlock. It snaps open with a sound like the report of a pistol. He opens the lid and removes an ancient-looking bottle)* Hand it here. *(Johan gives him the bottle)* The key, too. *(Johan returns the key, which Malachi pockets)*

MARIKA: So that's absinthe, then.

MALACHI: *(Looking proudly at his precious contraband)* The medicine of choice for Ossian Borg. It transformed what in another man would be suspicion, envy, jaundice, into vision. It made the shames that he experienced as resonant as holy revelations. It forced him to give voice to what he knew. It showed him he was set about with enemies and had to fight them off by naming and exposing them.

MARIKA: The wormwood gave him phantom foes to grapple with?

MALACHI: Not phantoms. His dead mother, the professor —who's to say they *weren't* his enemies? All of us are threatened by the people we depend on. They have us at their mercy, and they know it very well. The sentimentalists among us hope their loved ones won't abuse their power. Ossian knew better. With the help of the wormwood, he wrote what he knew.

MARIKA: Does he know less now that he doesn't drink wormwood?

MALACHI: What he knows, he knows—he can't know less. But he can know the same things less disruptively. He can know but not let knowing determine the course of his life. Ossian's stopped writing. He's gotten married. That's the life he's chosen, for the present. Have you made a choice? Are you equipped to make a choice? Do you know your alternatives? *(He has extended the bottle an inch or so towards her)*

MARIKA: Your wormwood wouldn't give me new alternatives.

MALACHI: No, but it would bring the old ones out. It would show you who your husband is. Isn't that the knowledge that you've come to seek?

MARIKA: I have enemies. I know I have. I don't need to drug myself to feel their hatred. You're my enemy.

MALACHI: I take that as a compliment.

MARIKA: You may. It is a compliment. Johan, for example, is my friend.

JOHAN: I hope so, Marika.

MARIKA: You are. But your employer knows that friends are paltry things compared to enemies.

MALACHI: Is Ossian your friend?

MARIKA: I'd hardly call my husband paltry.

MALACHI: It's for such as you that absinthe was distilled. Think of it seeping through the charcoal, clear as crystal, and then turning faintly greenish as the oil of wormwood started bleeding in.

MARIKA: Ossian is due home. He lives according to the clock, and that makes sense to me, and more sense now I've seen the way he used to live.

MALACHI: Johan, get her to stay.

JOHAN: How can I if she wants to leave?

MALACHI: You'd best persuade her. It's your job if you don't.

MARIKA: I'm going, but don't worry, Johan. If I hear you've lost your job because of me—or for any other reason—I'll report your boss for keeping back contraband liquor.

JOHAN: *(To Marika)* You don't have to . . .

MARIKA: I say this much for Malachi's own good. You're an excellent waiter, I'm sure. I wouldn't want to think he'd lost you on account of me. After all, aren't he and I the best of enemies? *(She goes unhurriedly out the door, leaving it open behind her)*

MALACHI: *(With sudden violence slams his hand on the table)* Damnation!

JOHAN: What's the matter?

MALACHI: What's the matter? You idiot, I wanted her to stay here!

JOHAN: Why? Before you found us, I was scared you'd fire me for bringing her.

MALACHI: I ought to. She says I can't fire you. All right, I'll put you back to running errands. You've got Axel's job.

JOHAN: Axel's job? What about Axel?

MALACHI: Axel's through. I'm getting rid of him.

JOHAN: What for?

MALACHI: *(Putting the bottle of absinthe back in the crate and snapping shut the padlock)* Because he didn't deliver my note in time. He dawdled on the way. I told him Ossian would leave his office punctually.

JOHAN: You sent Axel with a note for Mr. Borg?

MALACHI: That's what I just said.

JOHAN: What was in this note?

MALACHI: I told Ossian his wife was in the Back Room with a young man.

JOHAN: You suggested . . .

MALACHI: I suggested nothing. I told him the state of affairs.

JOHAN: All right, he didn't come, though, did he? He must not have believed you.

MALACHI: He didn't get the message. He'd believe me. Ossian knows that I don't lie.

JOHAN: How would he know such a thing as that?

MALACHI: I don't lie. You probably haven't noticed. You assume malicious people must be liars. But I've found the truth is much more damaging than any falsehood, so I always speak with perfect honesty. Ossian knows that.

JOHAN: But he hasn't come.

MALACHI: Axel must have stopped to have a pastry. I'll have his hide. You'll have his job.

JOHAN: I don't want his job.

MALACHI: I don't want his hide, but he does, so I'll have it. I did stretch one point in the note. I said the young man was a painter. That's more than an exaggeration. Yes, I must admit, that just may be an outright lie.

JOHAN: It just may be.

MALACHI: But it should have brought Ossian running. It would have. Axel dawdled.

JOHAN: Axel wouldn't dawdle. Axel's too afraid of you to dawdle.

MALACHI: Ossian would have come. I can't be wrong. I'm *not* wrong. I know Ossian. Why isn't he here? *(A man's voice*

—incisive and arresting—is heard through the open doorway; we can't see the speaker)

VOICE: I am here, Malachi. You're not wrong. *(Ossian Borg appears in the doorway. He is twenty-nine, and dressed in frigidly correct dark clothes: a suit with vest and ribbon tie. Only his thick mane of hair, refusing to be tamed, betrays the wildness in the man)* You do know me, to my everlasting shame.

MALACHI: Hello, Ossian.

OSSIAN: Don't call me Ossian. Call me Mr. Borg.

MALACHI: You've just missed Mrs. Borg.

OSSIAN: When your message came I went straight home. She's always there to greet me.

MALACHI: Not tonight.

OSSIAN: No, not tonight.

JOHAN: You must have passed her on the way here, Mr. Borg. She was heading for your house to meet you.

OSSIAN: *(To Malachi)* Who is this? *(To Johan)* You're not by any chance a painter?

JOHAN: If you stretch a point.

OSSIAN: I haven't stretched a point in years. I made a practice of it once, when I was writing. I've reformed. Writing didn't only rob me of all self-respect—it put me in the company of painters. *(Without taking his eyes off Johan)* Malachi, get out of here.

MALACHI: Delighted, Mr. Borg. You have a right to turn me out, of course. This room is yours. So is the larder. I assume you've missed your supper. Would you like a chop?

OSSIAN: I'd like to see your back.

MALACHI: Will you have a drink, then?

OSSIAN: I'll have your last remaining twitch of life if you don't quit my sight!

MALACHI: *(Clearing his tray and Johan's glass)* I'm always glad to offer all support.

OSSIAN: *(To Malachi)* What's your painter's name?

JOHAN: My name is Johan Ekdahl, Mr. Borg. I'm a waiter here.

MALACHI: You'll want privacy. I'll close the door behind me. *(He exits, doing so)*

JOHAN: Mr. Borg, I met your wife by accident this afternoon. A former fellow-student had a show—we'd been all three at the Institute together. When I told your wife I worked here, she asked if I could show her the Back Room, which she was curious to

see—because of you, of course—well, why else? She was curious
to see it—Mr. Borg.

OSSIAN: You knew my wife before I met her.

JOHAN: At the Institute, that's right, sir. We were classmates.

OSSIAN: Back before I'd ever seen her, and before she'd ever
seen me.

JOHAN: I think she'd graduated, sir, before she'd met you. I
believe that's right.

OSSIAN: Are you a sapper and a miner, Johan?

JOHAN: Sir?

OSSIAN: Do you dig holes and plant explosives?

JOHAN: No.

OSSIAN: You've run a tunnel underneath my marriage, though,
isn't that so?

JOHAN: No, sir, that isn't so. I haven't.

OSSIAN: You knew my wife before I knew her. Nobody
should have known my wife before I did. Nobody should have
known me before she did. Don't you think that's the best basis for
a marriage?

JOHAN: Ideally I guess it is. But it hardly ever happens, does
it? It *couldn't* happen. There's the parents, in the first place.

OSSIAN: Yes, her father. He's got the jump on me, and don't
you think he doesn't know it.

JOHAN: I didn't really know your wife that well.

OSSIAN: You knew her. More importantly, she knew you.

JOHAN: She never really paid me any mind, to speak of.

OSSIAN: You say so, but you could be lying, couldn't you? Or
you could be mistaken. It's a subject for conjecture. Happily, I
don't conjecture anymore. I translate business letters—Swedish
into French and German, French and German into Swedish. I
improve on the originals in both directions. That's all the writing I
do now.

JOHAN: There's nothing to conjecture about Mrs. Borg and me.

OSSIAN: There's always something to conjecture. You're a
painter. Is there ever not something to look at?

JOHAN: No, but looking's not conjecturing.

OSSIAN: Painting is.

JOHAN: No, Mr. Borg. You just paint what you see.

OSSIAN: You look past what you see to what you know to be
behind it and you paint that. Else why paint at all?

JOHAN: Your wife's stopped painting.

OSSIAN: That's right. In the name of simple decency.

JOHAN: I paint. Is that indecent of me?

OSSIAN: Not if you're completely without talent, as I'd guess you are.

JOHAN: What's talent got to do with it?

OSSIAN: A painter, or a writer, uses the people around him. The more talented he is, the more cruelly he exposes them. He strips the skin off his nearest and dearest, then offers the skin up for sale. He vivisects people like rabbits. He cuts the tail off his dog, eats the flesh, and gives the dog the bone to chew. What could be more loathsome?

JOHAN: He exposes himself too, doesn't he?

OSSIAN: He exposes himself most shamefully of all. That's hardly compensation to the people he humiliates. I wrote two novels in this room.

JOHAN: I know.

OSSIAN: Of course you know. Everybody knows, to my disgrace. The first one showed a father and his son—his wife's son—in a wretched symbiosis. It revealed the old man's martyrdom as the cramped manipulations of a crippled weasel. At the same time, it revealed the child's ingratitude as no less vicious. No quarter. No prisoners. Art in full deadly career, scything all before it into severed limbs and torsos.

JOHAN: I'm happy I'm not talented, if that's what happens.

OSSIAN: So you should be.

JOHAN: Your wife is very talented.

OSSIAN: Of course she is. If she'd been a dabbler like you, she could have gone on painting till the earth ran out of pigment.

JOHAN: You stopped her, though.

OSSIAN: She stopped herself. Her motives were the same as mine had been. Of course, there'd been some damage done already. My books were in print and some people had ogled her self-portraits.

JOHAN: They were staggering.

OSSIAN: No one but I should have seen them, and not even I. Not even Marika herself should have seen them. You surely shouldn't have. Better I should find you back here drinking with her.

JOHAN: Your wife and I drank absinthe in your honor.

OSSIAN: Absinthe?

JOHAN: Anisette. Real absinthe has been outlawed.

OSSIAN: Yes, I know. Quite rightly, too. Did you sit in my place, or was this glass Marika's?

JOHAN: That glass was hers.

OSSIAN: She hardly touched it.

JOHAN: She took a taste.

OSSIAN: It looks as thin as water. Absinthe used to swell with winding layers of greenish oil ready to suck at your tongue like a harlot.

JOHAN: There's some absinthe in that crate.

OSSIAN: Not real absinthe?

JOHAN: Yes.

OSSIAN: With wormwood?

JOHAN: Yes, sir. Malachi's illegal stock.

OSSIAN: I should have known he'd keep some back. One of the notes he sent me hinted that he had. It had been a grace to think there wasn't any wormwood left in Sweden—like dreaming that this room had caught on fire and burned to cinders. Do you have the key?

JOHAN: No. Malachi.

OSSIAN: The Provider. If I drank a glass of wormwood, I might find out how you met my wife.

JOHAN: I've told you.

OSSIAN: You've told me too much and nothing at all.

JOHAN: I've told you all there is to tell.

OSSIAN: You've said you met at school, without my introducing you.

JOHAN: We met before you knew each other!

OSSIAN: Don't you see that only makes it worse? You were able to impress yourself on Marika before I'd even come into the picture. One person's consciousness has only so much space for unalloyed impressions. That space is filled early in life, before the gestures of the face have carved their creases. My image in Marika's mind lies over images of people she knew earlier. A former image might one day bleed through, and where will I be then?

JOHAN: I've told you Marika paid no attention to me.

OSSIAN: No attention to you?

JOHAN: None.

OSSIAN: What teachers did you both hate?

JOHAN: *(Automatically)* Mr. Elstad . . . how did you know? Does she still talk about him?

OSSIAN: There always is one teacher all the students hate. He's usually the best.

JOHAN: Mr. Elstad was a rotten teacher. He taught History of Art. When he explained a painting, I could hardly see the colors on the canvas for Elstad's description of them.

OSSIAN: Did you and Marika make fun of Mr. Elstad?

JOHAN: He had a stupid moustache. It stuck straight out sideways like the bristles on a pig. Marika said it would have made a fine pair of brushes.

OSSIAN: Did she?

JOHAN: Oh, she hated Mr. Elstad.

OSSIAN: Where were you when she joked about his moustache?

JOHAN: Where? I don't remember that.

OSSIAN: Of course you do. Think back. Were you at school?

JOHAN: Well, most likely we probably were.

OSSIAN: Only probably? Then you might have both been some-place else.

JOHAN: We might have.

OSSIAN: Where?

JOHAN: I don't know. What does it matter?

OSSIAN: It's grist for the mill.

JOHAN: What grist for what mill?

OSSIAN: You're hiding something, Johan.

JOHAN: No I'm not. I don't have anything to hide.

OSSIAN: Then tell me. Where did Marika make this moustache joke to you about poor Mr. Elstad?

JOHAN: *(Concentrates a moment)* I don't think she made it just to me. I think she might have made it to a group of us.

OSSIAN: A group of students?

JOHAN: *("Yes")* All of us clustered around her when she talked down the teachers. She'd get really very nasty.

OSSIAN: Where did all you students cluster, if not at the Institute?

JOHAN: Well, sometimes we'd go visit the museums together. Sometimes we'd go to the shore.

OSSIAN: The shore?

JOHAN: The beach, yes. During lunch, or in the evening.

OSSIAN: In the evening?

JOHAN: When the sun stayed out, in summer.

OSSIAN: On Midsummer Evening?

JOHAN: Maybe so. I don't remember.

OSSIAN: That's when the sun stays out the longest.

JOHAN: Yes, I think we all went to the shore together one year on Midsummer Evening. When our last class was dismissed, we all trooped over.

OSSIAN: Did you stay all night?

JOHAN: I stayed all night. There were bonfires and dancing on the sand.

OSSIAN: Some of the others stayed all night, too?

JOHAN: I think most of them.

OSSIAN: Did Marika stay?

JOHAN: I don't remember if she stayed till morning. She stayed pretty late. *(Explanatorily)* Midsummer Evening.

OSSIAN: It won't offend you if I drink from my wife's glass?

JOHAN: Of course not.

OSSIAN: If you drank from it, that would offend me very deeply. *(He sniffs the glass of anisette)* Your pseudo-absinthe smells invisible, just as it looks. *(He drinks. Disapprovingly)* It tastes like licorice.

JOHAN: I like having the taste come from something that's clear. It's almost magical.

OSSIAN: If I think the wormwood into it—the taste like blackened sulfur from a burnt match—maybe we can manage our Midsummer Night. Now—we have a group of students, all clustered around Marika.

JOHAN: That wasn't on Midsummer Night, though. At least, I don't remember that it was.

OSSIAN: *(Ignoring Johan's cavil, sips his drink, as he will continue to do at intervals)* Gradually the group got smaller, didn't it? The students fell away in couples. There were Marika and you, and there were others, fewer and fewer as time went by. They fell away in couples.

JOHAN: *(Assents, as he comes under the influence of the picture Ossian is developing)* It was Midsummer Night.

OSSIAN: You didn't fall away, though, did you?

JOHAN: I fell away.

OSSIAN: You fell away with Marika—and left the last few stragglers standing, young men and women making an odd number, a sad little number.

JOHAN: I didn't leave with Marika. I left alone, to walk along the water.

OSSIAN: And left Marika alone.

JOHAN: She was alone quite often. Yes, I think I see her standing up the bank a little way, alone.

OSSIAN: You'd been alone together, then, before you left.

JOHAN: She was comfortable with me. I wasn't jealous of her talent like the others.

OSSIAN: She stayed all alone while you went down to walk along the shore.

JOHAN: She liked to stand among the trees. She did a painting of them once—several paintings.

OSSIAN: She liked it there among the shadows.

JOHAN: Yes.

OSSIAN: What else?

JOHAN: What else?

OSSIAN: There's more.

JOHAN: There's more what?

OSSIAN: There's more to the picture.

JOHAN: That's all I can remember. It's *more* than I remember.

OSSIAN: *(Begins filling the vacuum)* There's the Midsummer sun. You must remember that. The sun rode sideways until, right around eleven, it eased into the ocean at an angle almost flat with the horizon. The radiance it left behind bled softly through the sky above the skerries and across the beach and up the wooded incline where she stood. She was alone. And then he came back.

JOHAN: Who came back?

OSSIAN: The young man.

JOHAN: Wait a minute. What young man?

OSSIAN: The painter. She was standing on the hillside by the shore and he came back.

JOHAN: Who was this painter? Was he me?

OSSIAN: Her fellow student.

JOHAN: And her fellow student's name was what?

OSSIAN: His name was Johan.

JOHAN: Mr. Borg, this story isn't true. You know that, don't you?

OSSIAN: What?

JOHAN: This story isn't true.

OSSIAN: Why not?

JOHAN: Why not? It isn't, that's all. I just isn't.

OSSIAN: Because it didn't happen?

JOHAN: Right, because it didn't happen.

OSSIAN: Aristotle knew two thousand years ago that history is inferior to poetry. History, he said, is just what happened. Poetry is what happens.

JOHAN: I didn't go to Marika on any hillside by the water.

OSSIAN: Why didn't you?

JOHAN: I *didn't*.

OSSIAN: But you might have.

JOHAN: No!

OSSIAN: Why mightn't you?

JOHAN: No reason, but . . .

OSSIAN: Why mightn't you have been a man of talent, even genius, a man whose will was just as strong as Marika's? You weren't, but that was purely accidental, just a random fact. It says nothing about anything. It doesn't help us fathom what the world is like.

JOHAN: I'm not a man of genius and I never was.

OSSIAN: You're like a cork that slips down in the bottle when I try to pop it out. Go get Malachi.

JOHAN: All right, I will, but . . .

OSSIAN: I don't want to hear you anymore. You've given me all that I needed.

JOHAN: Mr. Borg, I'm not the Johan in this fantasy.

OSSIAN: You're not, no. You're not worthy of yourself. You lack your own dimensions. I can't correct that with you standing here in front of me. Fetch Malachi and don't come back.

JOHAN: *(Starting out)* I'll go. Just so you know . . .

OSSIAN: I won't know what I don't *believe*. Don't bother me with facts. They lie like algae on a lake. I want the close green depths to swim in—or to drown in, as the case may be. Vanish. Send in Malachi.

JOHAN: *(At the door)* I'm gone, but . . .

OSSIAN: You *are* gone. You're not there. Don't say another word. You're on the shore. Midsummer Evening. *(He empties his glass at a gulp and pays no further attention to the literal Johan)* You're walking up the hillside from the beach with slow firm steps. You come to Marika, whose face, though it's addressed to you, seems not to see you. It's as if she heard you with her eyes. The color of her eyes has darkened, getting deeper in their fear of getting deeper which then makes them deeper still and still more fearful, then still deeper . . . *(Johan makes to speak)* You won't make another sound. You'll disappear and send in Malachi. *(Johan has only the strength of will to hesitate before silently obeying. He goes out and softly shuts the door behind him. Ossian moves to the case of absinthe and grasps it with both hands as if tasting the wormwood through contact with the crate. His nails scrape the wood. Malachi comes in. Without moving, not even looking at Malachi)* Did you bring pen and paper?

MALACHI: They're where we've always kept them. *(He opens a drawer in the table and takes out some paper, a pen and a bottle of ink)*

OSSIAN: Is our contract there, too?

MALACHI: We never drew one up. Not in writing. The commitment that we made was verbal.

OSSIAN: I'd have sworn there was a document, with my signature in blood.

MALACHI: Blood flakes and falls away. Paper turns to powder. Our agreement lives.

OSSIAN: Open one bottle. I want to see the color, if it still looks like a patina of tarnish on old silver. *(Malachi opens the lock, which makes the same violent snap as before, opens the box and lifts out a bottle. Ossian listens but he doesn't watch. Malachi breaks the seal and opens the bottle)* The glass is still damp from the substitute. Pour half an inch to rinse out the nothingness. *(Malachi puts a small amount of absinthe in Ossian's glass. Ossian holds it to the light)* The real green. A half-inch, deep as all the oceans. *(He swirls the liquor around in the glass, then flicks it broadcast over the table)* Will that lay the dust? The room remembers. The ceiling's lowering to concentrate the fumes. The walls are closing in a little—just three inches, three or maybe four, or maybe only two. There were nights when it pressed in the size of a coffin. *(He breathes in the bouquet of the empty glass)*

MALACHI: Shall I fill your glass?

OSSIAN: *(Makes a sign that he shouldn't. Malachi sets down the bottle)* I've always heard that the muses descended, but it isn't so. I've descended. You've stayed where you were.

MALACHI: So you could find me.

OSSIAN: *(Still without looking at Malachi, starts to speak. Malachi sits and takes down what Ossian dictates)* The air among the trees was full of hovering pockets of warmth. One seemed to burst —the gentlest of explosions—against her ankle. It sent a shudder up along her leg. Midsummer Night, when the sun, even during the few hours it was set, left a softly swelling crest of light as hostage for its swift return. She and Johan walked together down the incline toward the water. Day in night. The sky carried the sun's pledge —the grains of light the sun had left behind it, like pollen in the air above a bursting field. The coastline wound away on both sides as the lovers reached the sand. There were bonfires blaring in the distance. All around them women danced in pairs. The women spun each other, leaning back. Their hair, like torch flames, swept soft circles, and their mouths were gaped in silent laughter. With Johan leading her at one unbroken pace, they waded to, then past, the water's edge. Now they had moved into another element, more mysterious than air or earth or fire. The water, like the air, was warm. She scarcely felt a change. Before she was aware of it, the ocean swirled around her softly as a swaddling cloth and sweetly as a shroud and she was floating, lost and floating . . . *(The door opens. Marika is standing there)*

MARIKA: Johan came and told me you were here. I should have guessed that Malachi had sent for you, and that this time you'd come.

MALACHI: Johan left his station without asking me? I'll have his guts for garters.

MARIKA: No you won't. He saw me to the front door, then he went his way.

MALACHI: You mean he's left for good, right in the middle of a shift?

MARIKA: That's right.

MALACHI: Just like the young scarperer, to quit before I had the chance to fire him.

MARIKA: Ossian, it's odd, you know. He took this job because you'd been here. Now you're back, he runs away.

OSSIAN: There's nothing odd about it. Some people recreate battles with chessmen on maps. But when a real war breaks out, you don't expect them to enlist.

MARIKA: From what he's told me, I assume you're back to stay.

OSSIAN: You haven't left me any choice.

MARIKA: If you don't have a choice, then it's because you never wanted one. You wanted to come back here.

OSSIAN: Did I?

MARIKA: Yes you did. You wanted me to force you to come back here.

OSSIAN: I suppose, then, I arranged your assignation with your lover?

MARIKA: There was no assignation. For my "lover," I must say Johan Ekdahl is a rather far-fetched candidate. He told me that you're glorifying him to make him fill the bill, but that will take some doing, won't it?

OSSIAN: It wasn't I who chose him. It was you. I think he'll fill the bill quite nicely.

MARIKA: He's told you I came here in search of you.

OSSIAN: Yes, what a shame you missed me. I was at the office. I thought you knew.

MARIKA: You were here in spirit. You've been here for months in spirit. Your body has been at the office or at home or on the streets between, hewing strictly to its schedule. Your spirit has been here. Do you think I haven't noticed?

OSSIAN: It isn't true, so how can you have noticed?

MARIKA: From your growing distaste for our life together. "Distaste" is much too weak a word. "Disgust" is better. "Nausea" is better still.

OSSIAN: I can't even guess what you mean.

MARIKA: All right, I'll tell you if you'll listen.

OSSIAN: I'll listen, but I warn you. What you say is your responsibility. What I hear is mine.

MARIKA: Why don't you hear what I tell you?

OSSIAN: I will. But once I've heard it, it belongs to me. Fair warning.

MARIKA: Fair warning. Will your landlord kindly leave us?

OSSIAN: Why?

MARIKA: I'd rather speak with you in private.

OSSIAN: I don't keep any secrets from Malachi. Whatever I discover at the basis of my life, I reveal to him exhaustively. Before long, all the world knows.

MARIKA: *(Looking at Malachi's papers)* You've begun another book.

OSSIAN: I've finished it.

MARIKA: You've finished it? How can you have finished it?

OSSIAN: Women misconceive artistic creation the same way they misconceive sexual union. A woman thinks the act of love should be like a massage, but in its purest form it ought to be a flash of lightning. My third novel is written. It's a vile thing, a tumor, a putrescence. I regret having brought it into being. But I had no choice. You'd killed me. I had to wash my body for the coffin.

MARIKA: When did you write this book? It isn't true. You've been losing me and I've been losing you—we've both been losing this third thing, our marriage. But you hadn't started writing.

OSSIAN: Malachi and I have only just set pen to paper, but the book is written. All the rest is just mechanics.

MARIKA: *(Waving a hand at Malachi)* And now this creature's going to reap whatever profit's in this new thing you've created.

OSSIAN: I've *recorded* it, and truly that's degenerate enough. But you've created it. You're the book's first mover and its subject.

MARIKA: Make Malachi get out of here. *(To Malachi)* Ossian will repeat to you, in due course, everything I say that compromises either me or him. You'll make your money, but for now get out.

OSSIAN: I don't know who you think should profit from the book. Should I? I should be flayed until the shirt falls off my back in strips, and then my skin. You have some claim to some part of the profits. Do you want them?

MARIKA: Come away with me where we can talk, or make him leave.

OSSIAN: Go on, Malachi.

MALACHI: *(To Marika, fawning, but with genuine respect)* May I bring you a glass? I'll just leave it and withdraw again. Your husband's using yours.

MARIKA: *(To Ossian)* Are you drinking wormwood?

OSSIAN: Not yet.

MALACHI: Let me bring you a glass.

MARIKA: Get out and stay out.

MALACHI: *(As he backs out of the room)* You remind me of the days when, half a century ago, I was a waiter at the Grand Hotel. It was a pleasure taking orders from people who knew how to give them. At your will, then . . . *(He goes softly through the door and closes it behind him)*

MARIKA: Ossian, I don't know if you remember, but you said some very silly things when you proposed to me. I was touched that such a brilliant man should talk so foolishly. It showed me that your heart was full. You said that, in the little house we'd have, the coffee grinder wouldn't rasp and growl. All coffee grinders rasp and growl, but ours would play sweet music. For these last months, though, you couldn't bear to hear me grind the coffee. The only way that you could stand the noise was to grind it yourself.

OSSIAN: You ground it *at* me.

MARIKA: No, I didn't. Why would I do that?

OSSIAN: I don't know yet. I'll find out the reason when I've written it.

MARIKA: In our first year and our second year, you came into my room sometimes to sit with me—not share my bed but just to sit while I combed out my hair or sewed garments that I couldn't take outside into the parlor. You stopped coming in.

OSSIAN: I showed more modesty on your behalf than you yourself. You ought to thank me.

MARIKA: You've made me learn to walk on eggshells. I used to live quite comfortably inside my body.

OSSIAN: Yes. Your comfort was cacophonous.

MARIKA: The quieter I got, the sharper you pricked up your ears. Should I thank you for that?

OSSIAN: Should I have slit my eardrums?

MARIKA: During our engagement, you wrote me that you longed to kiss my milk teeth. In the past few months you've seen they *weren't* my baby teeth. They're the teeth that I'll have till they drop from my head. I use these teeth to chew with. That revolts you. You can hardly bear to eat with me.

OSSIAN: I've never liked eating in company. Eating is a functional necessity, and not a pretty one.

MARIKA: You used to like to share your meals with me.

OSSIAN: I did at first. Then, later on, I didn't. I couldn't help my changing feelings—or returning feelings—little as I welcomed them. Still, I take responsibility for how I feel. You can't help it, any more than I can, that you have to eat, but nonetheless you have to be responsible. The world demeans us by giving us animal needs, but we demean ourselves still further if we fight shy of our guilt for them. To do so is undignified.

MARIKA: It's human.

OSSIAN: *(As if she'd made his point)* It's human. That's the perfect word.

MARIKA: My "humanness" is in your novel, I suppose. No doubt quite prominently.

OSSIAN: You know it has to be. It is there, if I'm foul enough to leave it in. It belongs there.

MARIKA: If you feel it belongs there, then you'll dose yourself with wormwood till you think I crunched my radishes and slurped my soup just to offend your sensibilities.

OSSIAN: You chewed at me. You swallowed at me.

MARIKA: No I didn't, Ossian.

OSSIAN: Maybe not. It's possible that someone might, though, isn't it? It wouldn't be against the laws of nature?

MARIKA: Someone might. I didn't.

OSSIAN: Then perhaps you didn't. Perhaps it wasn't you. I only know that it was Marika.

MARIKA: I'm Marika. Marika is my name and I claim it.

OSSIAN: It's been used by other people. I can use it too.

MARIKA: You can use the name. I can't prevent you. You can use me too. You will. I only want to know that you know there's a difference between Marika and "Marika." *(She has used herself to illustrate the first, Malachi's papers to illustrate the second)*

OSSIAN: The distinction doesn't interest me. It confuses me the way a pair of ears confuses hearing, the way a pair of eyes confuses sight. Think how a nose confuses smell. Surely the world's fragrances are better served by recreation in the mind than being snuffed up through a fungus on the face.

MARIKA: What's the Marika you're writing like?

OSSIAN: She's someone to be reckoned with. She's helpless. She's a liar.

MARIKA: I'm not a liar, Ossian.

OSSIAN: Marika's a walking lie.

MARIKA: She's your lie. She's your fiction.

OSSIAN: She's my fiction, yes, but not my lie. She's the world's lie, and my only truth. The deepest truth I'm learning.

MARIKA: I married you because I knew it wouldn't last. I loved you, but I knew it wouldn't last. I didn't want it to. That's why we haven't had children. You kept on saying we should wait until we'd saved more money, but that wasn't your real reason. You were terrified of art's destructive power, and you made a grand spasmodic gesture toward escaping from it. Look at who you married, though. An artist. One as gifted as yourself, whose addiction was as fatal. You knew we'd both go back.

OSSIAN: You went back. You came here with a painter. Before that you'd been to a gallery. That was your true infidelity. You were going back to painting.

MARIKA: I always knew, for years before I met you, that I'd have to marry someone. I didn't have the courage to throw off all the things that I'd been raised to want. I couldn't leave my father's house and forge into the world to paint. I couldn't have my inmost feelings scrutinized in public.

OSSIAN: Yes, the public. Their praise is as degrading as their mockery. They have the right to criticize, of course—the clay we mold in is their flesh. But, still, they stare and we can't turn away our faces.

MARIKA: I loved you and respected you, but underneath I knew you'd force me out into the open on my own, the former wife of the notorious Ossian Borg. You'd leave me nothing to protect from the ravages of my own talent. I'd be a painter by default. No one could blame me for a choice I hadn't made. I would have had no choice. And now it's come to pass. Half Europe's going to read your book. I'll be an outcast, only fit to stand outside the world, at my easel. You've forced me into freedom. Deep down I always knew that's what would happen. Ossian, you knew too. I want you to admit it. Then I'll leave you here with Malachi and "Marika."

OSSIAN: If you'd been someone else than who you are, we would have stayed together.

MARIKA: You knew who I was the day you saw my paintings.

OSSIAN: You promised to reform.

MARIKA: I couldn't, any more than you could, and you knew it. Can't you see that?

OSSIAN: In the Back Room, I invent what I see. I don't choose what to invent, though. I invent according to the world's laws. The world being what it is, what I invent is what no one would choose.

MARIKA: I'm beginning to see how I should paint this room. Perhaps I've painted it already. Yes, the painting's finished. I haven't dabbed the oils on the canvas yet, but that's just mechanics. Next I'm going to paint you.

OSSIAN: No. I paint myself. I'm matter for my pen, not for your brushes.

MARIKA: You're matter for my brushes if I'm matter for your pen. I'll be painting you for years to come—perhaps as often as I paint myself. We'll paint each other searchingly.

OSSIAN: And shamelessly. And pitilessly.

MARIKA: Yes.

OSSIAN: It isn't any worse than we deserve.

MARIKA: We're invulnerable, aren't we, in a certain way. For ordinary people, people like Johan, any suffering they undergo is suffering and nothing else. They have no alchemy to turn it to advantage.

OSSIAN: *(Fills her liqueur glass with wormwood and slides it toward her)* You'll want to try this if you're going to paint me.

MARIKA: I don't need to drink delusion.

OSSIAN: It will let you see more clearly. Paranoia's no distortion when it only shows the truth. I *am* your enemy, as you are mine. When we pledged ourselves one to the other, we struck a truce. We laid our weapons at each other's feet. Maybe we disarmed ourselves to save ourselves from suicide. In any case, we made peace. One makes peace with one's enemies, not with one's friends.

MARIKA: To you, then, Ossian. *(She drinks half the absinthe and hands him the glass)*

OSSIAN: To you. *(He finishes the glass and sets it down. Marika picks up her hat from the table)* May I take a feather from your hat? *(She hands him her hat. He pulls out a large feather and returns the hat. Marika goes out through the door, leaving it open. Ossian takes a penknife from his pocket, makes a quill pen of the feather and substitutes it for Malachi's pen, which he puts back into the drawer. Malachi comes in. Ossian moves to his place at the table and sits facing downstage. Malachi, with soft, deliberate movements—calculated not to interfere with Ossian's train of thought—fills the glass with wormwood, recaps the bottle, and sits himself down with his writing materials. He dips the new pen in the ink and sits patiently waiting as Ossian continues to look outward. Slow fade to black)*

The End

Grace McKeaney
HOW IT HANGS

Grace McKeaney

Grace McKeaney's *How It Hangs* was one of the audience pleasers in Actors Theatre of Louisville's 1985 SHORTS Festival. In Miss McKeaney's comic play the meeting of "The Temporary Shelter for Battered Women Past and Present Looking to Get Better in Lusk, Wyoming" disintegrates as the members turn from commenting on the men in their lives to their own relationships and values. Responding to the original production, Dale Sandusky of the New Albany, Indiana, *Tribune* observes: "*How It Hangs* is basically comedic, but with dark undertones. The women are able to laugh at one another and hope for a better life, but only one of them, Girlene, seems able to do something positive with reasonable hope of changing her life."

Since 1983 Miss McKeaney has been an Artistic Associate with Baltimore's Center Stage and Artistic Coordinator of their Young People's Theatre Program. She is also the recipient of the Le Compt du Nouy Foundation Prize for contribution to the American Theatre, presented to her in 1983 by Andre Bishop, artistic director of New York's Playwrights Horizons. Earlier one of her full-length plays, *Last Looks,* was presented in a workshop at the O'Neill National Playwrights Conference in Waterford, Connecticut in 1981, followed the next year by a full production at Baltimore's Center Stage. In the summer of 1985 Miss McKeaney was a participating playwright in the Sundance Playwrights Institute at Salt Lake City, Utah, with her most recent play, *Deadfall.* The play was subsequently produced at Center Stage in 1986 and by Actors Theatre of Louisville in 1987. Her other plays include: *Fits and Starts, Who They Are and How It Is with Them, Percy and the Amazing Gorgon Queen, Chicks, The Coming of Mr. Pine,* and *On-the-Fritzz.*

Miss McKeaney did her undergraduate work at Northwestern University, and received an M.F.A. from the Yale School of Drama, where she was honored with the Molly Kazan Award for Best Original Play of 1976. She has also studied acting with Alvina Krause. Miss McKeaney is a member of New Dramatists, a recent National Endowment for the Arts Fellow, and is currently working on a new musical.

Characters:

SISTER SWANNEE, *late 40's to early 50's. A self-styled Evangelist; a former Vegas showgirl. Founder of "The Temporary Shelter for Battered Women Past and Present Looking to Get Better in Lusk, Wyoming."*

GIRLENE GILLESPY, *36, an unwed mother-to-be. Former captain of her high school basketball team. A battered teenager.*

DOLL FOX, *37, Daddy Fox's "little girl"; Lusk's poor little rich girl.*

ROWDY GAPP, *36, Wes Gapp's ex-wife; battered. A "floater" mechanic at Art's Parts, the garage the shelter meets in.*

B. "BOB" MOORE, *36, mechanic, a straight arrow, a good guy; responsible for the station's motto: "We'll turn your lemon into a peach!" In charge of the station while his boss Art Fergus is away this summer.*

Setting:

Art's Parts, a pretty tidy little filling station on the outskirts of Lusk, Wyoming.

Time:

Mid-morning, Sunday, July, the present.

At Curtain:

Lights pop up to reveal the cozy inner office of Art's Parts, a little filling station on the outskirts of Lusk, Wyoming. An impressive array of tools and parts fill one wall; posters for Rotary Club picnics, Kiwanis' breakfasts, rodeos and square dancing are tacked here and there. The rodeo poster for Cheyenne's "DADDY OF 'EM ALL" Rodeo is by the door, and particularly fetching. There's a soda machine with a large banner-like sign over it saying: "CLOSED SUNDAYS! SEE YOU IN CHURCH!"

Some spare tires are piled to one side . . . people can sit on them. There's a pile of bashed-in fenders and bumpers in another pile. There's a good-sized counter with a dry-sink and lots of cabinets overhead. There's a gumball machine and potato chip dispenser. There's a basketball hoop with no netting hung lopsided somewhere and about to fall off. In the center of the room, a fussy little glass-topped table sits with a box of doughnuts and Kleenex on it. Also an ancient, faded little side-lamp, with a frilly pink shade. Here and there five or six folding chairs have been set out.

Doll Fox takes a swig from a Big Red soda and gets her notes in order. Sister and Girlene animatedly discuss an article in a magazine featuring mothers and babies. Doll clears her throat, signaling the meeting's about to start.

DOLL: The Temporary Shelter For Battered Women Past and Present Looking To Get Better in Lusk, Wyoming is hereby called to order. Doll Fox, secretary, that's me, now presiding.

SISTER: *(A little piqued)* Land's sake, Doll, you can skip all that stuff this morning, it's just the three of us.

DOLL: You said we'd each take turns running the meeting and we could run it like we liked and I like everything spelled out.

SISTER: *(To Girlene)* Me and my big mouth. *(Approaching doughnut box with interest)* What's these here?

DOLL: Crullers.

SISTER: *(Sotto voce)* Well, I've known a few of these in my time.

DOLL: *(Happily)* I got three crullers, six of that new whole-wheat glazed for the girls that's watching their health *(Winks at Girlene)* and the rest—

SISTER: *(A prayer)* Tell me jelly!

DOLL: *(Pleased)* Jelly, Sister, like you like! *(Sister takes a doughnut. Doll organizes her folder)* I'd like to start off today by reading you all a little testimonial I've typed up which highlights an important love experience I had this last month on my way back from Gilley's.

SISTER: *(Suspicious)* This ain't another *poem*, is it?

DOLL: Well, it takes the form of a poem, yes, since that was my major in junior college.

GIRLENE: *(Shifting her weight in the chair)* Is this a *long* poem?

DOLL: Now, just you wait and see. *(Clears throat)*
"There was once this guy,
His name was Mike,
He was working at a restaurant/diner kind of place.
He was kind of cute
And not real bright,
And I thought it would be like—sublime
To give his lips a taste."
(Sister and Girlene exchange looks)
"When he come on for my order,
We were flirting up a storm,
And I said I'd like to wrestle
With a big roast beef on rye
And he said, "How did I like it,
Did I like it thick and warm?"
And I said, "Why sure,
Was there any other kind?""

SISTER: *(Interrupting)* You know, at this certain angle *(Takes binoculars from her purse),* we got just a wonderful view of Wink's Minuteman Moter Court, damn its existence.

GIRLENE: I hate that place with a passion.

SISTER: It's the source of a LOT of our problems. Men got some pretty funny ideas about love when they're up fornicating total strangers half the night.

GIRLENE: I'm gonna miss this town.

SISTER: We gonna miss you, too.

DOLL: I'm gonna go right on now with my poem.
"Now, this *real* cute guy
Whose name was Mike,
Which anyone could see,
It was sewed right on his shirt,
Took a stroll past the counter
Toward the apple pie,
And that strut on him, ladies,
It was surely made to hurt.
I was filled with admiration
For this put-together guy
I was getting that ol' green-light

To go and get involved.
I's a little light-headed
As I had not had a bite.
And this stimulating scene
Was only starting to evolve . . ."

GIRLENE: *(Interrupting, to Sister)* Walked by the gymnasium one last time on my way over.

SISTER: I don't guess there was a girl in all the county recognized for more physical achievements than our own Girlene Gillespy!

DOLL: *(Patting Girlene's belly)* Well, I guess you really done it now!

GIRLENE: I always was a sucker for contact sports. Before coming here to this group, I had trouble holding my own in most matters concerning men. I had trouble saying no. Now, I know it don't matter if I have a right opinion or not, I'm entitled to my opinion.

SISTER: *(Cheering her on)* Amen!

GIRLENE: *(Enthusiastic)* And if I don't like what I'm hearing from a man, I just get up and leave the room.

SISTER: Right on!

GIRLENE: And I enjoyed those karate classes, too!

SISTER: Well, in my experience, you gotta cover ALL the bases.

DOLL: If you girls are finished up interrupting, I'd really like to plunge ahead with this. *(Indicating poem)*

SISTER: By all means, Doll.

GIRLENE: We're listening. *(Spits suddenly, wipes a hand across her mouth)* I got a cobweb in my mouth.

SISTER: Art really ought to take a broom to that doorjamb, he's got spiders in here! Hey, you ever see how one of them little sacks open, how many come out, and *every one* fix straight to make a web?

GIRLENE: *(Looking around)* It ain't the Taj Mahal, is it?

SISTER: No, but the Temporary Shelter For Battered Women had to relocate somewheres, and this is somewheres. *(Doll starts to speak, but Sister continues)* I don't hold it against Art Fergus that he's got lots of money.

GIRLENE: He does a lot of good for people.

SISTER: Art Fergus got my eternal admiration for opening us his doors in our time of need, such as they are. We're a mighty unpopular association in this here town . . .

GIRLENE: . . . As that unexpected fire proved . . .

SISTER: We may not know who struck that match under us. We may not have enough finances to purchase even a "pardon-our-dust" sign. But we know it don't matter where we temporarily meet, so long as our hearts are open and we speak our true minds to one another!

DOLL: *(Jumping in)*
"Now, fact of the matter
I'm the *restless* type
I been burned too often
To stay on too long.
If I'm with a guy a while
Well, I kinda get my gripes.
Guess I don't know the tune to that
Ol' long-run song."
(Sister and Girlene exchange looks)
"The casual close encounter
Of a highly private kind
Is more what I have come now to revere.
For those with *extra* daring
'TO WED'S' the Classic Lasting Bind
But most warranties run out within a year."
(Speaking apologies to Girlene) That wedding part there . . . it just fit the rhyme.

GIRLENE: Yeah, I noticed.

DOLL:
"Getting back to the point,
Looked like one more roadside joint *(Sister grunts)*
And *me* with an attraction coming on.
Then, he's back all smiles,
Which just turned on *all* my *dials*
Seemed no way to keep what's left of my lid on!"
(Doll is gearing up for her favorite part, excited)
"And wouldn't you just know
He's got that sandwich fixed *just so,*
Now I *know* that he's a bonafide gourmand!
And I wonder how he'll treat it
When I say: I'd love to eat it—here—

But I'm gonna have to get it to go!
(Doll does the chorus like a cheerleader)
"Get It To Go,
Gotta Get It To Go,
Slip It Right In The Sack
For A Girl On The Go!
Get It To Go,
Gotta Get It To Go,
Wrap It Up,
Gotta Have It,
Take It Out On The Road!"
(Girlene interrupts with a long, extended yawn)

GIRLENE: Oh, I'm sorry, Doll. I was up half the night with this baby kicking me to Kingdom Come.

DOLL: *(Crestfallen)* I'm sorry to hear that.

SISTER: You got to watch your rest now, Girl, and no fooling. You keep your checkup with Doc Bertie?

GIRLENE: Yeah—*(Lights a cigarette)*—she says everything feels like it's supposed to, but if this feels like it's supposed to, I am purely amazed any of us got here in the first place.

SISTER: I understand from these women's magazines that it gets a whole lot easier the last two months.

GIRLENE: God, I hope so. I am slugged night and day by some stranger within. Sometimes, it really makes me mad!

DOLL: *(Peeved)* Excuse me, but I *was* talking.

SISTER: Well, you're finished, ain't you?

DOLL: No. *(Waves papers)* I only got half-way.

SISTER: Where'd you say you fell in love with this waiter? Did you say you were riding the Bull at Gilley's?

DOLL: No. I said I HEARD a lot of *bull* at Gilley's. This incident happened next door at the diner. *(Ruffled)* I don't know why I bother to put so much effort into my monthly testimonials when there's not a SOUL in this garage paying any attention.

SISTER: Well, you put so much effort in because you got so much time on your hands. Lay around your Daddy's house with a couple of mangy pets, content yourself with a big, fat charge account . . .

GIRLENE: Let's listen to her, Sister.

SISTER: Well, I'll listen, but I heard it all before. She fell in love with a waiter *last* month, whose name was *Bill*.

DOLL: *(Hurt)* This is completely different. This *poem* is completely different. It has completely different scansion. What I felt for this boy felt truly *new.*

GIRLENE: It *was* new, Doll. It's always new.

SISTER: *(To Doll)* You're a thrill junkie. Don't stick with nothing.

DOLL: Well, you're a fine one to talk.

SISTER: What do you mean?

DOLL: A woman with all your trials and errors with men.

SISTER: *(To Girlene)* Oh, I'm not going to talk to her no more. She's not ready to be serious.

(Girlene reacts to being kicked by the baby)

GIRLENE: *(Talking to her stomach)* Oh! All right, I know it's dark and cramped in there, but I am only the container!

SISTER: Will it be a girl, do you think?

GIRLENE: I don't know, Sister; I guess there's half a chance.

SISTER: God, I hope it's a girl, and I hope she gets your big eyes and your big smile . . .

DOLL: *(Under her breath)* Well, I hope it don't get Trot's love of travel.

GIRLENE: *(Talking to her belly)* Take it easy in there, you got the whole world ahead of you!

DOLL: You got to know already that's Trot Wiley's child because it already don't listen to reason!

SISTER: Oh, mind your own business!

DOLL: Sister, you can't teach us to stick up for ourselves and our opinions then just ignore what we are saying! I am supposed to be chairing this morning's meeting, and you all are chattering like a truck-load of magpies! I have got an issue on the floor!

SISTER: You are not the only one with something going on here today. Girl is leaving, and we are losing just about our prettiest member!

DOLL: We talked that all out last time: we know what she's gonna do. She's going there to catch up with Trot at the "DADDY OF 'EM ALL" Rodeo; they're gonna exchange their I-Do's before that baby's walking and talking and live happily ever after . . . but I have got an issue on the floor here, and I'd like to know how to proceed according to Robert's Rules of Order!

SISTER: We got somebody starting off a whole new life here today, and I think that Robert would understand.

DOLL: Girl's just your favorite.

GIRLENE: Sister don't have favorites, Doll.

SISTER: Of course she's my favorite!

DOLL: See!

SISTER: *(Evangelizing)* POWER! That's what she's found in herself! We got the power to create in us, as well as the power to corrupt. And I think before you say another word here this morning, you better contemplate the power that is functioning in *your life.*

DOLL: Oh, I guess I'm supposed to put this here away *(Waves pages)* without ever getting to the part of the story where my WHOLE LIFE turns around!

SISTER: *(Shaking her head)*
Your life ain't turned around, Doll.
*You done the same thing you always do.
You went out and fucked the waiter.
Ain't that what it comes down to?

DOLL: Not entirely.

SISTER: And you wanted us to know about it, so you wrote a funny little poem so we'd laugh, and it wouldn't sound so harsh as what you actually-truly done, which was go out and fuck the waiter.

DOLL: I didn't *just* fuck the waiter. There was more to it than that.

SISTER: Well, I don't need to know *more!*

DOLL: I think what I felt with him was love.

SISTER: Oh, God, I get nervous when I hear you use that word.

GIRLENE: You use it a lot, Doll.

DOLL: I fall in love a lot. Some people do. It's chemical. I got a lot of room in my heart.

SISTER: You got a lot of room in your *head!*

GIRLENE: Now, I don't think we should run nobody down here.

SISTER: Well, we can't go on babysitting these bad habits! I did not start this shelter two years ago so that young women could come in here on a Sunday after a Saturday Night Plunge with some new Mr. No-Count and call it "love". Facts is facts, and we're only interested here in the facts: and the fact is, you went to a diner, you shanghaied the waiter, you fucked like a monkey, and now you want our forgiveness and you ain't got MINE!

(Suddenly the door to the station opens, tripping a device that sets a radio playing. The radio is tuned to a Bible station: Red Sovine sings, "If Jesus Came To Your House, I Wonder What

You'd Do?" B. "Bob" Moore enters in neat, but worn Sunday clothes; he's a good-looking guy, with a pleasant combination of shyness and western "thoughtfulness" about him. He flashes a big smile)

B.: I said after Church. *(To Sister)* Didn't I say I'd come by after Church! Hey, Girl.

GIRLENE: Hey, B.

B.: Hey, Doll.

DOLL: *(Seductive)* Hey, B.

B.: Hey, Aunt Sis. *(Pecks her on the cheek)*

SISTER: B, O, B, bless your ol' sweet heart. Ain't he getting handsome?

DOLL: *(With appreciation)* And fit. He's just so fit.

B.: *(Embarrassed under her gaze)* Art's got the door rigged so the Bible station pops on, on a Sunday 'case anybody's breaking in here with the wrong idea. *(Turns off the radio)* You hens having a meeting?

SISTER: *(Zeroing back in on Doll)* And it ain't just that you fucked the waiter, Doll. *(B. nods, exits pulling off his shirt)* It's that *one more time,* in spite of all our talking, you are dreaming that it's something else and asking for the *hurt. (Beginning one of her favorite reveries)*

I was wayward.

I was mean.

I was wanton in extreme.

I drank with the best of them and laid down with dogs.

I had no recollection of entire months passing.

Are you listening to me, Doll? *(Doll nods)*

I'd wake up and be married to somebody I didn't even know.

I danced in chorus lines in Vegas because what I craved was adulation. I was headed for an old age laced with orthopedic socks, bursitus and gin.

I had no central theme to my existence.

My mind was a bus locker full of things others had forgot and left behind, and my poor heart was a bus station where any fool could buy a ticket and take a ride!

DOLL: Well, it's hard to find substance these days. *(B. re-enters)*

SISTER: No, ma'am. The good ones are out there. *(Pulling B. over)* There's good men of conscience left in the world!

B.: *(Modestly)* Oh, shut up.

SISTER: And what we gotta figure out is why time after time we keep returning to the men with the troubles and let the nice ones go.

DOLL: I think it's numbers.

SISTER: It ain't just numbers. Sure there's plenty of troubled men to choose from, but each of us got an uncanny radar for sniffing 'em out.

DOLL: Are you saying I am making my own problems?

SISTER: I am saying you got to think of a problem as your own in order to recognize a pattern. *(Pushing over next to B. as he sorts through a tool box)* Whatcha stalling for, B.? Jeez, you got a lot of different sized nuts in here.

B.: *(Shutting box on her)* Will you get your fingers out of there, you're messing up the order.

SISTER: Are you gonna get me out there to throw the good book around some this weekend or what?

B.: Oh, Aunt Sis, it's really too hot to get anything right.

SISTER: Don't poop around, give it to me straight: will the Red Tide run again?

B.: *(Lining up his tools)* Tell everybody how I named it.

SISTER: He was a little shaver, not doorknob high, a-playing at driving my ol' red station wagon, and he says one day real serious that the hood spread out over the land like the red tidal wave in the Bible. We think he meant the Red Sea. There was a while there we were real nice to him on account of we thought he had Higher Sight. *(Bops him on the head)*

B.: You ain't gonna like the sight I show you later on this charge pad. That heap is twenty years old. It ain't worth fixing up time and again. I want you to come out here and see how your whole underside is hanging ... *(He starts off, she follows)* If you speak up now, I can give you a real nice price on a completely reconstituted Honda ... *(He goes off)*

SISTER: *(Carrying tool box after him)* Don't talk to me in Honda, B., and don't speak ill of the "Studebaggah" Classic ... *(She goes off)*

DOLL: Sometimes I just hate her. *(Meek)* How come her to pick on me all the time.

GIRLENE: *(Moving to her)* She ain't really picking on you, hon, she's trying to get you to hear yourself.

DOLL: Well, all I can hear is her picking on me again.

GIRLENE: She was hard on me, too, when I first come here. Don't write her off altogether now, she's got some valuable things to offer. She sees a lot of herself in you and sometimes that gets in the way. What you got to do is find some way to use this group to your own advantage.

DOLL: *(Hugging her)* That's easy for you to say, you're getting out of here for good.

GIRLENE: Hey, I like that little table and lamp you brung, it's nice, it's homey. Ain't that your dog Pink's night light?

DOLL: *(Welling up)* Oh, what's the matter with me: I just keep losing the people I love. *(She cries)*

GIRLENE: What is it, honey? Something happen?

DOLL: I know being a feeling person you'll understand a lot by the next two words I say: Pink died.

GIRLENE: *(Handing her Kleenex)* Oh, Doll, No. You must feel awful . . .

DOLL: I picked up the keys to the Cougar and drove all the way to Texas, so you know I wasn't in my right mind. I been so much in grief, Girl, I don't know what I'm wearing. *(Blows nose)* And I *don't* think I can take no more roughing up today.

(B. enters, followed by Sister)

SISTER: I don't want to hear no excuses, B. That is my Mobile Mission Of Mercy you got up on your jack out there, and I'm due in Camp Stool no-later-than-noon to pray over somebody's lingering grip.

B.: Oh, Aunt Sis, nobody gets the grip anymores.

SISTER: That's what you think, Mr. Smarty: people get grips of all kinds, it would purely astonish you.

B.: *(Ceremoniously unwrapping a part)* There's your part. It's a universal joint and it come all the way from Wayne.

SISTER: It's from Wayne? *(Taking it)* Ain't it pretty? What I like's a joint that's guaranteed to work. Has it got a guarantee?

B.: Sister, only guarantee I know is once you think you got something fixed, it's guaranteed to come apart again.

GIRLENE: *(To Sister)* Pink died, Sister. Doll feels bad.

DOLL: Now, don't all start in with the questions, I'm a little besides myself on account of I had to help it along some . . .

SISTER: Did you have to give her the Big Shot?

DOLL: *(Nods, sobs)* Well, she couldn't lift her little fuzz-head off the rug to eat no more . . . I wish you could have seen the hurt look on Teeny's face struggling to get them "Ocean Bits" down her throat this morning . . .

SISTER: *(Trying to be helpful)* Did you put water on 'em?

DOLL: *(To an insane person)* Well, of course I put water on 'em . . . It was loneliness affecting Teeny . . . there's Pink's bowl where it's been sitting nineteen years . . . there's Pink's bowl sitting and no Pink. Now I got a cat without a dog just like I always knew it would be . . .

B.: You can get yourself another pooch.

DOLL: That's what Doc Voltz thinks I should do. He says I'm going through the change and this business with Pink has triggered some very emotional issues.

GIRLENE: What kind of issues, Doll?

DOLL: *(Breaking)* Why I get so attached to animals and can't find myself a man.

B.: Well, animals is easy to love, Doll. You can make up what they're thinking.

DOLL: But I do that with men, too, trying to figure out what they mean. Like this waiter told me he'd been waiting his whole life for me to come walking through the doors of that diner. Way he said that seemed like the whole and simple truth. He was prompt. And attentive. And I wanted to love somebody . . .

GIRLENE: Maybe, hon, what you liked so much was just *him* liking *you* . . .

(Sister looks at the charge pad she's been holding)

SISTER: *(Agog)* Two hundred and sixty-seven fifty?

B.: *Before* labor.

GIRLENE: *(Laughing)* Oh, B., don't use that word, I'm trying to forget. *(Shifting her weight)* Doc Bertie says this is a boy I've got, the way I'm hanging. Had this dream last night this was a boy and when he got here I didn't know what to say to him!

B.: *(Hugging her)* You gonna leave these arms, soon, hmm, and run off with a fugitive from a bull pen?

SISTER: This very morning, Mister, so get your licks in quick.

B.: Oh, I am devastated thinking of you married and gone. *(He hugs her tightly, pushes away suddenly, apologetically)*

B.: Does that hurt you if I do that? Will that hurt the baby?

GIRLENE: *(Pulling him back)* Don't you go away with those arms, they're the nicest things I felt all day.

B.: Gonna take a fun honeymoon after? *(Girlene shrugs)* Gonna have a big wedding with a cake?

GIRLENE: *(Rubbing her belly)* I don't guess we'll make a fuss, conditions being what they are. Trot and me been together since Prom Night, glory sake, off and on.

B.: You excited?

GIRLENE: Scared.

SISTER: Oh, it's only a wedding. I did it six times and never got it right.

GIRLENE: Well, some people only do it once, Sister.

DOLL: How come everything just always works out so nice for you? First, you're gonna have a baby, now you're getting married to the boy you always loved . . .

SISTER: *(To Doll)* She got a plan for her life!

GIRLENE: Now, Sister, I never said I had the answers!

SISTER: *(Pressing on)* She knows that if we're looking for love and commitment, it takes TWO people that's truly up to it, and nothing gets accomplished by a roll in the hay except heaping emptiness on top of emptiness 'cause it just ain't answer enough to the ache!

B.: Now, don't be so hard on Doll, Sister; far as I can tell, everybody's just trying to get one foot in front of the other . . .

SISTER: But a girl like Doll who's had all life's great advantage . . .

GIRLENE: Nobody knows 100 percent what's right. I know I don't know for sure what I'm getting into. I just said, "Trot, you're gonna marry me. I don't think I can do this all alone." But I never tried nothing so important in life before.

B.: Well, there's no time like the present to start learning . . . and I think people kinda learn things as they go.

GIRLENE: Oh, I almost forgot, my car!

B.: That yours with the U-Haul-It parked outside?

GIRLENE: I been having some trouble starting, nothing major, I hope, but I thought I'd wait for Rowdy to look at my ignition when she come in.

B.: She called in sick.

GIRLENE: Oh?

B.: Won't see her today.

GIRLENE: No?

B.: And points ain't my specialty, so I don't think I'm your man. There's a guy though I know on the road out to Cheyenne. I'll get you his number—he'll be glad to have the work. *(He goes off to the area by the jack)*

DOLL: *(Taking a cruller)* Well, I hate to bring this up, but I think Rowdy ain't here for a reason.

GIRLENE: I ain't heard nothing from her since last time, so I guess I ain't surprised.

SISTER: I heard she got drunk and threw a big scene the other night . . .

GIRLENE: Was it about me? About me leaving?

DOLL: It was more aimed at Sister. She says you been pushed into this decision and that Sister's all the one to blame.

SISTER: I heard about it, too. *(To Girlene)* Some people see their problems in other people.

DOLL: . . . Says Sister's got you headed for trouble one more time . . .

SISTER: *(Sharply to Doll)* And some people ain't got the courage to speak for themselves!

DOLL: Well, every time I do, you shut me down. I don't understand Girlene going back with him either. Not after all she's been through.

SISTER: Well, ain't it obvious: she's gonna have his child.

DOLL: Oh, a woman don't have to marry to have a baby anymores. Any qualified biologist will come right out loud and tell you that. Why don't she just go off and have it on her own. I know that's what I'd do.

SISTER: Oh, that's rich coming from you. You don't do nothing without your Daddy Fox saying so.

DOLL: Well, everybody's afraid of my daddy. I ain't the only one. Our homestead was right there on the phone book cover as a representation for ALL Wyoming of something really, truly OLD . . . He owns *everything* worth having in this town.

GIRLENE: You're the one most affected by his holdings, Doll—you can't make a clear decision for yourself.

SISTER: You hop from man to man and each time you think you found the right one—then you get home to that house and you get to worrying about what your daddy will think of this one, because you KNOW what your daddy thinks of all of them, none of them are good enough for Doll. Only Daddy is man enough for Doll . . .

DOLL: *(Edgy)* My daddy has never raised a hand in hatred to me! I don't have anywhere near the problems you girls have in this group.

SISTER: He don't have to raise a hand. He don't have to raise his voice. He knows the fear of him you got there deep inside. You won't ever have a relationship of consequence with anyone so long as you are living under that man's roof. That's battery, dear, as sure as I'm sitting here. Only some scars don't show.

(Pause)

DOLL: *(To Girlene)* Didn't Trot break a arm of yours once?

GIRLENE: *(Taken back a little)* That year I was a roller guard at the Skateaway? Yeah . . . I think so.

DOLL: *(Indicating she must get Sister off her back)* Well, I hope you know, I hate to bring this up.

GIRLENE: We were really just kids . . . and it was my fault as much as his, just standing there in the middle of the floor. We'd just had words.

DOLL: What kind of words?

GIRLENE: I didn't want to skate no more . . . Last thing I wanted when I got off working was to skate some more but Trot, he really wanted to skate that night and . . .

DOLL: He was half-cut as I remember . . .

GIRLENE: *(A little deflated)* Yeah—he'd had something to drink and bumped into me when he come around the curve cracking the whip. It was an accident.

DOLL: Well, I guess what I want to know is what you're gonna do the next time he comes around the curve cracking the whip about something he wants you to do you don't want to do . . .

GIRLENE: It was an accident. It got blowed up forever after by everybody way out of size . . .

DOLL: Yeah, I guess that time he struck you in the face was a little accident, too.

(Pause. Girlene is stung by this)

GIRLENE: *(Stung)* No. That was no accident. That was what brought me to this group two years ago. But it only happened *once,* and it caused me to stop and think just what might be behind it.

DOLL: I think it's pretty obvious what it meant, now, ain't it? He is capable of violence to a woman. I think that's pretty loud and clear.

GIRLENE: What did it mean when I struck right back, Doll? What does that say about me?

SISTER: *(Severely, to Doll)* Why are you determined to make trouble for this girl her last day here?

DOLL: She's making her own trouble going back with a man she ain't too sure of.

SISTER: We are trying to say goodbye and wish her luck! *(Sister goes to a box tied with a bow)* Look what I found in that pawn shop in East Flaming. *(Sister helps Girlene unwrap it. Sister lifts a small athletic trophy from the box. Girlene is delighted. Sister reads the inscription)* "GIRLENE GILLESPY, BEST ALL-ROUND SPORT."

GIRLENE: *(Handling it gingerly)* I was winning those trophies on the field and getting conked on the head with them later by Daddy when he was drunk. Wake up the day after a big victory and find this sitting in some pawn shop window . . . I learned to watch my step awful early . . .

SISTER: But just look how you come around—putting your foot down with Trot, making him face his responsibilities.

DOLL: I don't see where she's found no answers in herself.

SISTER: Why should she have to face this all alone?

DOLL: All she's doing is pushing that man into marrying her.

GIRLENE: I didn't push nobody into nothing, Doll. He and I got a situation to face together here and he's willing. He quit the rodeo this week. Went and got himself an actual job. Going on Monday with the National Rivet Company out there in Cheyenne.

DOLL: How long you think he'll last at that?

SISTER: None of us knows what the future holds, Doll. We got to take care of the here and now.

(B. enters with a little bouquet of wildflowers)

B.: Found these growing out behind the station. *(Gives them to Girlene)* I don't know if you got your bouquet together yet.

GIRLENE: *(Kissing him)* Oh, B.

DOLL: Where's my flowers? Don't I get no flowers?

B.: Well, why don't you and Sister go out and catch this bouquet for the next in line.

DOLL: I guess I can't get too choked up about another marriage.

SISTER: . . . You made such a mess of the first one . . .

DOLL: . . . That's 'cause I just did it to spite Daddy Fox like I hear you recommending now. He said come on off the back of that cowboy's Palomino Pony or don't you never set foot in my fine house again. So I didn't. I married Flynn instead of going back in the house!

SISTER: How long did you say it lasted—about six weeks?

GIRLENE: I don't think we should be running nobody down here. We're all talking about the same problem—if we don't support each other, I don't know what this group's about. *(To B.)* I got something I want to leave with the shelter, if you don't mind it sitting around. *(Taking her keys, going. Sister catches her arm)*

SISTER: You got your wedding gown out there in the U-Haul-It? *(Girlene nods)* Won't you give us-that-can't-be-there a little sneak preview of the happy thing to come?

GIRLENE: *(Going)* Oh, sure. Why not?

SISTER: *(To Doll)* That Girl makes me so proud—makes me feel like there's hope for all of us. *(Doll opens a bag of potato chips, eats. Sister takes a doughnut, eats throughout her monologue)* First husbands should be lasting things. I remember mine. He was a dentist. Took care of everybody's teeth in town, just a whole town full of teeth. And when he run out with his assistant, I never once bothered with my teeth again. I didn't care what I put in my mouth. Just everything went in there: chocolate eclairs, peanuts in the shell, pecan pie with whipping cream piled as high as it would go . . . He left an awful hole behind him I just kept trying to fill.

DOLL: You're still trying to fill it as far as I can tell.

SISTER: *(Wiping her hands)* What do you mean?

DOLL: *(Flustered)* Just pushing that girl right back into trouble in some oversized wedding gown . . .

SISTER: I didn't push nobody into nothing . . .

DOLL: . . . See your own problems in everybody else. See your problems in me and try and break me down . . .

SISTER: *(Rising)* Why, you spiteful, miserable thing . . . *(Inadvertently reaching out to shake her)* Don't you dare talk to me that way . . .

B.: Sister, what are you saying . . .

SISTER: She's got no right to talk to me that way . . .

DOLL: I am sick of some born-again whore with no true self-knowledge working things out through other people . . . I am tired coming here every week to this Doom and Gloom Club where my progress is ignored and my experiences don't impress nobody and I go away thoroughly disenthused about myself!

(Rowdy Gapp has entered unbeknownst to anyone through the offstage jack entry. She is messy and looks hungover. She wears a torn T-shirt advertising some kind of beer, and jeans and high tops. Her left hand is heavily bandaged. She carries an old basketball in the other hand. She bounces the ball)

ROWDY: Now, that's what I like to see: you girls handling your problems. Hey, B., how's it hanging?

B.: Oh, pretty much the way it was the day before. Thought we weren't gonna be seeing you today. Thought you was sick.

ROWDY: No, I'm just miserable. Ain't you ever had a day where you ought to eat a worm and die? *(Holds up bandaged hand)* I can't do no work today. But I can put in my two-cents like anybody else around with half-a-brain.

(Girlene enters holding a withered palm in a pot, and carrying her wedding gown draped over one arm)

There she is—ol' Great-With-Child—see you all packed out there and ready to start a whole new life. You're fucking crazy, but I guess you know that.

GIRLENE: Come here to make sure and depress me before I go?

ROWDY: *(Lying back on the tires)* Well, you know me, Girl. I'm small-minded. God just give me a little wind-up mind to work with. I don't understand a lot of things people do here with their lives.

GIRLENE: How come we can't just say goodbye like we ought to.

ROWDY: You're right, Girl, we should. I can't stand having a truly stupid person for a friend. *(Tosses ball and catches it)*

GIRLENE: *(Handing plant to B.)* Thought a change of scene might do it good.

B.: Well, ain't that nice. Ain't that a nice touch for the place. *(Peering closer)* What *is* that kind of plant?

GIRLENE: More dead than anything else. It's a pony-tail palm Rowdy give me once when we were getting along.

ROWDY: Leaving some things behind you?

GIRLENE: Well, I can't really look at it no more with you and me acting this ugly way...

ROWDY: I'm sure glad somebody got somewhere faroff to go today... I'd run away, too, if I could...

GIRLENE: I ain't running from nothing...

ROWDY: No? I thought that's what you told me after last meeting.

GIRLENE: ROWDY!

ROWDY: Didn't you say how glad you'd finally be to leave Sister and talking things to death far behind...

GIRLENE: *(Embarrassed)* Thanks-a-pant-load! I didn't think you'd be repeating it first chance you got!

ROWDY: *(To Sister)* But ain't that why we come here, Sister, to speak our true minds to one another?

GIRLENE: *(To Sister)* It ain't all one-sided way she makes it sound . . .

SISTER: I thought I'd been a big help to you, Girl, sorting through your questions . . .

GIRLENE: You were, Sister . . .

SISTER: I believe in people talking to one another—that's why I started this shelter—I thought if we were all talking about our problems, we might not feel so all alone . . .

GIRLENE: I needed your support when I first come here because I was feeling pretty low . . . I been looking all my life it seems for somebody to lean on and tell me which way's right . . . And it helped to hear your thoughts on things because it made me realize we're . . . two different people . . . and we can talk on it forever . . . but nobody knows better than me what I should be doing with my life . . . *(She presses Sister's hand, smiles)*

SISTER: *(Smiling)* Oh, put your gown on, I'd like to see you in it.

GIRLENE: *(Going to get into the gown)* Everybody ready for a sight!? I bought this gown three weeks ago, thinking I couldn't expand much more! *(Girlene slips out of her dress, and into her gown during the following exchanges)*

ROWDY: *(Dreamily)* Boy, I wish I could get myself knocked-up here. Then, I'd have just all my problems solved. Wouldn't have to work in this ol' gas station no more. Wouldn't have to think about nothing . . . Just get in there and fold them diapers on the diagonal and look out the window, and wait . . . just for hours . . . for my reason to come home.

SISTER: *(To Rowdy)* What's this I hear about you telling Bertie Bean I'm full of shit? *(Rowdy laughs a rough laugh)* She said you had a snootful the other night over there at Everybody's Country and run me down in front of a whole lot of people that didn't like hearing it.

GIRLENE: *(Calling to Rowdy)* So, you're drinking again . . .

ROWDY: *(To Sister, in a fierce whisper)* Well, ain't you full of shit? Ain't you got this one talked into marrying a man once broke an arm for her?

SISTER: *(Quietly to Rowdy)* That was a long, long time ago.

ROWDY: Some things you don't forgive. *(Pushing past Sister)* Excuse me. *(Bouncing ball: calling to Girlene)* This is Trot's ol' ball from when he lent us it for practice. Thought you might like to take it along for your new baby to bounce, providing it's a boy!

Hey, don't *never* let me tell you what I had to do for Trot to get this ball on loan!

DOLL: *(Hushing her)* Rowdy!

GIRLENE: Don't never tell me, okay?

DOLL: She's just jealous cause she loved him herself. Everybody loved Trot. He looked like Little Joe on Ponderosa.

ROWDY: Yeah, I loved him, what I knew of love. I loved looking at him. 'Cause he excited me. And when I couldn't have him, I found one I thought was like him. But what I found in my experience is that funny feeling between your legs tends to kinda fade a little bit the more times you get your fool head knocked up into the parlor window sill.

(Girlene turns and enters their circle, radiant in her wedding gown. It is still unzipped and she wobbles a little bit, twirling her bouquet)

SISTER: *(Applauding lightly)* Don't you look sweet?

DOLL: Here. Let me help you. *(Attempts to zip it up without success)* This *is* tight. Well, I guess you just wear it once and toss it to the moths!

(Girlene turns to Rowdy for some approval. Rowdy tosses the ball to her hard. Girlene passes the ball to Doll)

DOLL: Lusk's Lovely "Leaping Lizards"! We were pretty good!

ROWDY: Oh, Doll, you were the worst guard we ever had. Just never had the heart back then to cut you.

GIRLENE: You don't mind cutting people now, do you?

ROWDY: I'm all growed-up, now, Girl. I know everybody just takes their lumps.

DOLL: *(Tossing ball to Rowdy)* My daddy wants to know about that rent check.

ROWDY: Well, you tell your daddy I ain't got that rent check. *(Tosses the ball back to Doll. Doll lobs the ball to Girlene)*

GIRLENE: *(Holding ball)* Where'd you come upon this after all these years?

ROWDY: Well, I had my marriage, Girl. Now, I'm getting my yard sale together. Got rare items and curios of every kind. Hey, you know why they call 'em curios, don't you? 'Cause after you buy 'em and bring 'em home and watch 'em sit there about fifteen years, you're curious as hell why you wanted 'em in the first place.

DOLL: I don't think that's where that word comes from.

ROWDY: Oh, Doll, you're so slim in the wit department . . . And they'll tell you right there on television that a mind is a terrible thing to waste.

DOLL: Ain't that Gapp's ol' shirt? Whatcha still wearing that relic for?

ROWDY: I wear it cause it fits, Doll. Don't make something where there ain't nothing.

DOLL: You sure got awful smart since your man run off with Lyla Fergus. That what it takes to get so damn awful smart in love these days.

GIRLENE: We don't run nobody down here . . .

DOLL: I'm just saying . . .

ROWDY: We don't run nobody down here, Doll, get that through your thick head!

DOLL: Nobody's an expert.

ROWDY: No, but you're a true professional, Doll. We know it ain't easy staying active president of the Man-a-Month-Club.

GIRLENE: She don't mean that, Doll.

ROWDY: I don't mean that, Doll. Nobody here means anything they say. *(Laughs a rough laugh)* Well, come on, girls! Let's have some SERIOUS laughs, and get all our Men Troubles straightened out. You know, there are times I lie between them sheets and think it was almost worth assault and battery to get this chance to come and laugh like hell at you all every month.

DOLL: Your trouble's lying between them sheets so long alone . . .

ROWDY: I got things running just according to Hoyle, Doll. That's 'cause I been following Sister's fine advice here. When I first come here with my arms all black and blue, that's all I heard: Get out from under a man if he's hurting you . . .

SISTER: That's the first step, hon, to see how much you been hating yourself all along . . .

ROWDY: *(Tossing the ball hard to Doll)* Well, what's the fucking second step, Sister? Cause I ain't been able to figure that one out. *(Putting change in the soda machine)* I read all the books you give me. And I tried to stop my drinking. And I didn't go try to get him back. And I'm just as miserable now as I ever been before. *(No soda comes out; she hits the machine violently)*

SISTER: *(Quietly)* That don't work, hon. I lost fifty cents in it yesterday. *(Rowdy hits the machine again)*

B.: *(Offstage)* Don't hit it!

ROWDY: *(Growling)* Well, I lost my change.

B.: *(Offstage)* Well, it ain't working!

ROWDY: Well, I didn't get a soda!

B.: *(Offstage)* Well, I'll call somebody Monday, but it don't help it to be hit.

(Rowdy slumps against the machine, holding her hand which pains her in the air)

GIRLENE: What happened to your hand?

ROWDY: I had a window to get in my way.

SISTER: Rowdy, sit down if you got something valuable to offer. I been so anxious for one of us to work things out with a man we love . . . I might of made things simpler-sounding than they are . . .

ROWDY: *(Laughs)* I ain't gonna sit . . . I'll sit on the tires if I want to sit . . . Hear the same stream of bullshit wherever I sit . . . People telling lies . . . people making up happy endings . . .

GIRLENE: It ain't the same for everybody, is it, just 'cause things didn't work out for you. I'm thirty-six years old and I'm gonna have a child . . . *(Pause)*

ROWDY: Oh, I'm gonna go. *(To Doll)* Give me the ball.

DOLL: *(Tossing her the ball)* I don't understand why you come here in the first place.

(Pause)

ROWDY: I come because I put my fist through a window this morning, Doll. I come because I got scared thinking about that. I come because we all used to know each other in better days and I didn't have nowhere else to go.

SISTER: Sit down, Rowdy.

ROWDY: What for, Sister? I got a big mouth and say a lot of things nobody wants to hear. There's nobody here who *can* hear. We're all just damaged goods, that's what those books will tell you. *(To Sister)* And you. For all your good intent, you can't even get it straight. First, you tell us to flee the circumstance of violence we're ALL so good at finding, then next thing, you're pushing some scared somebody right back in the door. If that had been me, that little problem would have gone right down the toilet. *(To Girlene, with emotion)* You ain't got enough sense yet to have a child. But if you listen to Sister, she'll tell you to get blind and hope, hope, hope for the best . . .

SISTER: I know hope ain't enough . . . I know girls don't grow to women by a clock. Some of us stay children a long time past the time we ought to, and before we know it, we're in there raising children of our own . . .

GIRLENE: I can't do nothing about that, Sister, can I? It's a late day for regrets.

SISTER: I know hope ain't enough . . .

DOLL: Well, fear ain't much to go on, either, *(Softly)* 'cause I know, Girl, you must be afraid.

GIRLENE: *(Trembling)* Of course I'm a little afraid. This is the most important thing I've tried to do in my life. But I ain't afraid of Trot no more.

ROWDY: *(Wild)* You know two-thirds of America's citizens believe there's Intelligent Life somewheres else and it's gotta be, too, 'cause it sure as hell ain't in this garage!

GIRLENE: You think you got it figured out for everybody, don't you? You got the darkest view of life I ever seen.

ROWDY: *(Bearing down on her)* If a man raises his hand to a woman once, he'll do it twice, if he does it twice, he'll do it again, and you got more than your damn self to think about—bring another little kid into the world to get bashed around!

GIRLENE: . . . I'm not gonna stand here and listen to this. He and I worked hard these last years to put our difference behind. He's changed and so have I!

ROWDY: *(Pushing over a chair)* They don't change!

GIRLENE: . . . He's got us a big ranch house out there by his Uncle Burns' he's been working on while we're standing here fighting . . .

ROWDY: . . . Just cross him someday . . .

GIRLENE: He's out there in the hot sun doing all the repairs himself . . .

ROWDY: . . . See what supporting him gets you . . .

GIRLENE: Got new drains, new gutters, new gables . . .

ROWDY: And it's just one-more-something he'll stick with for awhile! He struck you once!

GIRLENE: And I struck back, 'cause just like you I couldn't see no other way!

ROWDY: Well, the Bible will tell you there's a place for righteous anger . . .

GIRLENE: . . . And the Bible will tell you to love each other, too. But I wouldn't expect you to understand that 'cause you can't love nobody 'til you get some self-respect. *(Through her own pain)* Look at you. You don't care nothing for yourself—how can you expect anybody else to care?

(Long pause. Rowdy's eyes fill)

ROWDY: I don't expect anybody else to care. *(Sets the chair she's pushed over upright)* I don't have no friends here . . . We were just girl friends together long ago . . . *(Weary)* You go on out there to Cheyenne, Girl, and see how long he comes in regular hours, see how tired you get trying to hold him, and you see how much love you can keep alive in your heart for his child . . .

GIRLENE: Ain't you tired, Rowdy? I'd rather be tired loving somebody than hating myself. I cried my heart out when I knew I'd be having this baby, because I know nothing in life got a guarantee. *(Touching her belly)* But I got somebody on the way that's gonna need some love soon and I'm clearing out the pain to make a way . . . *(Turning to Sister)* Sister, you said the power within us for good don't mean much unless we're connected to one another. You said men and women were supposed to go on having children and trying to help each other grow . . . You told me that . . . *(Through her tears)* . . . and I thought that was pretty fair advice.

(Sister turns, walks to the table, lights a cigarette)

SISTER: I can say it, honey. I can't do it.

(Girlene looks around. Doll, Rowdy, Sister are each in their separate worlds of isolation)

GIRLENE: Well, I can do it. And I'm gonna do it. *(Begins taking off the dress)* I don't see where any of you got an answer but being poor in spirit and alone. I can't tell you how much I've missed him, or what my place has felt like with him gone. I hate my room. I hate its hollow sound. I hate the way the clock sits on the mantel. I hate the furniture waiting for people to come fill it. People ain't meant to live alone and I'm sorry everybody's been so damn hurt by someone that should have loved them better. But I'm gonna finish something up here I started with a man . . . I got a chance to start somebody all brand new.

(She has removed her dress and put on her regular clothes)

ROWDY: Well, don't never be lonesome, Girl, I can't imagine a worser fate . . . I woke up from a dream of my mama this morning . . . she was dead, like she is . . . but in this dream, she was trying to get warm . . . "Hold my hand," I said . . . "I can save you." And I wake up, and I'm holding my own hand . . . I saw myself looking into that pane of glass by my bed there . . . and I hated what I saw so much, I just thought I'd break it forever . . .

SISTER: You got to leave the past behind you, Rowdy . . .

ROWDY: Tell me where to leave it, Sister, and I'll gladly put it down . . . My mama gets dumped and she takes it out on me and I go out looking for that same kind of love . . . which is no kind of love . . . and I always find it with some man that's got more anger inside him than even I do . . . Had to walk in by her place this morning . . . had to see that ol' porch swing bumping in the breeze . . . you come in alone and go away alone . . . I remember her saying that to me, that's all she had to offer . . . but I think she got that pretty close to right . . .

(Girlene moves toward her)

GIRLENE: I ain't alone . . . We're none of us alone . . . *She places Rowdy's bandaged hand on her swelling belly. Rowdy feels the movement of the baby)* We each come from one another . . . how much plainer can that be? *(Rowdy cries)* Everywhere I look I see women with their children . . . I see a lady in a grocery line, studying her child . . . loving that child with her eyes . . . and I think that must be what God's love feels like . . . where there's no fear yet, no hurt, no holding back . . . *(Happy)* I'm gonna know what that is soon, isn't that wonderful? *(She takes Rowdy's face, turns it to her)* I can't unlearn your sorrow and I can't teach you love . . . but one day . . . I hope you get finished with the pain. *(They embrace, a long, tender embrace. Doll cries out suddenly)*

DOLL: *(Crying)* I miss Pink. Now, I got a cat without a dog just like I always knew it would be.

(Rowdy laughs a loud, hard laugh. The others join in laughing. Rowdy grabs the ball, bounces it)

ROWDY: Oh, that dog lived long enough. That dog had an embarrassing longevity. That dog lived longer than most people in the Bible. *(Despite Doll's sorrow, they are all having trouble not laughing)*

DOLL: She was the keeper of all my secrets and dreams. *(Even Doll manages a smile)*

SISTER: *(Rising, to put her arm around Doll)* Maybe God got something different in store for your secrets and dreams, now, Doll. I'll tell you one thing: He cooks in funny pots. *(They laugh)* And anyone who says they understand Him, ain't got a steady leg to stand on . . .

DOLL: *(Drying her eyes)* Life's sure cruel to her dumb animals.

GIRLENE: Well, some things got to die, so others can live. We got to believe that . . .

ROWDY: *(Bouncing ball)* I hate Sundays. Makes me realize how fallen away I truly am. You know this morning, I couldn't remember how to start up the Lord's Prayer.

GIRLENE: How come you think of starting up the Lord's Prayer?

ROWDY: I locked my keys in the car.

(They laugh)

DOLL: You ain't supposed to pray just when you want something.

GIRLENE: Got to pray when you believe. You must believe in something.

(Rowdy's eyes twinkle. She passes the ball to Girlene just like she used to for the pre-game warm-up. Girlene bounces the ball a couple of times, her old captain-self for a moment)

GIRLENE: Something big. *(She passes the ball to Rowdy who catches it)*

ROWDY: *(Catching it)* The World. Something flat. *(Passes ball to Girlene who catches it)*

GIRLENE: *(Catching it)* Doll's Head. Something pointy. *(Passes it to Doll who catches it)*

DOLL: *(Catching it)* Rowdy's Head. Something you have to cut. *(Passes it to Rowdy who catches it)*

ROWDY: *(Catching it)* A fart. *(Sister laughs)*

SISTER: Oh, Lord!

(They are warming up and the passing of the ball becomes faster as they get into it)

ROWDY: Something that runs. *(Passes the ball to Sister)*

SISTER: *(Catching it)* Me, away from Chester Burns . . . A kind of fruit. *(Passes to Girlene who catches it)*

GIRLENE: *(Catching it)* Ronald Crax. Something round. *(Girlene passes it to Rowdy who catches it)*

ROWDY: *(Catching it)* Doll's heels.

DOLL: Hey!

ROWDY: Something wet. *(Passes to Girlene who catches it)*

GIRLENE: *(Catching it)* No comment. Something hard. *(Passes it to Sister who catches it)*

SISTER: *(Catching it)* No comment. Something good to eat. *(Passes it to Girlene who catches it)*

GIRLENE: *(Catching it)* No comment!! Something French. *(Passing it to Doll who catches it)*

DOLL: *(Catching it)* Eau de Cologne. Something that bounces. *(Passing it to Rowdy)*

ROWDY: *(Catching it)* Sister's checks.

SISTER: Hey!

ROWDY: A kind of machine. *(Passes it to Girlene)*

GIRLENE: *(Catching it)* Bill Berwin's Privates! Something unpredictable. *(Passes to Rowdy)*

ROWDY: *(Catching it)* A date with Al Larson. Something predictable. *(Passes to Girlene)*

GIRLENE: *(Catching it)* A *second* date with Al Larson. Something to remember! *(Passing ball to Rowdy, but all scream the response)*

EVERYONE: DON'T GO OUT WITH AL LARSON!

(They are laughing)

ROWDY: Something to dribble. *(Passes to Girlene)*

GIRLENE: *(Catching it)* The Ball. Something to pass. *(Passes it to Doll)*

DOLL: *(Catching it)* The Ball. Something to win. *(Passes it to Rowdy)*

ROWDY: *(Catching it)* The Game. The way to do it . . . *(Passes ball to Girlene)*

GIRLENE: *(Catching it)* Score.

(She tosses the ball in the overhead basketball hoop in a neat hook shot. They cheer. The ball bounces to a slowdown; she picks it up and sets it on the counter. She looks around at each of them. Picks up her wedding gown and bouquet. She embraces Doll. She embraces Sister. She approaches Rowdy and looks into her eyes)

Hey!—wish me luck!

(She tosses Rowdy the bouquet, which she catches with a big smile. Girlene exits, as Doll suddenly remembers she's left the trophy on the counter. Lights down as the three watch the door, the trophy held high in the air)

The End

Louis Phillips

GOIN' WEST

Louis Phillips

Louis Phillips is a widely-produced playwright whose works have been performed in New York City and at regional theatres throughout the United States. Playwrights will recognize Mr. Phillips as the author of numerous poems that have appeared in *The Dramatists Guild Quarterly,* and New York theatregoers will recall his quizzes on theatre topics which have appeared in the Broadway theatre program, *Playbill.*

Among his published plays are: *Warbeck, The Envoi Messages,* and *The Last of the Marx Brothers. The Envoi Messages* won first prize in the State University of New York Playwriting Contest in 1972, and was given its world premiere four years later at the Indiana Repertory Theater under the direction of Ed Stern.

For four years, Mr. Phillips was playwright-in-residence at the Colonnades Theatre Lab in New York City, where his plays *Who Here Has Seen the Color of the Wind, Warbeck,* and *The Ballroom in St. Patrick's Cathedral,* were performed under the direction of Michael Lessac. Another of Mr. Phillips's plays, *The Great American Quiz Show Scandal,* was directed by the late Alan Schneider at the University of Southern California at San Diego. In recognition of his talent Mr. Phillips received a Fellow in Playwriting Award from the National Endowment for the Arts in 1981.

Mr. Phillips's poems have appeared in numerous poetry and literary magazines. In 1985 a number of his poems were published in a collection of his works entitled *The Time, the Hour, the Solitariness of the Place.*

Currently Mr. Phillips teaches creative writing at the School of Visual Arts in New York City. He is married to Patricia Ranard and is the father of twin boys, Ian and Matthew.

Goin' West, published here for the first time, is a wild burlesque of the American dreams of fame, fortune, and happiness, which meet an inevitable disillusionment despite being preserved forever by the fantasy of the movie industry.

Characters

VOICE OF "THE OREGON TRAIL"
ARCHIBALD MONTH
AMY MONTH
APRIL MONTH
CAMERAMAN (HENRI CHATILLON)
PREACHER
CAPTAIN
SHAW
SCRIPT GIRL
INDIAN
DESLAURIERS
ROGERS
ALFRED MONTAIGNE
MAY MONTAIGNE
AMY MONTAIGNE
STRANGER (FREDERICK JACKSON TURNER)
NEWSPAPER GIRL
MAN WITH MICROPHONE
EXTRAS: PIONEERS, INDIANS, VAGRANTS, MOVIEGOERS

Setting:

The stage consists of a single wooden table. The table will be used to represent, at various stages of the journey goin' west, a raft, a small wagon, a steamship or whatever is needed to transport the Month family from east to west.

In the dark we hear a voice reading the opening paragraph of Francis Parkman's THE OREGON TRAIL.

VOICE: "Late spring, 1846, was a busy season in the city of St. Louis. Not only were emigrants from every part of the country preparing for the journey to Oregon and California, but an unusual number of traders were making ready their wagons and outfits for Santa Fe. The hotels were crowded, and the gunsmiths and saddlers were kept constantly at work in providing arms and equipment for the different parties of travellers. Steamboats were leaving the levee and passing up the Missouri, crowded with passengers on their way to the frontier."

(As the lights come up we see a man, a woman, a young child holding a rag doll, and a young man in the dress of the early 1900's trying to set up a very crude motion picture camera mounted upon a tripod. The man, Archibald Month, is dressed in buckskins; his wife, Amy, is dressed in homespun calico, as is the daughter, April. The daughter is about eight years old, with her hair in braids.

We hear the sound of swirling water. The man holds a long pole and struggles heroically as he tries to get the tiny raft down the river)

AMY: We're going to capsize!

ARCHIBALD: No, we ain't. No, we ain't.

CAMERAMAN: Gonna make a wonderful movie, Mrs. Month.

ARCHIBALD: No, it ain't. No, it ain't.

CAMERAMAN: Sure, it will. The raft capsizing and all of us falling into the water.

APRIL: *(To Doll)* Don't you worry, Marzipan. I know how to swim.

ARCHIBALD: We ain't goin' to fall into no river. Get that out of your mind.

CAMERAMAN: Make a wonderful movie for my Uncle Cecil. We'll sell it and make a lot of money.

AMY: I don't want my daughter and me to fall into the water just to make you a lot of money.

CAMERAMAN: Of course you do. Of course you do. Why else would any normal person want to go West. Especially to California.

APRIL: *(To Doll)* Don't listen to him, Marzipan. We ain't goin' into that nasty river.

(Sound of waterfalls)

AMY: What's that sound, Archibald.

CAMERAMAN: Why, that's Death's-Head Falls.

(Cameraman cranks his camera furiously)

ARCHIBALD: No, it ain't. No, it ain't.

CAMERAMAN: *(Produces a map)* Sure it is. It was marked right out on this map.

ARCHIBALD: Why didn't you mention it before?

CAMERAMAN: I just thought it would make a wonderful picture.

ARCHIBALD: Don't seem fair to me. To spring a surprise like that. You said this river was as gentle as a baby's breath.

APRIL: Marzipan and I always wanted to see waterfalls.

CAMERAMAN: No one's ever gone over these falls and lived.

(April stands up)

AMY: April, you sit down. There's nothing to be gained by dying standing up.

CAMERAMAN: Thank you, Lord!

APRIL: What are you thanking God for?

CAMERAMAN: Because God has reached into his hip pocket and pulled out my big chance. When we go over Death's-Head Falls, Documentary Photography is going to come of age!

ARCHIBALD: Put down that camera, and pole, you bastard!

APRIL: Look how white the water is.

(Roar of the falls drowns out further human sounds. Lights out. In the darkness we hear the sound of a man's voice. As the lights come up we see a scarecrow of a travelling preacher standing with his head bowed, his large black hat at his side. Under the table are three white wooden crosses. On the table is Marzipan the doll. Standing next to the preacher is the Camera-man. He takes films of the ceremony in progress)

PREACHER: Dearly beloved . . . *(He looks around; then to Cameraman)* I guess that means you . . . We are gathered here today to bury the bodies of the Month family—Archibald, Amy, and April. Some say April is the cruelest Month, but, being that she is so young, I doubt that it is so . . . They were goin' West, Lord, and their journey was swift. The river was goin' West, and its journey was swifter. For as it saith in the book of Isaiah, "For as a young man marrieth a virgin, so shall thy sons marry thee; and as the bridegroom rejoiceth over the bride, so shall thy God rejoice over thee." Amen.

CAMERAMAN: Preacher, I don't know how that verse of yours about the bridegroom rejoicing over his bride was appropriate to the occasion.

PREACHER: *(Puts on his hat)* It's got to be . . . It's the only one I know.

CAMERAMAN: Maybe you should have read from the Bible. Something like "Dust to dust . . . "

PREACHER: Can't. Can't read. Can't write. I'm only fit to be two things—a preacher or a movie producer . . .

(Sounds of a coyote howling in the distance)

CAMERAMAN: If you loan me your *Bible*, I could read something over them.

PREACHER: Traded my *Bible*.

CAMERAMAN: Traded your *Bible?*

PREACHER: Traded it for a picture of Betty Grable. I mean *Bible* is *Bible*, but legs is legs.

CAMERAMAN: Nobody can dispute with you on that.

PREACHER: *(Spits)* Nope.

(Sound of a coyote howling)

CAMERAMAN: You goin' West, too ?

PREACHER: Yep. Everybody goes West. Nothing in the East. They don't even make TV shows there.

CAMERAMAN: Maybe our paths will be crossing then.

PREACHER: Paths are crossing all the time.

(Preacher holds out his hand. The Cameraman puts a silver dollar into it. The Preacher bites it)

PREACHER: Lots of counterfeiting going on lately. Don't know who to trust.

(Preacher exits. The cameraman discovers Marzipan, and props the doll against the smallest of the three white crosses)

CAMERAMAN: I guess we should have buried the doll with you, child. But now it will just have to stand guard. Lord, let it guard all these lives. All these lives lost goin' West. And the wind will come and the dust. Then maybe somebody will find you, and they'll know. *(He picks up his camera and exits. Lights down)*

VOICE: "One day, after a protracted morning's ride, we stopped to rest at noon upon the open prairie. No trees were in sight; but close at hand a little dribbling brook was twisting side to side through a hollow . . . Henry Chatillon, before lying down, was looking for signs of snakes, the only living things he feared, and uttered various ejaculations of disgust at finding several suspicious-looking holes close to the carts."

(When the lights come up, we see two men lying underneath the table—Shaw and the Cameraman. Henri Chatillon is looking for snakes)

CAMERAMAN: If there's one thing I can't stand it's snakes.

SHAW: You'll love California then.

(A man in a cavalry uniform enters. Scene from the Oregon Trail)

CAMERAMAN: 'Lo . . . Here comes the Captain!

CAPTAIN: See that horse! . . . There! By Jove, he's off. That's your big horse, Shaw.

SHAW: Hey, that's my horse!

CAPTAIN: Go catch your horse, if you don't want to lose him.

(Shaw bolts off, trying to buckle his trousers and run at the same time)

CAPTAIN: I tell you what it is, this will never do at all. We shall lose every horse in the band some day or other, and then a pretty plight we'll be in. Now I am convinced that the only way for us is to have every man in camp stand horse-guard in rotation whenever we stop. Supposing a hundred Pawnees should jump up out of that ravine, all yelling and flapping their buffalo robes in the way they do! Why, in two minutes, not a hoof would be in sight.

CAMERAMAN: If a couple hundred Pawnees jump out of a ditch, a few horse guards ain't goin' to stop them.

CAPTAIN: At any rate, our whole system is wrong; I'm convinced of it; it is totally unmilitary. Why, the way we travel, strung out over the prairie for a mile, an enemy might attack the foremost men, and cut them off before the rest could come up.

CAMERAMAN: We're not in enemy country yet. When we are, we'll travel together.

CAPTAIN: Goin' West, ain't we?

CAMERAMAN: I'm goin' West. That's for certain.

CAPTAIN: Then we're in enemy country. They're the goddamndest Philistines out there. Just as you think you've got it made in the shade, you get attacked in your camp. We've no sentinels. We camp in disorder; no precautions at all against surprise. My own convictions are that we ought to camp in a hollow square with the fires in the centre, and have sentinels and a regular password appointed every night. Besides, there should be vedettes, riding in advance . . .

CAMERAMAN: Vedettes?

CAPTAIN: I don't write it. I just read it.

CAMERAMAN: Who in the hell knows what vedettes are?

CAPTAIN: Script girl!

(Script Girl enters)

SCRIPT GIRL: Please! Let's not have any more arguments about the script. We've got to shoot the scene before we lose the light.

CAPTAIN: Light! That's what we're always losing around here! That's all we ever lose. I want to live someplace where I can lose something else beside light!

CAMERAMAN: Nobody knows what vedettes are.

SCRIPT GIRL: Shall I ask the writer?

CAPTAIN: He don't know. He just puts them in because it sounds good. Big long word like that.

SCRIPT GIRL: It's only eight letters.

CAPTAIN: Shouldn't be no words in a Western. A Western is action. It's shoot 'em up, bang, bang. The good guys chasing the bad guys all over the landscape and roundin' 'em up. But no, play-wrights have got to have us stand around and talk.

(During the above a savage Indian has snuck up on the crew. He lets out a savage cry and leaps. The Captain pulls out his pistol and shoots. He catches the savage in mid-air, the Indian falls dead in a heap)

CAPTAIN: Now that's what people pay to see. That's what a Western is. If movies are goin' to survive, it's got to have more action in them than in real life. In the East, people ride about in little vehicles; in the West we stand free and unafraid. We move. We revel in action. We take meetings!

(The Cameraman walks to the savage and kicks him)

CAMERAMAN: You know what I think? . . . I think we're runnin' out of Injuns.

(Lights out. In the dark we hear the song "She Wore a Yellow Ribbon." The song fades. We hear a voice in the dark)

VOICE: "On the next morning we had gone but a mile or two when we came to an extensive belt of woods, through the midst of which ran a stream, wide, deep, and of an appearance particularly muddy and treacherous. Deslauriers was in advanced with his cart . . . In plunged the cart, but midway it stuck fast."

(Lights up. A French Canadian stands on the table with a whip. Behind the wagon; two other men are trying to use poles to help the cart out of the mud)

DESLAURIERS: Sacré . . .

ROGERS: Drive on! Drive on!

CAPTAIN: My advice is that we unload; for I'll bet any man five pounds that if we try to go through we shall stick fast.

DESLAURIERS: Mud! That's all this country is . . . from one end to the other. Mud.

ROGERS: Drive on! Drive on!

CAPTAIN: Well, I can only give my advice, and if people won't be reasonable, why, they won't, that's all.

DESLAURIERS: Mud . . . What good is mud?

CAPTAIN: Mud.

ROGERS: Drive on! Drive on!

DESLAURIERS: Can't you say nothin' else?

ROGERS: I don't write it. I just read it.

CAPTAIN: That's the attitude that's going to make you a star, boy! . . . Look at this mud. You know what I predict? I predict that someday there's goin' to be a great motion picture palace, and in front of it there's goin' to be lots of mud. Tons and tons of mud, and people are goin' to lie down in the mud . . . They're goin' to stick their noses and legs and faces and moustaches right into it . . . It'll be the biggest thing to hit the West since the Buffalo.

ROGERS: Sounds like a great idea, Captain.

(Enter the Cameraman, carrying a motion picture screen)

CAPTAIN: What's that blockhead bringin' with him now?

CAMERAMAN: I've got this idea. We're goin' to line up all the covered wagons around this movie screen and we'll show movies under the stars. It will change our whole attitude how we look at movies.

(Sound of Indians)

ROGERS: Sounds like the Pawnees, Captain.

CAPTAIN: Deslauriers, would you run away if the Pawnees should fire at us?

DESLAURIERS: Ah! Oui, oui, monsieur.

CAPTAIN: Good. If there is one thing disastrous to the human race, it's reckless courage.

ROGERS: They're comin' over the ridge, Capt'n.

CAPTAIN: Men, prepare to fire.

(Sound of an Indian attack. Rifle shots. Lights out. Lights up on the Captain who stands alone in a circle of light)

CAPTAIN: Four or five horsemen soon entered the river, and in ten minutes had waded across and clambered up the loose sandbank. They were ill-looking fellows, thin and swarthy, with careworn anxious faces, and lips rigidly compressed. They had good cause for anxiety; it was three days since they first encamped here, and on the night of their arrival they had lost a hundred and twenty-three of their best cattle, driven off by wolves, through the neglect of the man on guard. This discouraging and alarming calamity was not the first that had overtaken them. Since leaving the settlements, they had met with nothing but misfortune. Some of their party had died; one man had been killed by the Pawnees; and about a week before they had been plundered by the Dakotahs of all their best horses, the wretched animals on which our visitors were mounted being the only ones that were left. They had encamped, they told us, near sunset, by the side of the Platte, and their oxen were scattered over the meadow, while the horses were feeding a little farther off. Suddenly the ridges of the hills were alive with a swarm of mounted Indians, at least six hundred in number, who came pouring with a yell down towards the camp, rushing up within a few rods, to the great terror of the emigrants; when, suddenly wheeling, they swept around the band of horses, and in five minutes disappeared with their prey through the openings of the hills.

(Lights down. Lights up on a family in their wagon goin' West—a man, a woman, and a young child. They should remind us of the family we met in the opening scene. The man —Alfred Montaigne—is dressed in buckskins. His wife, Amy, is dressed in homespun calico, as is their eight year old daughter, May. They are singing the children's song, "The Tailor and the Mouse," their voices lifting high and carrying over the wide expanse of prairie)
MONTAIGNE FAMILY: (Singing)
"There was a tailor had a mouse,
Hi-diddle dum cum feed-a.
They lived together in one house.
Hi diddle dum cum feed-a,
Hi diddle dum, cum tin-trum, tantraum,
Through the town of Ramsey,
Hi diddle dum, come over the lea,
Hi diddle dum cum feed-a."
ALFRED: Onward, Old Paint. We have to go to California. That's where the money is. Heaps and heaps of it, piled all the way up to the sky. All you have to do is sell your life story to the movies and you're on easy street forever. Onward, Old Paint. To Beverly Hills and Rodeo Drive.
MAY: I don't like the way you call the horse "Old Paint," Poppa. Can't we call him something else.
AMY: Hush, dear. Don't talk while Daddy is driving.
ALFRED: Look at it, Amy. The whole prairie is clogged with covered wagons.
AMY: I guess everybody's got the same idea we've got.

ALFRED: Goin' West. Everybody and their uncle goin' West. Because the West is a dream, and we're pushing our horses hard, and our families hard, and ourselves hard to get a piece of it. If you get up on that silver screen, it's immortality. Onward, Old Paint!

AMY: I want to call him something else, Poppa.

ALFRED: Anything you want, my darlin'. Anything you want, my dear. Why do you think we're risking starvation, risking sandstorms, risking mud, risking Indian attacks—so my little girl can grow up in Hollywood.

AMY: All right, May. You go ahead. What do you want to name the horse?

MAY: Can we call him "Giddy-up?"

ALFRED: Can't call a horse "Giddy-up."

MAY: Why not, Poppa?

ALFRED: Well, suppose I want it to "Whoa" and I have to say, "Whoa, Giddy-up." Now "Whoa, Giddy-up" is goin' to be pretty confusin' to a horse. Old Paint won't know whether to stop or to plunge forward. The poor horse will have a nervous breakdown, and it's not easy to find a good animal psychiatrist out on this freeway.

AMY: Lot of animal psychiatrists in Los Angeles.

ALFRED: I know, but we ain't there yet.

MAY: Then let's call him something else.

ALFRED: OK, giddy-up, Something Else.

MAY: I gotta go to the bathroom.

AMY: We just left Fort Leavenworth.

ALFRED: All right. But make it quick. And be on the lookout for snakes.

(The wagon stops. May hops off and goes offstage. A man appears. He is Frederick Jackson Turner, author of The Frontier in American History. *He is dressed in simple black and wears spectacles. He carries with him a satchel filled to overflowing with notes and papers and books)*

AMY: Look, Alfred. There's a man standing there!

(Alfred Montaigne reaches for his rifle)

ALFRED: Howdy, stranger!

STRANGER: Howdy.

ALFRED: What are you doin' out here on foot? Shank's mare is no way to travel, especially if you're goin' West. You've got to enter California first class, or they don't pay no attention to you at all.

STRANGER: My horse was stolen by the Pawnees, so I'm hoping some West-goin' family will offer me friendly transportation.

ALFRED: Well, we're right friendly enough. I'm Alfred Montaigne, this is my wife, Amy . . . Our little girl, May, has gone off into the bushes.

STRANGER: Pleased to meet you all. I'm Frederick Jackson Turner.

ALFRED: You're not dressed to be a frontier scout, Mr. Turner.

TURNER: Well, I am a frontier scout in a way.

(He climbs onto the wagon table)

TURNER: You see I'm doing a study of the "Significance of the Frontier in American History."

ALFRED: A professor, uh. Now ain't that interesting . . . Ain't that interesting, Amy?

AMY: Our family don't know much about book larnin'.

TURNER: It's my thesis, ma'am, that " . . . the frontier is the outer edge of the wave—the meeting point between savagery and civilization."

AMY: What do you mean by savagery, Mr. Turner?

TURNER: Savagery? Oh, I suppose, killing, looting, violence, and, pardon me, ma'am, rape, in a savage sort of way.

(Alfred Montaigne takes up a jug of corn liquor)

ALFRED: And civilization?

TURNER: Civilization? Oh, I suppose, killing, looting, violence, and, pardon me, ma'am, rape, in a civilized sort of way.

AMY: What's taking that girl so long . . . *(She stands up and calls)* May!

ALFRED: It's refreshing to talk to a man of ideas, Professor, because that's all our great country is, a land of ideas from one coast to the other. Ideas piled up like boulders, like rocks, like mountains, and we got to dynamite our way through.

AMY: May! You answer me! You hear me, girl?

TURNER: I agree with you, Mr. Montaigne. "The most important effect of the frontier has been the promotion of democracy here and in Europe." The frontier produces individuals.

AMY: May!

ALFRED: I'll go fetch her. I guess she's playing games with us again.

TURNER: Can I be of any help?

ALFRED: *(Jumping down)* You just sit here, Professor, and think your great thoughts. Our daughter's just angry with us because I wouldn't let her change the name of the horse.

(Alfred goes off)

AMY: I should have gone with her.

TURNER: Oh, it's a great opportunity goin' West, ma'am. We're goin' to expand westward and develop all sorts of new opportunities . . . Whatever pressures build up in the East, we've got the West . . . It's a safety valve. We blow off steam by movin' West.

(Alfred emerges from the undergrowth. He carries his dead daughter in his arms. An arrow sticks from her breast)

AMY: *(Horror stricken)* May!

ALFRED: Savages!

(Lights out. In the darkness we can hear the melancholy song of a lone harmonica. As the lights come up, we see Alfred and May standing beside a small white cross. With the man and wife is the scarecrow of the travelling Preacher, and the Professor with his satchel of papers by his side)

PREACHER: "For as a young man marrieth a virgin, so shall thy sons marry thee: and as the bridegroom rejoiceth over the bride, so shall thy God rejoice over thee." Amen.

OTHERS: Amen.

(Preacher holds out his hat and takes up a collection. One by one, he pulls out the coins and tests them with his teeth)

PREACHER: Sorry it couldn't be more elaborate . . . but you know how it is. All this dying hardly gives a man time to prepare. It's hard to see the significance of it all when there's so much space to traipse around in . . . Too much space for the eye to behold, and it all comes down to a few feet of earth.

(Preacher exits)

TURNER: The wilderness masters the colonist. It finds him a European in dress, industries, tools, modes of travel, and thought. It takes him from the railroad car and puts him in the birch canoe. It strips off the garments of civilization and arrays him in the hunting shirt and the moccasin. It puts him in the log cabin of the Cherokee and Iroquois.

ALFRED: Will you shut off your yap . . .

AMY: Alfred!

ALFRED: Goin' West ain't no theory . . . it's no big words from educated men . . . Oh no, Goin' West is living and dyin' and scrapin'. It's holdin' your family together by the sweat of your brow . . .

AMY: *(To Turner)* Don't mind him. He's out of his head with grief.

ALFRED: Out of my head with grief! Well, let me tell you somethin'. When you look at that horse there, you call him 'Giddy-up' and nothing else . . . Because that's what its name is, for now and forever! Amen and Giddy-up!

(Lights out. Sound of people singing "Shall We Gather by the River." *When the lights come up we see Alfred Montaigne standing on the table with his wife, Amy. Around Amy's neck is a halter of rope. Alfred holds the end of the rope. A crude sign reads:* AUCTION THIS MORNIN'. *A few people, including the Cameraman [Henri Chatillon] stand lazily about)*

ALFRED: Sure, she's got a few lines on her . . .

(The Captain crosses to Henri Chatillon)

CAPTAIN: What's goin' on, Henri?

ALFRED: A few miles on the old speedometer, but that don't mean she don't have some good years left.

CAPTAIN: Another one of your publicity stunts?

ALFRED: She may not give you any more children, but what are you goin' to do with children anyway? They aren't writin' movies for children.

CAMERAMAN: Auctioning off his wife.

ALFRED: How about an openin' bid of a hundred dollars?

CAPTAIN: You kiddin' me, Henri?

CAMERAMAN: Nope.

ALFRED: One hundred dollars, and you take this woman home with you.

CROWD MEMBER: How about a thirty-day guarantee?

(Laughter)

CROWD MEMBER: If we take her off your hands and it don't work out, can we return her to you?

ALFRED: Guarantee? Why, I'm givin' this woman the highest recommendation a lovin' husband can give . . . When you snore or come to bed without washing the mud off your boots, she don't make no piss and moan about it.

CROWD MEMBER: Seventy-five and a bottle of hootch.

ALFRED: One hundred or nothing. This old lady loves the hanky-pank so much, she's worth her weight in gold. In fact that's what I should be asking—her weight in gold.

CROWD MEMBER: What do you need all this money for, friend?

ALFRED: I won't lie to you. I need the money to start my own movie company. I've got a blockbuster of a film deal cooking with 20th Century Coyote. So there's got to be a little trade-off involved. Look at me, ladies and gents. I ain't done much in my life, so don't let this big chance pass me by just because you got a few twinges of conscience. When it comes to goin' West, conscience can have nothin' to do with it. It's a once in a lifetime deal. A chance to rub elbows with Eddie Polo and all the big name movie stars. If you don't bid on this woman, I'm goin' to kill myself, because I was born to make movies, I was born to take meetings and to talk deals. When I was born, The Good Fairy of the Expense Account was hovering over my cradle. It's her wand that has touched me.

CROWD MEMBER: Touched you in the head, you mean.

ALFRED: Oh, no, friend, we're all in the same boat. We wanna talk money. We don't wanna talk buffalo dung, that's for sure. I wanna talk money in seven figures. I wanna plaster dreams up where everybody can see 'em. Everybody stands in line waiting for the big dream, the beautiful bodies to be flashed.

CROWD MEMBER: Flash us some of those beautiful bodies, and maybe you've got yourself a deal.

ALFRED: A beautiful body don't bring you no peace of mind the way this woman brings you peace of mind . . . It's getting late. The Decline of the West is setting in. What are we goin' to do?

CROWD MEMBER: I bid one hundred pound sterling!

ALFRED: Let me tell you this. Whoever buys this woman here . . . when I go on the Academy Awards show, and everybody in the whole world is watching, I will speak that person's name . . . speak that person's name in front of the whole world, thanking that person for making my great success possible. How about that?

(The bidding increases)

CROWD MEMBER: One hundred twenty-five.

ALFRED: I hear one hundred twenty-five pound sterling.

CROWD MEMBER: One hundred and fifty.

CROWD MEMBER: One hundred and sixty.

CROWD MEMBER: One hundred and seventy.

ALFRED: One hundred and seventy, once . . . How about her weight in gold?

CROWD MEMBER: One hundred and eighty.

CROWD MEMBER: Gol' durn it. Let's stop this pussy-footin' around. *(He tosses up some bags of gold dust)* I offer her weight in gold.

ALFRED: Gents. Anyone want to beat that offer? . . . Going once, twice, gone. Sold! I tell you, sir, you've made a wise decision . . . Now I can start my search for a new Rhett Butler and a new Scarlett O'Hara.

(Winner jumps to the table and grabs the woman, lifting the woman's dress)

CROWD MEMBER: *(Winning bidder)* Come here, woman. Let's get down to the hanky-pank.

(Lights out. We hear the voices of whippoorwills and the voices of quail. And then the flash of lightning. The sound of rain)

VOICE: "But all our hopes were delusive. Scarcely had night set in when the tumult broke forth anew. The thunder here is not like the tame thunder of the Atlantic coast. Bursting with a terrific crash directly above our heads, it roared over the boundless waste of prairie, seeming to roll around the whole circle of the firmament with a peculiar and awful reverberation. The lightning flashed all night, playing its livid glare upon the neighboring trees, revealing the vast expanse of the plain, and then leaving us shut in as if by a palpable wall of darkness."

VOICE #2: How are ye, boys? Are ye for Oregon or California.

VOICE #3: California.

VOICE #4: California.

VOICE #5: California.

VOICE #2: Everybody in the whole world is goin' West, headin' to California!

(Music—"California, Here I Come." Lights up. A Newspaper Girl stands on the table, hawking her wares)

NEWSPAPER GIRL: Extra, extra, read all about it! California sinks into the ocean! . . . Extra, Extra, read all about it! California sinks into the ocean!

(Man with a microphone appears)

MAN WITH MICROPHONE: This is Burt Ellis from Station KLO reporting on the events of the day.

NEWSPAPER GIRL: Movie studios destroyed. Economists predict great depression.

MAN WITH MICROPHONE: The stock market plunged today when news reached the East Coast about the apparent demise of California. It seemed that four billion persons of all nations, weights, and sizes, descended upon California today to take part in the worldwide search for the new Rhett Butler and Scarlett O'Hara. Early reports suggest that the combined weight of all the hopefuls was just too much for the state to bear. The entire United States shifted toward the West, and California simply broke off and sunk into the Pacific. It is too early to say whether there are any survivors.

NEWSPAPER GIRL: Read all about it! "California Sinks Into the Ocean." No more movies to be made.

MAN WITH MICROPHONE: Stay tuned, ladies and gentlemen. We'll bring you an update as soon as we get it, and now back to our studios for a little mood music.

(Lights down. Mood music is the "Hallellujah Chorus." *When the lights come back up, the table now holds a life-sized cutout of the woman, May Montaigne, who had been auctioned off. She is dressed in sexy lingerie and strikes a suggestive pose. Next to the cutout is a movie poster that reads:* "Today only. Hollywood's Final Film—May Montaigne in *The Palpable Wall of Darkness.*" *We hear the rain. The lightning flashes. Two patrons of the movies enter. They check the skies and hoist their umbrellas.*

Under the table are vagrants, bums, the down-and-out. All members of the cast are there dressed in rags. They warm their hands by a small fire. They cook soup in cans)

MOVIEGOER #1: How did you like the movie, darling?

MOVIEGOER #2: I'm tired of Westerns, Alfred. They're all the same. Shoot 'em up, bang, bang.

BEGGAR: *(Henri Chatillon)* Take your picture for a quarter?

MOVIEGOER #1: Go away.

MOVIEGOER #2: The good guys chasing the bad guys all over the landscape. It's always the same.

VAGRANT: *(To his daughter)* Get up there, daughter, and sing for the nice people.

MOVIEGOER #2: You would think the last movie would have had more imagination . . .

VAGRANT GIRL: *(Sings)*
"There was a tailor had a mouse,
Hi diddle dum cum feed-a.
They lived together in one house,
Hi diddle dum cum feed-a."

MOVIEGOER #1: Didn't you like the part about the family goin' over Death's-Head Falls?

MOVIEGOER #2: Too sad. Movies should let us forget our troubles . . . *(Pauses in front of the life-sized cutout)* I don't know why they never once let May Montaigne make any comedies. I bet there was a secret sadness to her life, something the fan magazines were afraid to reveal.

VAGRANT: *(To his daughter)* Do a little dance for the nice people, darling.

MOVIEGOER #1: You know what I was thinking about when I saw that family go over Death's-Head Falls?

MOVIEGOER #2: What?

MOVIEGOER #1: I was thinking Documentary Photography had finally come of age . . . Too bad California had to fall off into the ocean.

(One of the beggars removes a harmonica and starts to play a melancholy tune. As the Moviegoers exit, the man with the daughter turns and calls to them)

VAGRANT: If things had been different, my daughter could have been another Shirley Temple! Yes, she could! Another Shirley Temple!

(The Moviegoers exit)

VAGRANT GIRL:
"Hi diddle dum, cum tin-trum, tantram,
Through the town of Ramsey . . .
(Lights out)

The End

Shannon Keith Kelley

PRACTICAL MAGIC

Shannon Keith Kelley

Practical Magic by Shannon Keith Kelley is the third play in a trilogy of one-acts under the collective title *Hope of the Future,* which premiered at the Denver Center Theater under the direction of Randal Myler in March of 1986. Reacting to the evening of plays, *Variety* reviewer Young reflects, "As that unusual item in contemporary theatre, Kelley's plays show gentle persuasion in their glimpses of young people and their relationships over a period of time. . . . In each of these, Kelley enriches ordinary conversations with the pulse of life, its small laughs and deep sorrow, but the stress is on the casual remark that wells up with startling emotion." Teri Micco, covering the play for *Westword,* comments on the characters: "Willing to look beyond the often harsh (and sometimes Mickey Mouse) realities of a world moving too quickly to be interested in even the simplest dreams of one man, Kelley's characters dare to pause. They dare to question, and in questioning themselves, each other and society, to have faith not just in the slick wisdom of the empirical (the observed and proven), but in the magical wisdom of the soul."

In *Practical Magic* the author probes the contrast of reactions between a young couple with a robust new baby and another couple whose infant needs medical attention in order to examine the need for faith, and rituals which confirm that faith, in a society preoccupied with material comforts. The two other plays in the trilogy, *Dennis and Rex* and *Rapid Transit,* explore episodes in the earlier lives of characters who share the background and values of the couples in *Practical Magic.* Additional productions of the three plays, either together or separately, have been presented in New York City at the Manhattan Punch Line, Theatre at St. Clements, the W.P.A. Theatre, and the Circle Repertory Theatre.

Other plays by Mr. Kelley which have been presented at regional or college theatres include: *Time Was, Ever After, Headsets, Blind Home Coming Near,* and *Big Apple Messenger.* Among the additional theatres which have produced Mr. Kelley's work are the Actors Theatre of Louisville, the Arena Stage in Washington, D.C., the Mark Taper Forum in Los Angeles, the Pennsylvania Stage Company in Allentown, and the South Coast Repertory in Costa Mesa, California.

A native of Cape Girardeau, Missouri, Mr. Kelley now lives in Springfield, Illinois, with his wife and son. His writing projects recently have included scripts for video productions for the State of Illinois. Also a poet, Mr. Kelley has had frequent publication in literary magazines and anthologies, and has a collection of poems in a chapbook entitled *About in the Dark.*

Prior to living in Illinois Mr. Kelley spent a decade in New York. During that time he worked for a Manhattan messenger service as phone man and dispatcher, held a variety of temporary jobs, and for five years worked on the staff of *Popular Mechanics* magazine. Also during his New York years he was a member of the Circle Repertory Theatre's Playwrights Lab. He holds an M.F.A. in playwriting from Ohio University and is a two-time recipient of the university's Alumni Performing Arts Award for the plays *Time Was* and *Big Apple Messenger.* Other awards for his work include a 1986 award in playwriting from the Illinois Arts Council and an award in the Illinois State University Fine Arts Competition for the play *Ever After,* which the college produced in March of 1987.

Last year *Practical Magic* was published with its two companion plays in *PrimaFacie 1986, An Anthology of New American Plays.* Mr. Kelley dedicates *Practical Magic:* "in memory of Dolph Sweet."

Characters:

> ARNIE
> ROBERT
> CAROL
> DIANE

(All the characters are around thirty years of age.)

Time:

> *The present.*

Scene I:

> *A small park near Manhasset General Hospital, Manhasset, Long Island. Arnie and Robert enter, followed by Carol and Diane. It is spring. Carol and Diane are both in the third trimester of pregnancy.*

ARNIE: *(To Robert)* In Oregon, I've heard, they do it with Jell–O.

CAROL: *(To Diane)* Hold it under warm running water and beat it with a knife handle.

ROBERT: *(To Arnie)* With Jell-O?

CAROL: *(To the men)* That's not confirmed.

ARNIE: It's rumored.

CAROL: *(To Diane)* Works every time. You have to beat it counter-clockwise, of course. Clockwise you're just tightening it.

DIANE: Warm water, beat counter-clockwise. I'll remember.

ROBERT: That sounds interesting.

ARNIE: Yeah, it does.

DIANE: Lids.

ROBERT: What about lids?

DIANE: That's how you loosen them.

ROBERT: Another fantasy down the drain.

CAROL: *(Laughs)* Is he always like this?

DIANE: Only since I'm pregnant. Can't keep his hands off me or his mind off sex.

ARNIE: What else is there? I mean, up to a certain point, you understand. For the male.

ROBERT: We're all obviously beyond that point. *(To Carol)* I'm always like this.

CAROL: *(To Diane)* Lucky girl.

ROBERT: Diane never noticed until after she became pregnant.

ARNIE: I know what you're going through. I can sympathize. I hate the feeling of working alone.

CAROL: Continue in this vein and you can continue "working alone."

ARNIE: Carol, I've held my end up.

CAROL: That's right, Arnie, *you* have.

ROBERT: *(To Arnie)* Is she always like this?

ARNIE: Only since June, 1975. We were married in June of '75.

CAROL: June what, dear? Go on, June what?

ARNIE: I remember the date of our anniversary.

CAROL: Every other year.

ARNIE: The twelfth. We were married June twelfth.

ROBERT: Atta boy, Arn.

DIANE: Marvelous, isn't it, the way men remember when they want to remember?

CAROL: *(Sitting at a bench)* Alicia's going to be one disappointed little girl.

ARNIE: Oops.

CAROL: Alicia's our daughter. You remember, don't you, Arn? *(To Carol and Robert)* Alicia was born on June twelfth.

(Sound of an ice cream truck)

ARNIE: The twenty-second is our anniversary.

CAROL: There are no second guesses.

ARNIE: I always get those numbers mixed up, you know that.

CAROL: You work with numbers.

ARNIE: Numbers as inches, as feet, as yards. Not numbers as dates.

ROBERT: You set our cause back a hundred days.

ARNIE: I'm the one who will suffer.

CAROL: Got that right, first guess.

ARNIE: I hear the tinkle of an ice cream truck. Want a malted, honey?

DIANE: *(Crossing to near the bench)* The appetite tactic.

CAROL: I'm aware.

ARNIE: How 'bout a sundae? Float?

CAROL: How about diamond earrings on June twenty-second. See Lucille at Fortunoff's. She knows the pair I want.

ARNIE: Six weeks to our anniversary and already I'm paying.

ROBERT: Why is it that men bear the burden of proof when it comes to anniversaries and birthdays?

CAROL: *(To Diane)* He's a lawyer? *(Diane nods)* You can always tell.

DIANE: Because men are the partners who invariably forget. *(A beat)* Me, too.

CAROL: Men you can always tell.

ROBERT: How about you, babe? Want something?

DIANE: *(Sitting at the bench)* Diamond earrings. I'll let you know which ones after I've consulted with Lucille.

(The men exchange glances)

ARNIE: I'm having a cone. And I'm buying for the group. What's your pleasure, Diane? I ask you because my wife has to flip through her mental rolodex before she arrives at a decision.

CAROL: Sundae. Mint chocolate chip. Double chocolate sprinkles.

DIANE: Sounds delicious. Make that two, thank you.

ARNIE: Coming with me?

ROBERT: I'm not staying here alone. I'm already out a set of earrings.

ARNIE: At least you don't have to shop.

(The ice cream truck starts leaving)

ROBERT: He's pulling out.

ARNIE: Yo, calorie man!

(The men jog off)

DIANE: Thanks for the earrings.

CAROL: I'm glad to be of help. He'll get them for you?

DIANE: Probably. Robert's a romantic. He *thinks* he'll surprise me with them one night. He'll use joint savings. Robert's also extremely practical.

CAROL: What do you care as long as your ears dazzle. *(They laugh)* When's your due date?

DIANE: The fifth of next month.

CAROL: Mine's the eleventh. If I deliver on that date, Arnie will really get confused.

DIANE: Did you have Alicia with Lamaze?

CAROL: Are you kidding? I had trouble getting him to the hospital waiting room. Arnie had a dream. In his dream, there were all these men in the waiting room, pacing shoulder to shoulder. Each smoking a pack of Marlboros a minute.

DIANE: *(Laughs)* Oh, no.

CAROL: It gets better. Arnie couldn't get in line with them to pace. Said it was like rush hour on the L.I.E. No room left on the floor for him to walk. In the dream, he said everybody walked in the same direction, don't ask me why. He's compelled to pace. So he jumps up on the furniture and goes stride for stride with them. He's on the couch, he's on the end table, he's on the arm chair. He takes a *carton* of cigarettes from his coat pocket—somehow it fits in his breast pocket ...

DIANE: Marlboros?

CAROL: He didn't say. He doesn't smoke.

DIANE: That's good. Neither does Robert.

CAROL: Except in the dream he does. So Arnie's frantically trying to keep up with the others while digging in his pockets for a light. He realizes he has no lighter and no matches. he gets hit by this huge nicotine fit—body starts to shake, hands tremble ...

DIANE: This is a full-fledged nightmare.

CAROL: Arnie screams, "Will somebody give me a light. Anybody." *(A beat)* The men stop all at once. Arnie looks at them. And they now have these identical green gargoyle heads from a Japanese movie. In unison, all the gargoyle people pull identical red Cricket lighters, strike them, push their matching green monster hands at him.

DIANE: What does Arnie do?

CAROL: He lights up from one of the gargoyles. And then— this is where it gets weird—he takes a couple of puffs, they all start marching ...

DIANE: In unison?

CAROL: Unh-hunh. And Arnie says all of a sudden he feels this instantaneous change come over his body. He knows he's become one of the gargoyle men.

DIANE: This is right out of *Twilight Zone*—no, *Outer Limits*.

CAROL: He looks down at his hand ...

DIANE: And it's slime-colored with leathery skin and warty knots all over. Oh, that's awful.

CAROL: Yes, that is. But no, that's not what he sees. His hand is now feathers, the tip of a wing. Arnie goes berserkers. Stumbles over the end table, the chair, the couch to a mirror and in it is this exotic, white-plumed bird. With kind, pearl-like, skyblue eyes. And that bird is him.

(Pause)

DIANE: That's wonderful. Wonder what it means?

CAROL: He woke up. *(A beat)* Arnie's come a long way since Alicia was born. *(A beat)* Robert wanted to go natural?

DIANE: Never any question for either of us. It seems much healthier for the baby than other methods.

CAROL: Also for the mother.

DIANE: I suppose so.

CAROL: I *know* so. With my daughter, I was loopy from medication twenty-four hours after. My eyes wouldn't focus more than a couple of seconds . . .

DIANE: Light-headed?

CAROL: Light-headed—to say the least. When they brought my baby to me first time, I thought the nurse was bringing in a basket of cellophane-wrapped fruit—that pinkish tint, you've seen it. Alicia did have a banana head at birth, I hate to say.

(The men enter carrying four mint chocolate chip sundaes with double chocolate sprinkles)

ARNIE: No table, no birthing chair, nothing but this womb temperature gelatin mattress.

ROBERT: What's the purpose?

CAROL: They're back in Oregon.

ARNIE: Supposed to relieve pressure for the mother and simulate a womb-extension experience for the infant, a bridge from the womb to the world.

ROBERT: I thought the baby needed the shock of an extra-uterine environment to get him to breathe.

ARNIE: Apparently this is enough shock.

ROBERT: Interesting.

ARNIE: They're very progressive in Oregon.

ROBERT: *(Handing the sundae to Diane)* Sounds similar to Leboyer, but with the emphasis on the mother.

ARNIE: Yeah, she even gets to choose the flavor of gelatin.

CAROL: The *color* Arnie, the *color*.

ARNIE: I heard rumored flavor.

CAROL: The gelatin isn't for eating, it's for cushioning. It has no flavor.

ARNIE: Seems like a waste. All that Jell-O.

CAROL: It's not *really* Jell-O, Arnie.

ARNIE: Then why do they call it Jell-O?

CAROL: It's a synonym.

ARNIE: Oh.

ROBERT: The Zuñi Indians of Western New Mexico scoop out the ground right after delivery, rub clean wet sand between hot stones, spread the warmed sand in the hole, and place a heated cloth over that. Sand beds, they're called. One for the mother, one for the newborn.

(A beat)

DIANE: Robert's intrigued by various birth rituals.

ROBERT: There's a link, don't you see, between the Jell-O method and Zuñi sand beds?

(A beat)

ARNIE: Possibly.

(A beat)

CAROL: Know much about birth-related dreams, Robert?

ROBERT: Afraid not.

CAROL: *(To Diane)* Anyway, don't expect your baby to look like an ad for Pampers.

DIANE: Oh, I know they can appear pretty roughed-up right after delivery.

ARNIE: Alicia was a bruised banana the first couple of days.

CAROL: He called her Chiquita till I made him stop.

ROBERT: As long as he's healthy.

(All knock wood on the bench)

ARNIE: You know it's a boy?

DIANE: We know it's an it. He hopes it's a boy.

ROBERT: I'd be satisfied with a healthy girl.

ARNIE: Ibid. all around.

(All knock wood)

ROBERT: I find it difficult at the median point of the third trimester to call our baby an "it." I don't know how you can.

DIANE: I'm only trying to keep an open mind—and to keep you from being disappointed.

ROBERT: I won't be disappointed as . . .

THE OTHERS: Long as it's healthy.

(All knock wood)

CAROL: Arnie?

ARNIE: Yeah?

CAROL: Give me my sundae.

(He gives her the sundae, sits on the end of the bench)

DIANE: *(Rising)* Robert, sit down.

ROBERT: Don't be ridiculous.

DIANE: You're the one with swollen feet. I'm pregnant, his feet swell.

ROBERT: I have sympathy feet. *(Motioning her to sit)* I'll scrunch in.

(All squeeze in on the bench. They begin eating the sundaes slowly, then voraciously, then with abandon)

ARNIE: *(In between bites)* Another thing, Robert, make sure Diane practices her Kugel exercise. That's important for later.

CAROL: You're a piece of work, aren't you, hon?

DIANE: Kugel?

CAROL: He means Kegel.

(Diane tries not to laugh)

ARNIE: Kugel, Kegel, who cares as long as you do it.

CAROL: Your mother. According to her, she makes the best kugel in her Hadassah, if not all of Long Island.

ARNIE: That's what she's always going on about?

CAROL: Among other things.

ARNIE: I thought that stuff was deep dish knish.

CAROL: How can you not know kugel? You grew up in a Jewish household.

ARNIE: As soon as I was old enough to leave home, I ate out. My point is, the workbook says the Kegel is the most important exercise *for the rest of a woman's life.*

CAROL: Your concern touches me.

ARNIE: I paraphrase from the workbook: good muscle tone in the pelvic cavity enhances sexual pleasure by narrowing the vaginal canal.

CAROL: For both partners.

ARNIE: What?

CAROL: Enhances sexual pleasure for both partners.

ARNIE: That goes without saying.

CAROL: Sure it does.

ROBERT: Have you been practicing your Kegels?

DIANE: Robert.

ROBERT: Have you?

DIANE: Yes.

ROBERT: Atta girl.

DIANE: When I watch *Magnum, P.I.*

(A beat)

ROBERT: Okay, I get the message.

DIANE: Good.

(All eat in silence for a moment)

ROBERT: I think we have a more than competent instructor.

DIANE: I'm glad she's a registered nurse at Manhasset General.

ARNIE: And that she actually delivered her child by Lamaze.

ROBERT: Yes.

DIANE: Unh-hunh.

CAROL: I don't know. Something about her.

DIANE: She does seem a bit remote.

ROBERT: Tends to recite the information at times, as if she'd rather be somewhere else.

ARNIE: She could give more individualized instruction when we practice the breathing. When I did effleurage, for instance . . .

CAROL: You know I'm ticklish . . .

ARNIE: That's the point. She could maybe have given you some tips on concentration.

CAROL: I can't concentrate when I'm being tickled.

ARNIE: If, in your mind's eye, you had established a proper focal point, you wouldn't've noticed.

CAROL: Effleurage is intended to induce relaxation, to block out discomfort.

ARNIE: So?

CAROL: If I don't notice it, how can it help me?

ARNIE: I give up.

CAROL: The idea of you moving your fingertips slowly in a pattern from my pubic bone to my stomach is *funny*. With Arnie, foreplay is more like three-play.

ARNIE: Don't mind me, I'm only sitting here. *(A beat)* Think of *Magnum, P.I.* when I do it.

CAROL: *(Suggestively)* Oh, I couldn't do that.

ARNIE: I'm talking natural childbirth, fulfilling my responsibility as husband and coach—your mind's in Teen Sexland. I want to participate in this as much as I can. If it's not going to happen for us, tell me now and we can skip the last two meetings.

CAROL: *(Seriously)* I'll try harder. I won't laugh anymore.

ARNIE: Even if you have to?

CAROL: I'll do my best. *(A beat)*Next session, I'll take the instructor aside for us.

ARNIE: I'd appreciate it.

CAROL: Even though she has no hips.

ARNIE: That's what you don't like about her?

CAROL: The woman has no hips, how can she be a mother?

DIANE: She wears that necklace with the boy figurien.

ROBERT: I don't think she'd deliberately lie about that.

CAROL: She isn't under oath.

ROBERT: That's true.

CAROL: She has no hips now, imagine her thighs before.

ARNIE: Number two pencils. *(Arnie and Carol laugh. All eat)* Do you spend much time in court, Robert?

ROBERT: Never, practically. I do estate law. Diane's a regular Joyce Davenport, though.

CAROL: Really? We never miss it.

ARNIE: *Hill Street Blues* is our favorite series. You're a public defender?

DIANE: I work in immigration law. That involves court time.

ARNIE: I see.

CAROL: Arnie's a designer.

ARNIE: Furniture is where my heart is.

CAROL: But he's doing fashion.

DIANE: You design clothes?

ARNIE: I know. You never would've guessed. Me either. What I design, you wouldn't want to wear. Rags for Punks and East Village-types.

ROBERT: I can't imagine people with pink and orange hair buying designer clothes.

ARNIE: There's always a market. And the stuff I do is moderately priced. Like I said, you wouldn't wish it on your worst enemy.

DIANE: Where do you get your ideas?

ARNIE: Nightmares. *(Women exchange glances)* There's good money in it. A few more years, I go strictly furniture. Traditional lines, classic looks with an up-tempo twist. That doesn't sell right now. Everyone's out for one of two things in furniture today. One, comfort, or two, non-commitment. How often have you gone to someone's home, they say have a seat, and you don't know what you're supposed to sit on?

ROBERT: I know precisely what you mean.

ARNIE: Sure you do. Armchairs resemble wrecked golf carts, couches look like giant rumpled bagels.

ROBERT: Last week, I was at a client's. We're in his den. I almost sat on a lamp. It was suspended from the ceiling like a wicker swing. What saved me from embarrassment, if not electrocution, was that he started folding up these pillows strewn on the floor and when he finished, it was a chair.

ARNIE: I ask you, isn't that sad? Non-commitment. Furniture with no sense of objective. Am I a chair? No, I'm a pallet. Or if you wad me to the left and turn me on the perforated line to the right, I'm a toaster.

CAROL: Arnie's designs make a statement.

ARNIE: Well, let's say they imply a strong moral code.

DIANE: That can be done with furniture?

ARNIE: It's possible with a sofa. Maybe with a chair grouping. But a bed is always and only a bed.

ROBERT: I'd like to see your designs sometime.

ARNIE: I can do better than that. I've got a basement full of prototypes.

CAROL: You have to sit in his recliner.

ARNIE: That is one of my better ones.

CAROL: With the lever in third position, you're transported to heaven.

ARNIE: Want to come over now? We only live ten minutes from here.

ROBERT: Actually, I'm hungry. I thought we'd go to the Imperial Diner for a bite.

DIANE: Robert, you're eating a sundae.

ROBERT: This is dessert. I want dinner. Unless you're against it?

DIANE: I'll pick at a salad.

CAROL: The Imperial has a great chef's salad.

ROBERT: Tonight's the lobster special. Had my heart set on a lobbie. Come on, Diane, go for a lobbie. You know you want to suck on those tentacles.

DIANE: *(Placatingly)* All right, I'll have lobster. Ever since the E.P.T. brown ring, he's been fattening me up.

ROBERT: I want substantial poundage on this little boy of ours.

DIANE: And if our little boy is a girl?

ROBERT: She goes right on a diet.

DIANE: Hunh-unh. No guilt trips at birth. My child will be reared guilt-free.

ROBERT: That'll be a first. You'll join us?

ARNIE: Why not?

CAROL: What about your mother?

ARNIE: You call her from the diner. Tell her to show Alicia how to make kugel. It's getting dark. We can eat on our way to the cars.

CAROL: Let's pick up some lox for later.

ARNIE: The deli two doors down from the Manhasset Twin has good Nova.

DIANE: Rothstein's. We've tried them.

CAROL: Delicious, right?

DIANE: Let's buy for tomorrow.

ROBERT: I was thinking the same thing.

(All continue eating at the bench)

CAROL: Who'd doing your layette?

DIANE: Denny's in Baldwin.

ARNIE: *(To Robert)* Being a parent is life's greatest pleasure.

CAROL: We used them for Alicia.

ARNIE: You have a load of wonderful experiences ahead of you.

CAROL: They have the best prices on the island.

ROBERT: I'm prepared for it.

DIANE: *(To Carol)* All our friends recommended them. They carry quite a selection.

ROBERT: If I'd known, we would've gone to a lingerie party sooner.

CAROL: You'll be more than satisfied.

ARNIE: I don't follow.

ROBERT: Our next door neighbors threw a lingerie party. You know, Tupperware for the bedroom.

CAROL: *(To Robert)* I can't get Arnie to one of those.

ROBERT: I was not enthralled by the idea, but they are our neighbors.

DIANE: We had a great time.

ROBERT: And our child was conceived because of it.

CAROL: Really? What did you buy?

DIANE: Nothing. With Robert, the names of the products did the trick.

ROBERT: I'll let that pass.

DIANE: Joanne's Joy Rub.

ROBERT: Nastassia's Nipple Cream.

DIANE: Burt's Bare Assence.

ROBERT: That one didn't do anything for me.

CAROL: Hon, next time we're invited to one, we have to go.

ARNIE: We agreed on *two* children. Besides, I'd be bored.

ROBERT: Take my word for it, you wouldn't be.

ARNIE: For me, that kind of thing is on the order of a busman's holiday.

DIANE: You wouldn't believe some of the appliances.

ARNIE: Yeah?

ROBERT: Especially those of Chinese derivation.

CAROL: Really? The inscrutable Chinese?

DIANE: *(Beginning to laugh)* Not inscrutable at all. *(Laughs)* They're just very, very content—particularly the women.

CAROL: Arnie, next time we're going.

ARNIE: *(Rising)* Speaking of going. *(The others rise; all slowly amble toward the exit)* Nastassia's Nipple Cream?

ROBERT: Edible. Eight flavors.

ARNIE: *(To Carol)* And *not* for cushioning.

ROBERT: The Arapesh of Papuan New Guinea have a unique belief. Once the wife is sure she's pregnant, the husband and she, as the Arapesh call it, "work together to make the child." For the next six weeks or so, every night the couple makes love. When the wife experiences the normal changes in her breasts that accompany pregnancy, they then know that the child has become a round egg and their work is finished. They have "built" the child.

ARNIE: I'd say so.

ROBERT: Then they do not make love again until after the infant walks.

ARNIE: I bet Mr. Arapesh has little Johnny on his feet in a couple of months.

ROBERT: This is sacred with them.

ARNIE: It would have to be.

(A beat)

ROBERT: So, Carol, tell us your birth-related dream.

CAROL: Not me. Arnie.

ARNIE: Me? I don't remember any dream.

CAROL: Before Alicia was born.

ARNIE: You're not going to bring that up.

DIANE: I've already heard it, Arnie.

ARNIE: Great.

DIANE: I think it's fascinating.
ARNIE: Yeah? It was different.
ROBERT: Now my interest is piqued.
DIANE: Robert, do we have enough cream cheese?
ROBERT: Depends on what you have in mind.
CAROL: He's always like this?
ARNIE: Does that Nastassia cream come in mint chocolate chip?
(They exit. Blackout)

Scene II:

The park. The following spring. Robert sits on the bench, smoking. After a long moment, Arnie enters wheeling a baby carriage. On either side of the carriage, tucked upright, are two brightly colored balloons attached to limber, unfinished wood sticks. Arnie sees Robert, starts to say something, realizes Robert is lost in thought. Arnie crosses the stage. At the other side, he wheels the carriage back around to near the bench.

ARNIE: Robert. *(A beat)* Robert?
ROBERT: *(Looking at him)* Oh. Hi.
ARNIE: Hi. *(A beat)* How's Diane?
ROBERT: She's at Rothstein's.
(A beat)
ARNIE: Great deli, Rothstein's.
ROBERT: Yes.
ARNIE: How are things?
(A beat)
ROBERT: We'd been meaning to call. You know how it is. No time.
ARNIE: *(Nods)* Same here. I can't tell you how many times Carol or I said we've got to call you two. But with a four year old and little Kiwi, it's midnight before we have a chance to . . .
(Robert has risen and is crossing to the carriage)
I call her Kiwi. She slid out with this perfectly shaped noggin. Gold-brown fuzzy spikes of hair—sort of a mini-Punk look. I said to my wife, she's a little Kiwi. And she is. Anjela's her name.
ROBERT: Anjela's a beautiful name. *(Looking in the carriage)* All people are made of three things, so say Greenland's Polar

Eskimos. A body, a soul, and a name. They believe a name is magic. It suits her well. She's precious.

ARNIE: And a *good* kid. I've never seen a baby this good. Smiles all the time, hardly ever cranky. Three weeks old she was, I'm coochy-cooing her, she cackles right in my face. A regular laugh-o-meter, this one. *(Robert has begun rocking the carriage)* Carol has Alicia and her playmate at the Manhasset. Disney's "Cinderella." Some things never go out of style. I get to guard their balloons. Could've put them in the car, I guess.

ROBERT: Among the Arapesh, a child is not named until it laughs in its father's face. You would be a very proud father to have named your daughter so soon. *(A beat. He now realizes he has been rocking the carriage)* She sleeps so peacefully. *(He crosses to the bench, pulls out a cigarette)* Mind?

ARNIE: Not in this air. This air is terrific. *(Robert lights up)* How was Diane's labor?

ROBERT: Long. Fifteen hours.

ARNIE: That's tough.

(A beat)

ROBERT: We have a son. Jonathan.

ARNIE: *Mazel tov.* Carol will be thrilled to know.

ROBERT: Born on his due date.

ARNIE: That never happens. She's the fourteenth. Weighed in at seven-nine.

ROBERT: Six pounds, one ounce.

ARNIE: That's a good size.

ROBERT: Small.

ARNIE: Labor was a snap. Three hours, eleven minutes. We got to the labor room, they told us to skip shallow breathing, forget effleurage, go straight to pant-blow. *(A beat)* I had my dream again. *(Robert looks at Arnie)* The gargoyles and the bird. Three nights before her birth. It was exactly as last time, except . . .

ROBERT: He's in the hospital. *(A beat)* Diane's calling from Rothstein's. I had to get out of those . . . antiseptic white rooms. Waiting. Waiting for days. Tests. More tests. The same tests again. A valve in his heart. It doesn't function properly.

(Pause)

ARNIE: I'm sorry. They'll operate?

ROBERT: We're waiting to hear. Jonathan's eleven months old, he's been in and out of there three times. Each time they keep him longer. *(A beat)* They don't like to put an infant under . . . to administer anesthesia until after it's at least a year old. There's always the chance it won't wake up. They'll have to operate. If not now, soon.

ARNIE: You have our prayers.

ROBERT: Thank you, Artie.

(A beat)

ARNIE: Arnie.

(A beat)

ROBERT: Of course. *(A beat)* We were going to invite you to the *bris,* but Diane figured you'd either had your child or were about to. *(A beat)* That's when I first suspected something was wrong. The *bris.* After the circumcision, Jonathan whimpered, no scream, no real crying. Small tears. He slowly turned blue. Rhetta, our nurse, tried to reassure us. Said she'd seen this kind of thing before. That helped Diane. She trusted the nurse. When he turned blue three days later, Rhetta said we'd better contact our pediatrician. The tests began. *(A beat)* Jonathan looks up at me with eyes my own, and I can do nothing, say nothing, to comfort him .. to ease whatever flutterings, fits and starts of blood pulsing through his heart. When he looks at me—he has my eyes, Diane says—I almost wish . . . At home he sleeps with wires attached. Our civilization is inadequately prepared. Earlier societies had customs, practices to guard against the . . . possible mistakes of birth. The Greeks went among themselves saying a male was ill-favored, thereby avoiding the envy and wrath of jealous gods. On the fifth day of the infant's life, the father ran naked around the hearth fire with his son in his arms, burning off the *strangeness* of the newborn, cleansing him by fire. The Arapesh father took a stick with the bark stripped, rubbed it over the backs of village children to capture their magic power, their *goodness,* then transferred that magic we call health to his child's back. Rubbing, soothing it in with a chant from beyond tribal memory. Even God-forsaken, nineteenth century Fuchau China *revered* any son—no matter how malformed—as "a great, great happiness." A daughter was only "a small happiness."

(Pause)

ARNIE: I can imagine what you're going through. Every parent has those fears.

ROBERT: Those fears are our reality! And they never cease.

(Pause)

ARNIE: I think I'd better leave you, now.

ROBERT: Yes.

ARNIE: If you . . . let's talk when you want to. *(He starts to leave)*

ROBERT: What we call faith, we've abdicated to machines and men wearing sterilized masks. The price of our technological wonders was the *loss* of wonder—the healing salve of superstition. I order my life on facts and codicils and parties of the first whereas. *(A beat)* You're right. I should be alone. I'm not company now. I'm talking crazy . . . If there is a God-like power in this world, and if it sent me a sign, some sort of omen, I wouldn't recognize it. Who among us would? That trait has been bred out. We've been educated to discount such possibilities. If I could, I'd gather up my son and run naked with him around any fire. I couldn't take him from that prison if I tried. I . . I just want the . . . chance to . . . do, *do* for my son. *(A beat)* An idle dream. *(A beat)* Stillborn dreams are what remain. You had no dream. What you had was a nightmare, a nightmare brought on by festering anxiety.

ARNIE: *(Softly)* I had a dream.

ROBERT: Cigarette-smoking, 3-D monsters that goosestep on cue?

ARNIE: It was a dream. *My* dream.

(A beat)

ROBERT: It doesn't matter. Fine, it's what you say it is.

ARNIE: No, Robert, it is what it was. I said this time it was exactly as before. That's true. Except this time, I didn't wake up —right away—when I looked in the mirror. We stared at each other. I mean, I, the bird, stared at my bird reflection. I became calm. Filled with calm. Everything was going to be all right. That's what the dream was telling me, was trying to tell me four years ago with Alicia. *(A beat)* I'm going to miss that dream. I wish I could give it to you.

(Pause. Diane enters)

Robert told me about Jonathan's . . . I'm sorry.

(She nods, takes his hand)

ROBERT: What do they say?

DIANE: Wait and see.

ROBERT: *Five days* they've been saying that.

DIANE: *(Releasing Arnie's hand)* I think that's encouraging.

ROBERT: Why?

DIANE: Because they . . . because I choose to. Because our child will not undergo surgery today.

ROBERT: It's inevitable.

DIANE: But not today. *(Pause. She looks in the carriage)* I see pink trim on that outfit, so this must be Anjela.

ARNIE: You have a good memory. Anjela she is.

DIANE: She's adorable, Arnie.

ARNIE: I call her Kiwi. Because of her hair.

DIANE: Carol must love that.

ARNIE: She tolerates it.

(A beat)

DIANE: Send her our love.

(A beat)

ARNIE: I will. Medical science today . . . Manhasset General's a great hospital. I'm sure he'll be fine. I mean that, Robert. *(He begins leaving)*

DIANE: Let's go home.

ROBERT: Let me finish this cigarette.

DIANE: I wish you would stop.

(She sits by him At stage right, Arnie halts. He takes a balloon from the carriage, snaps the stick in half)

ARNIE: Robert?

(He holds the stick toward Robert, keeping the balloon in his other hand. A moment. Arnie lifts the light-weight blanket covering Anjela, places it on the handle of the carriage. He begins rubbing the stick across the sleeping infant's back)

I've never seen a baby this good.

(A moment. Robert crosses to Arnie. Arnie hands him the stick. Robert reaches inside the carriage with the stick. He begins moving the stick)

DIANE: *(Looking from Robert to Arnie)* One of the rituals. *(Arnie nods)* Arnie.

ROBERT: How am I going to get this past them in the hospital?

DIANE: *(Crossing to the men)* We'll find a way.

(Robert continues with the rubbing as Arnie and Diane look on. The lights fade)

The End

Martin Epstein

HOW GERTRUDE STORMED THE PHILOSOPHERS' CLUB

Martin Epstein

How Gertrude Stormed the Philosophers' Club by Martin Epstein was one of the hits in the annual SHORTS Festival produced by the Actors Theatre of Louisville (A.T.L.) in 1985. With a novel twist on the theme of women's liberation, the playwright offers his view of what happens when a sanctuary for philosophic males is invaded by a progressive female. Reviewing the play for the Louisville *Courier-Journal,* William Mootz writes: "Epstein's comedy is anything but conventional, and the destiny of Edgar and Edward is anything but predictable. By play's end, Epstein has taken them on a bizarre and surreal journey toward self-enlightenment . . . [The play's] dramatic progress is accompanied by a series of time bombs, whose explosions focus our attention and warn us to tread warily through Epstein's labyrinthian deceits and complications." The reception of the play prompted A.T.L.'s artistic director Jon Jory to revive the play for the 1986 Humana Festival of New American Plays. An earlier play written by Mr. Epstein, *Autobiography of a Pearl Diver,* was presented in A.T.L.'s 1981 Humana Festival.

Mr. Epstein also has worked closely with The Magic Theatre of San Francisco, which has given productions to a number of his plays, including *Autobiography of a Pearl Diver, Charles the Irrelevant, The Man Who Killed the Buddha, Off Center,* and *Possum Song*—the last three directed by the author. In its San Francisco production, *The Man Who Killed the Buddha* received the Dramalogue Award for the best play of the 1981 season.

Other groups which have produced Mr. Epstein's works include the Odyssey Theatre in Los Angeles, the Round House in Silver Spring, Maryland, the Detroit Repertory Theatre, the New Theatre of Brooklyn, and the Bay Area Playwrights Festival in Mill Valley, California.

From 1980 through the present, Mr. Epstein has been a playwright-in-residence at the Padua Hills Playwrights' Festival, where he teaches workshops and has directed the premieres of a number of his plays. Additionally, in the summer of 1985 he supervised the Playwrights' Workshop at the Bay Area Playwrights Festival. Sharing his professional expertise with students, Mr. Epstein teaches Creative Writing and Literature at the New College of California and the San Francisco School of Dramatic Arts.

Mr. Epstein's plays have been published in *West Coast Plays*, *Plays from Padua Hills*, and in the *Plays in Process* series from the Theatre Communications Group. His playwriting efforts also have been rewarded recently with a Rockefeller Fellowship in Playwriting. Mr. Epstein dedicates *How Gertrude Stormed the Philosophers' Club:* "For Ellen."

Characters:

EDGAR, *a philosopher, fortyish, corduroy jacket, pipe*
EDWARD, *a philosopher, fortyish, tweed jacket, pipe*
JASON, *a waiter, fortyish*
GERTRUDE, *the right fielder for the Queen Kongs, thirties*

Setting:

The Philosophers' Club.

Time:

Now.

Scene One:

The Philosophers' Club: a comfortable reading room. Two large dark leather arm chairs. A small table near each. Rear wall: floor to ceiling bookshelves with fine old hardback editions. Upstage left, a bust of Socrates on a pedestal. Upstage right: a waiter in a cutaway white tux. Edward in arm-chair, down right (the Nietzsche Chair). Edgar, up left in the Wittgenstein Chair. The names, Nietzsche, Wittgenstein are present on small tags on the chairs to identify them. Lights up. The men smoke their pipes.

EDWARD: You know, I'm glad there are places in the world like the Philosophers' Club, where a man can go solely to think.
EDGAR: There we agree.
EDWARD: What a privilege to be able to come here and check one's body at the door, so to speak.
EDGAR: You make it sound a lot simpler than it is.
EDWARD: You find it difficult to check your body at the door?
EDGAR: Sometimes.
EDWARD: Hm.

(Edward signals the waiter for another round of drinks. Waiter exits. Edward and Edgar smoke)

EDWARD: There's one other thing, you know, I love about this club.

EDGAR: What's that?

EDWARD: Read my mind.

EDGAR: *(Smiles)* Yes, I agree with you there, too. If they want to have a Philosophers' Club of their own, they have every right, of course, to get together and start one.

EDWARD: Yes. But can you imagine one of *them* even conceiving such an idea?

(They smoke)

EDGAR: Well, you know, they *are* making progress.

EDWARD: Oh yes! On my way over here, I passed through the park. There was a softball game going on, and though I've never been all that interested in the sport, I found myself strangely *compelled* by some irregularity I couldn't quite put my finger on. It took me almost a full inning before I realized there wasn't a single man on either team.

EDGAR: They played that well, did they?

EDWARD: They looked damn attractive in their uniforms, too. Cleats and everything.

EDGAR: Cleats.

(They smoke)

EDWARD: They're also learning how to fix cars.

EDGAR: Um.

EDWARD: It's a veritable revolution, I think . . .

EDGAR: Therefore, I am.

BOTH: *(Smiling)* Um.

(Jason, the waiter, enters, carrying a tray loaded with drinks)

JASON: Gentlemen, your drinks.

BOTH: Ah!

JASON: *(Placing a drink on Edward's table)* One cognac, up.

EDWARD: *Merci.*

JASON: *Pas de quoi, Monsieur. (Placing drink on Edgar's table)* And one gin and tonic with a twist of lime.

EDGAR: Thank you, Jason.

JASON: You're very welcome, Sir. *(He sets the tray on the serving stand)* And for myself, seven double martinis. I hope you don't mind if I join you in a little toast. *(He takes a martini)*

EDWARD: I think I do mind, Jason.

JASON: Oh?

EDWARD: You're an employee here, are you not?

JASON: Yes, sir.

EDWARD: Well, why don't we just keep it that way. Go drink in the kitchen if drink you must. *(He sips his cognac)*

EDGAR: I'll be glad to join you in a toast, Jason.

JASON: Thank you, sir.

EDGAR: Why don't you propose it.

JASON: *(Lifting glass)* To my last day of bogus freedom on this soon-to-be-extinguished planet.

EDGAR: I'll drink to that.

(They both drink)

EDWARD: I'm afraid that little toast may cost you your job, Jason.

EDGAR: Oh come off it, Edward.

EDWARD: Edgar, I don't like disturbing the natural order of things. The man is a servant! *(Jason lifts a toothpick and olive to his mouth)* Jason, if you so much as nip a corner of that olive in my presence, your waiting days at the Philosophers' Club are over.

(Jason nips the olive. Edward rises. Jason pulls a Saturday-night special from his cummerbund)

JASON: Sit down, sir. Please.

(Edward sits)

EDGAR: *(Laughs)* Bravo, Jason!

JASON: *(Turning the gun on him)* Hush!

EDGAR: *(Raising his hands slowly above his head)* I have no money on me . . .

(Pause. Jason turns the gun back to Edward)

JASON: These olives are a little off. *(He eats the rest of it)* You know, many years ago I took an extension course in philosophy. We read Plato's *Symposium.*

EDWARD: A splendid little book.

JASON: Yes? I remember there was a lot of talk about love. Queer love, as I recall. Fag love. But nowhere in the whole of that splendid little book does old Socrates ever discuss what to do with a faggot downstairs neighbor who refuses to turn down his stereo in an apartment complex where the walls are already paper thin, and just the sound of him munching his morning cornflakes is enough to drive me off my conk! *(He has polished off a second double; eats the olive)* Notice how quietly *I* chew, gentlemen! *(He chews)* That is because I am basically a conscientious person. I respect the privacy of others. *(He takes third double)* But for the last seven years—and I am now going to drink one double martini for each of them—*(He drinks)* For the last seven years, I have had to endure— Christ, these olives are positively rancid! *(He chews)* Gentlemen, do you have any idea what it's like to have that disco beat in your head for six, eight, sometimes twelve hours at a stretch?

EDWARD: No.

EDGAR: Have you tried communicating with him?

JASON: Yes. I have. Tried. Communicating. *(He drinks a fourth double)* I have also tried pounding on the floor with a broom handle, a steel claw hammer and a bowling ball. But all he does, gentlemen, is turn the volume up, *up,* UP! He slams his doors, talks for hours on the phone in a shrieking tone of voice, in which he is joined three to five nights a week by a whole chorus of his "friends" who sit around through the wee hours of the morning doing their Tallulah Bankhead imitations. *(He eats an olive, makes a face)* Or if they happen to be in a more serious mood, he'll play his "Great Moments in the Life of Hitler" album, and let us not speak of how *that* scene usually ends. *(He takes a fifth drink)* Gentlemen, I want to make one thing perfectly clear. I am not *(exhaling hard)* ho—mo—pho—bic! I'm not going to kill my downstairs neighbor because of his sexual politics, or his putrid taste in music. I'm going to kill him because I can no longer tolerate the *quality* of his life. *(He raises an olive in front of his face, looks at it)*

EDGAR: Jason?

JASON: *(An olive into his mouth)* Hm?

EDGAR: What is it, exactly, you'd like from us?

JASON: *(Picking up sixth drink)* Confirmation.

EDGAR: Confirmation?

JASON: Gentlemen—*(He lays gun down on the arm of Edgar's chair, picks up seventh drink in his other hand, looks from one to the other)*—I need to *know,* from a purely objective point of view— does a man not have an *obligation, regardless of the consequences,* to rid the earth of a life he *knows* is absolutely the shits? I shay he does, what do you shay?

(Edgar picks up the gun and fires point blank. Jason falls. Pause)

EDWARD: Edgar?

EDGAR: Yes?

EDWARD: What have you done?

EDGAR: I answered his question.

EDWARD: You realize there'll be consequences?

EDGAR: No matter. I did what had to be done. *(He fires four more shots)*

EDWARD: You're something of a perfectionist, aren't you?

EDGAR: Edward?

EDWARD: Yes?

EDGAR: I feel sick.

EDWARD: Mentally or physically?

EDGAR: *(Trying to think)* Physically.

EDWARD: No one's ever thrown up in the Philosophers' Club. Not even on the steps. Is there anything I can do?

EDGAR: Help me think.

EDWARD: Therefore, we are?

EDGAR: Yes!

EDWARD: What would you like to think about?

EDGAR: My immediate paralysis.

EDWARD: What about it?

EDGAR: I'm not sure. But if a man shoots another man once, and then shoots him four more times, it seems to me he should know for sure that he's accomplished something.

EDWARD: Well, you did put him out of his misery.

EDGAR: It doesn't seem like enough.

EDWARD: Perhaps we should think about your options, then?

EDGAR: I can't seem to focus on any.

EDWARD: It seems to me there are basically two.

EDGAR: Yes?

EDWARD: A) You can turn yourself in. B) You could make a run for it.

EDGAR: Could you elaborate a bit?

EDWARD: A) Should you turn yourself in, you'll be processed in the usual manner and most likely you'll be found incompetent to stand trial.

EDGAR: *Incompetent?*

EDWARD: Assuming you play your cards right with the psychologists.

EDGAR: They'll turn me over to the psychologists?

EDWARD: Inevitably.

EDGAR: Let's move on to B.

EDWARD: B) If you make a run for it, you'll be a fugitive.

EDGAR: A fugitive?

EDWARD: Haven't you ever seen any movies about fugitives?

EDGAR: I can't remember any at the moment.

EDWARD: To begin with, you'll never be able to use your Visa or MasterCharge again. You won't be able to take books out of the public or university libraries. You'll have to give up the apartment you've been holding up in for the last sixteen years and "take it on the lam."

EDGAR: Take it on the lam?

EDWARD: It means running, hiding, slinking. It means everyone from your parents through your friends would be a potential enemy.

EDGAR: No more casual conversations with the checkout girls at Safeway . . .

EDWARD: An immediate lien on your grandmother's trust fund.

EDGAR: No more money from the National Endowment . . .

EDWARD: And you'd be hunted round-the-clock.

EDGAR: Hunted?

EDWARD: By a group of dedicated professionals with electronic equipment beyond your wildest imaginings. Not to mention what would happen to you in your dreams.

EDGAR: My dreams?

EDWARD: Where I assume you'll be pursued by "forces" far beyond anything the police or F.B.I. could possibly send after you. *(Pause)*

EDGAR: Well, I refuse to have anything to do with the psychologists!

EDWARD: Then you *choose* to be a fugitive?

EDGAR: Yes! *(He tries to rise, falls back into chair)*

EDWARD: Edgar?

EDGAR: What?

EDWARD: You'd make a lousy fugitive.

EDGAR: Well, then, there's always a third option. *(He raises the gun to his temple)*

EDWARD: Are you thinking of killing yourself?

EDGAR: There's one bullet left.

EDWARD: There's also a fourth option, you know.

EDGAR: A fourth option?

EDWARD: Suppose I were to take the blame.

EDGAR: You?

EDWARD: Um.

EDGAR: *(Lowering the gun)* Would you really do that for me, Edward?

EDWARD: Don't be absurd.

EDGAR: *(Raising the gun)* Oh.

EDWARD: I would, however, do it for myself.

EDGAR: *(Holding gun to his temple)* Explicate.

EDWARD: Suppose an innocent man confesses to a crime he did not commit . . .

EDGAR: And confesses sincerely enough to be believed, go on!

EDWARD: The psychologists ask him questions. From his answers, they determine: A) that he is not only competent, but B) that the crime was also premeditated, and even C) that the killer is unremorseful, as well as D) thoroughly pleased with himself! What do you think they'd do to such a man?

EDGAR: They'd sentence him to death, obviously!

EDWARD: And they'd be *so hopelessly wrong,* wouldn't they!

EDGAR: Would you really sacrifice your life just to make fools of the psychologists?

EDWARD: Yes! And while I'm at it, I'd also enjoy giving my wife and children a little something to broaden their outlook a bit.

EDGAR: Explicate.

EDWARD: My family takes an almost sadistic pleasure in constantly reminding me what a predictable guy I am. *(Pointing to Jason)* And suddenly the method is at hand wherein I could turn their little bourgeoise world upside-down! *(Reaches for gun)* Edgar, I would definitely like to take the blame. Provided, of course, you agree.

EDGAR: *(Handing him gun)* I agree.

EDWARD: Good. The crime is mine, then, *(He fires the last shot into Jason's body)*

EDGAR: Christ!

EDWARD: What?

EDGAR: Do you realize the implications of what we're doing?

EDWARD: *(Shakes head)* Nnnnn.

EDGAR: We're destroying the whole concept of the philosopher as a being who checks his body at the door.

EDWARD: *We?* Excuse me, but whose ass is actually on the line?

EDGAR: Literally, yours. Philosophically, mine.

EDWARD: ALL YOU'VE EVER DONE IS PLAY WORD GAMES, YOU SON-OF-A-BITCH!

EDGAR: I beg your pardon?

EDWARD: Sorry. That was way out of line.

EDGAR: I'll just pretend I didn't hear it. *(Pause)* So what happens now?

EDWARD: You return to your apartment a free man.

EDGAR: And you?

EDWARD: I take our former waiter and this weapon to the nearest police station.

EDGAR: You won't change your mind once you get there?

EDWARD: *(Hoisting Jason onto his back)* Edgar, in the twenty-six years we've known each other, have you ever known me to change my mind?

EDGAR: Can I help you with him?

EDWARD: You can help by getting on your own way!

EDGAR: Shall I visit you in jail, then?

EDWARD: Edgar, I think . . .

EDGAR: Therefore . . .

EDWARD: It would be better if the two of us never saw each other again!

EDGAR: Yes, well, I'll follow the case in the papers.

EDWARD: I'm sure you will.

EDGAR: Good luck.

EDWARD: Good luck to you, too.

EDGAR: I go this way, I guess. *(He exits left)*

EDWARD: And I go this way. *(He exits right. Lights dim quickly to black)*

Scene Two:

Spot up. Enter Gertrude. She wears a softball uniform, the name of her team across the front: "The Queen Kongs." She carries a baseball bat in one hand, the other is gloved. She addresses the audience.

GERTRUDE: Hi. I'm Gertrude, and I think it's time I put in an appearance, seeing as how my name dominates the title of this play. I guess that last scene demonstrates once for all that whenever men gather together to think, inevitably they kill. *(Pause)* If you're wondering what women do when they gather together to think, I can tell you that, too: I've just come from our team locker room. I play right field for the Queen Kongs, and we lost our season opener to the Green Barettas. Seventy-four to nothing. And though I didn't play any sloppier than the other girls, I made the mistake of trying to cheer my fellow Kongs up: "Hey, Kids, come on, it's only a game!" Well, believe me, if I hadn't grabbed my stuff and run, I'd have ended up as dead as that waiter. Only it wouldn't have been as cleanly done. *(She moves about, taking in her surroundings)* Now the question still remains, what am I, Gertrude, doing in the Philosophers' Club? I suppose I can give you some possible answers: A) Maybe I'm fatally attracted to men with a certain quality of m-i-n-d. B) Perhaps I heard that the Philosophers' Club has a "men only" policy, and that kind of *thinking* gets me in my t-w-a-t. C) I might have been on my way back from the ball game and I had to find a bathroom, quick. D) Maybe I don't know what I'm doing here. *(Sound of door slam)* Anyway, I think I hear someone coming. I hope it's a philosopher so I can get to the bottom of this mystery. Shhh. I'll just plop myself down here in the Wittgenstein chair and pretend I'm asleep.

> *(She does this. Enter Edgar. He crosses to spot where Jason fell, gets down on his hands and knees, whispers "Bang" and falls. Edward enters, closing door. Edgar scrambles to his feet)*

BOTH MEN: It's you!

EDWARD: I thought we agreed never to see each other again!

EDGAR: We did agree!

GERTRUDE: *(Aside)* I'm in luck. It's *two* philosophers!

EDWARD: So what are you doing here, then?

EDGAR: I don't feel right about what happened here a short while ago.

EDWARD: Refresh my memory, will you?

EDGAR: I *did* shoot that waiter, didn't I?

EDWARD: We both shot him.

EDGAR: But I shot him first. And I shot five times.

EDWARD: So?

EDGAR: So I've been thinking . . .

EDWARD: Therefore?

EDGAR: I'd like my crime back.

EDWARD: Why?

EDGAR: Because even though you took the blame, I still feel guilty, damn it! I *feel* like a fugitive!

EDWARD: Well, perhaps you'd best learn to live with it.

EDGAR: Why?

EDWARD: Stop and think a moment about something beside your own existential five-and-dime sized universe, and you might ask me how it is I happen to be standing here, rather than sitting in a jail cell surrounded by the psychologists! *(Gertrude snores lightly)*

EDGAR: Edward, I don't give a shit why you're standing here. I just want my crime back!

EDWARD: And suppose I told you there was no crime?

EDGAR: I fired five bullets into that waiter, Edward!

EDWARD: But suppose it wasn't any of those five bullets that killed him, Edgar!

EDGAR: What else could have possibly killed him, Edward?

EDWARD: Botulism!

EDGAR: Botulism?

EDWARD: The martini olives were contaminated.

EDGAR: The martini olives?

(Gertrude snores a bit louder)

EDWARD: According to the computerized police autopsy report, our waiter died of botulism forty-three hundredths of a second before your first bullet hit him! *(Pause)* We're both innocent!

(Gertrude snores louder)

EDWARD: What is that horrible sound?

EDGAR: It's coming from theWittgenstein chair. *(They both move toward it, discover the sleeper)*

EDWARD: Who is this?

EDGAR: Don't know. Never seen him before.

EDWARD: Well, whoever he is, he has obviously not checked his body at the door! *(Gertrude moans)* And what's he doing in a baseball uniform?

EDGAR: He plays for a team called "The Queen Kongs."

EDWARD: Shouldn't it be "The King Kongs"?

(Gertrude mumbles)

EDGAR: Shhh. He seems to be dreaming.

GERTRUDE: Oh, Papa . . .

EDGAR: About his father.

GERTRUDE: *(Rising)* I have to find it, Papa.

EDWARD: Edgar . . .

EDGAR: Shhh . . .

GERTRUDE: *(Moving)* I found it once, I'll find it again.

EDGAR: He's sleepwalking.

(Gertrude turns toward the bookshelves. Her name is in large black letters across her back, together with the image of a Kong-type gorilla face)

EDWARD: His name is Gertrude.

EDGAR: Impossible. Gertrude is a woman's name.

GERTRUDE: Please help me find it, Papa.

EDWARD: Edgar . . .

(Gertrude takes a book from shelf, opens it, drops it)

GERTRUDE: It's not here.

EDWARD: Edgar, there's a woman in the Philosophers' Club.

EDGAR: Impossible. We pay dues to keep them out.

(Gertrude flings a handful of books)

GERTRUDE: Not here!

EDWARD: Use your eyes, for Chrissake! She's going after our books!

GERTRUDE: *(Flinging books from shelves)* Not here! Not here! not here!

EDWARD: Damnit, she'll destroy our entire library!

EDGAR: *(Holding him)* Shhh. It might be even more dangerous to wake her!

(Gertrude tears into library, sending books out by the armful)

EDWARD: What do you propose we do?

EDGAR: We should ease her into consciousness, obviously.

(Gertrude has begun to climb the bookcase)

EDWARD: Ease one of them into consciousness? Oh, go on, Edgar. You ease her into consciousness. I'll observe.

EDGAR: *(Moving closer)* Gertrude?

GERTRUDE: *(Stops)* Papa, is that you?

EDGAR: Yes, dear.

GERTRUDE: *(Climbs back down)* Oh, Papa.

EDGAR: How are you, sweetheart?

GERTRUDE: I'm in so much trouble, Papa.

EDGAR: What's wrong, my darlin' girl?

GERTRUDE: I can't find it anywhere, Papa.

EDGAR: Find what, Gertrude?

GERTRUDE: It.

EDGAR: It?

GERTRUDE: Oh, Papa, softball did not come easy to me.

EDGAR: Softball?

EDWARD: See if there's any link between softball and *it*.

EDGAR: Shhh . . .

GERTRUDE: I was always afraid the ball would disfigure my face.

EDGAR: One has to have courage, daughter.

EDWARD: It!

GERTRUDE: But everyone could smell my fear. They always chose me last. They put me in right field.

EDWARD: That's where they used to stick me, too. Ask her what *it* is?

GERTRUDE: But nothing ever happened in right field . . .

EDWARD: Thank God. It gave me lots of time to think!

GERTRUDE: Until that incredible afternoon when Coco Butterwrack connected!

BOTH MEN: Coco Butterwrack?

GERTRUDE: She hit the ball almost as high as the sun. Oh, Papa, for a small eternity, it seems to hang there. Then it began to fall . . .slowly . . .toward me . . .the right fielder. And I thought: here it comes! here comes doom! and there's nowhere to run! So I stuck out my glove and—*smack!* There it was, the ball . . .

EDGAR: It felt good, Gertrude?

GERTRUDE: Good doesn't begin to describe it, Papa. Later that day, I came home, you were sitting in the living room, smoking your pipe. You looked at me, and you knew something was *different*. And you said, "Hi, Gert, what you been up to?

EDGAR: *(Soft)* Hi, Gert, what you been up to?

GERTRUDE: And I said, "I've been playing softball, Papa." And you said, "Oh, yeah?"

EDGAR: Oh, yeah?

GERTRUDE: And I said, "Yeah. And I been playing hard!" And you said, "Oh, yeah?"

EDGAR: Oh, yeah?

GERTRUDE: And I said: "Yeah. And I got real dirty, Papa." And you said: "Oh, yeah?"

EDGAR: Oh, yeah?

GERTRUDE: And I said, "Yeah!" And the two of us were beaming so hard we couldn't look at each other we were that embarrassed. And even poor Ma, who never wanted me to do anything more than spell properly and stay clean, Ma stood at her ironing board nodding and smiling, even though she didn't know what the hell was going on!

(Gertrude, leaning back, lets her full weight rest against Edgar, who doesn't quite know what to do with his hands, which have come up under her arms. Edward relights his pipe, watching)

EDGAR: What was going on, Gertrude?

GERTRUDE: I was filling up with *it*, Papa!

EDGAR: It?

EDWARD: Will you establish the identity of *it*, for Chrissake!

EDGAR: What *it*, Gertrude?

GERTRUDE: I was filling up with The Secret Exaltation, Papa!

BOTH MEN: The Secret Exaltation!?

GERTRUDE: *(Nodding)* Yes, because I knew for a fact that if I could catch that ball, I could catch *anything!* *(She folds his hands gently in her own)* Oh, Daddy.

EDWARD: Edgar, don't you think this little masquerade has gone far enough?

EDGAR: Shhhh.

(Edgar and Gertrude walk together in this position)

EDWARD: *(Insistent whisper)* Edgar, in the language of the psychologists, you may be exploiting this woman's Oedipal proclivities!

EDGAR: Edward, in the language of the psychologists, perhaps she's exploiting mine!

(They continue to walk this way. The scene should build with a real and dangerous heat)

EDWARD: May I remind you what happened the last time you put your mind at the mercy of your trigger-finger?

EDGAR: Nothing happened. We got off scot-free!

EDWARD: You may not be as lucky this time.

EDGAR: I'll take my chances. *(They continue walking)* Come, Gertrude.

GERTRUDE: Where are we going?

EDGAR: Someplace deep, someplace soft: the Nietzsche Chair. *(He stops by the Nietzsche Chair. They kiss)*

GERTRUDE: Wait.

EDGAR: What is it?

GERTRUDE: You're not really my father, are you?

EDGAR: *(Pause)* No.

GERTRUDE: *(Turning back for another kiss)* Well, okay, then. *(Edgar moves in for the kiss. Gertrude ducks under, comes downstage to audience, her hands making the time-out sign. Edgar and Edward freeze)*

GERTRUDE: Time out! I'm afraid I really can't stomach the little scene that's coming up. The author would just love Gertrude and Edgar to tumble into the Nietzsche chair and go at it hot 'n heavy.

EDGAR: Yeah.

GERTRUDE: I personally don't get off on the idea of being fucked in my sleep. By *anyone! (She backs up)* So we've decided on a little compromise. *(Whispers to Edgar, while pushing him onto the Nietzsche Chair)* Okay, play ball.

EDGAR: *(Falls into the chair and begins making love to it)* Oh, Gertrude! Darling Gertrude!

GERTRUDE: *(Standing to the side, she plays)* Go on, do it to me, baby!

(Edward moves in, watching Edgar make love—tenderly—to the chair. He moves off, crosses toward the bust of Socrates, addressing it)

EDWARD: I had an erotic experience once.

GERTRUDE: Ummm!

EDWARD: I was thirty-two at the time. *(Edgar and Gertrude sounding)* Just completing my Ph.D. at U.C.L.A. *(Sound)* Newly married. *(Sound)* Preparing for my orals. *(Edgar does a hand stand, his legs straight up in the air)* I remember I was on line in the student cafeteria, standing next to a young lady in a paisley dress. Lying on the tray next to her turkey sandwich, Kant's *Critique!*

GERTRUDE: Oh, you dirty dog!

EDWARD: On my tray, Hegel's *Phenomenology* and a bowl of watery borscht.

GERTRUDE: Oh, you dirty, filthy, sweetheart dog!

EDWARD: Our eyes met!

GERTRUDE: AH! *(Gertrude can participate with mimetic gestures)*

EDWARD: The recognition was immediate. "We must talk," I said. "Before or after we screw, you choose," she replied. "After," I said.

GERTRUDE: OH!

EDWARD: We got to her apartment, we took off all our clothes, she handed me her hairbrush, "Brush," she said.

GERTRUDE: OU!

EDWARD: "Go on, baby, brush!" And so I brushed. *(He combs her invisible hair, perhaps the bust's head)* And I brushed! And I brushed!

GERTRUDE: Oh, baby!

EDWARD: *(Brushing)* Her hair was thick and black and henna rinsed.

GERTRUDE: Oh, honey!

EDWARD: And as I brushed, I could feel the darkness sift from her body to my own . . .

GERTRUDE: Oh, sugar!

EDWARD: And as I brushed, something in me darker still began to throb and stretch—to show its ivory teeth and claws.

GERTRUDE: It's happening . . .

EDWARD: And as I brushed, I wasn't Edward anymore, I was all fur and throbbing darkness staring at the back and shoulders and buttocks of a girl whose scent was urging me to spring!

GERTRUDE: It's happening!

(Edward purrs)

GERTRUDE: It's happening!

EDWARD: And I knew if I let that beast break from the cage of my existence, it was goodbye my new wife, goodbye my Ph.D., goodbye my academic career, goodbye western civilization—*(With each of the above named, Gertrude lets out an equivalent sound)* —and with the beast already en route through the air, I performed what I consider still to be the single most definitive act of my life—I grabbed my pants and ran! I grabbed my shoes and socks and ran! I grabbed my *Phenomenology of the Mind* and I ran! *(Gertrude orgasmic. Edward pushes the statue over with a cry)* Fool! Idiot! Coward! Why! *(Slapping himself)* Oh, hypocrite, why! Why! Why! Why! Why! Why! Why did you run away? Oh, why? *(More Gertrude)* Because if I had stayed, I'd have devoured her, that's why! If I had stayed, I'd have eaten her alive!

(Edgar has descended, slowly, his legs folding down and the rest of his body crumpling up on the floor. Edward, too, on his hands and knees, regarding the broken pieces of the statue)

EDGAR: Edward?

EDWARD: What?

EDGAR: Help me think.

EDWARD: What about?

EDGAR: Gertrude.

EDWARD: Gertrude?

EDGAR: Am I dreaming her, or is she really out there?

(Edward crawls across books and over to the Nietzsche Chair. He observes)

EDWARD: You're dreaming her.

EDGAR: Merciful God, please, let me go on dreaming. *(He collapses on his side, curls up. Edward, staring at the empty chair, purrs)*

EDGAR: What was that?

EDWARD: That was panther language.

(Gertrude sings a very haunting, wordless melody)

EDGAR: Edward?

EDWARD: *(Staring at the chair)* What?

EDGAR: My dream is singing. *(A light purr from Edward)* I'm afraid to move, I'm afraid to breathe.

EDWARD: *(Rising on his knees, leaning over the chair)* Well, I'm not afraid. *(He purrs loud. Gertrude stops singing, screams as though waking from a nightmare. Edward does a double-take; Edgar sits up, wide awake. Edward growls at Gertrude. She grabs baseball bat, makes as though to strike)*

EDWARD: No! Don't hit me! I didn't do anything! Hit him. He's the guilty one! He's the fugitive!

GERTRUDE: You, fugitive! What the hell is going on here?

EDGAR: Gertrude, I love you.

EDWARD: Gertrude, he had congress with you on the Nietzsche Chair!

GERTRUDE: Congress?

EDGAR: Marry me, Gertrude.

GERTRUDE: I must still be dreaming.

EDWARD: Maybe we're all still dreaming. *(He turns his gaze back to the Nietzsche Chair, and from this point on he will continue to look at it as though she were still lying there)*

EDGAR: Oh, Gertrude, I've listened to your theme.

GERTRUDE: My theme?

(Edgar sings a bit of Gertrude's theme)

EDWARD: You sang it for us in your sleep.

GERTRUDE: I don't remember.

EDGAR: Oh, Gertrude, before I heard your theme, I lived like a one-man Diaspora.

GERTRUDE: A one-man who?

EDWARD: He lived alone.

GERTRUDE: Oh, yeah, alone.

EDGAR: I lived for no one but myself.

GERTRUDE: Sure. I know that scene.

EDWARD: We all know that scene.

EDGAR: No one knows that scene the way I know that scene!

EDWARD: He always has to be the king!

EDGAR: That's right.

EDWARD: Why?

EDGAR: Becaue I *am* the king, goddamnit!

EDWARD: King of who, sir? King of what?

EDGAR: I am the Fugitive King of the Earth!

EDWARD: Oh, really?

EDGAR: Oh, Gertrude, before I heard your theme, I ruled over my whole imaginary universe like a crazed despot! Because I felt like a fugitive, I wanted everyone else to feel like a fugitive! Yes, I sat upon my mental throne, and I banished all the people! I banished the cities! I banished the nations! I sent the sun and the moon and the stars into perpetual exile!

EDWARD: His Fugitive Majesty is raving!

(This scene can turn operatic, with Gertrude catching Edgar's fever, so that she bursts into a refrain: "COME HOME, COME HOME, COME HOME, ETC.")

EDGAR: *(Singing Gertrude's theme)* But now that I've heard your theme, Oh, Gertrude, I want my kingdom to come home! *(Singing)* Mother, Father, come home! Baby Sue! Brother Tom! Come home! Childhood playmates and friends of my youth, come home! Office Workers, Insurance Salesmen, Secretaries, Real Estate Agents, come home! *(All this, of course, to the house)* Plumbers, Doctors, Hat-check Girls, Salad Chefs, Taxi Drivers, home! Farmers, Garbage Men, Physicists, Movie Stars, home! Thieves, Pimps, Prostitutes, Congressmen, home! CIA Agents, come home! Moscow! London! Peking! Dallas! Los Angeles, *please—(Or whatever city the play is being performed in)—Come home! (Gertrude continues to sing as he speaks)* No one need ever pay another dollar to the psychologists! All your fugitive guilt is hereby forgiven! Edgar, King of the Fugitive Earth declares a universal amnesty! *(Spoken)* Oh, Gertrude, rule with me! Say you'll be my queen!

EDWARD: *(Still focused on the Nietzsche Chair)* Gertrude, the Fugitive Queen!

EDGAR: No, no! Be Gertrude, Queen of the Secret Exaltation!

GERTRUDE: Queen of the Secret Exaltation? *(Edgar sings. She sings. They sing. She slides to her knees beside him)*

GERTRUDE: Oh, Your Fugitive Majesty, that's a very hard offer to resist!

EDWARD: Resist it anyway!

GERTRUDE: Why?

EDWARD: Because as pretty as it sounds, it's basically a crock! *(He mimics Edgar's singing)* That's the way all fugitives sound when they think they've fallen in love!

EDGAR: I think I'm in love, therefore, I *am* in love! Gertrude, I have a comfortable income. We'll honeymoon in Mexico!

EDWARD: Don't say yes until you've heard my proposal!

BOTH: Your proposal?

EDGAR: You can't propose, Edward. You're a married man! The father of three. Old Predictable, they call him!

(Edward roars)

GERTRUDE: Why do you keep roaring that way?

EDGAR: He thinks he's a panther.

EDWARD: I think I'm a panther, therefore, I *am* a panther!

EDGAR: Marry me, Gertrude!

GERTRUDE: Shhhh.

EDWARD: Gertrude?

GERTRUDE: Yes?

EDWARD: How would you like to nourish the beast of your choice?

GERTRUDE: Nourish the beast . . .?

(Edward purrs)

EDGAR: Gertrude, marry me.

GERTRUDE: Shhhh! Will you let him talk!

EDWARD: Yes, Edgar, let me talk. *(A light purr)*

GERTRUDE: Just what do you mean "Nourish the beast of my choice," Panther Man?

EDWARD: Listen, Gertrude, since the advent of our birth, the eye of the beast has been fixed on each single one of us. Fixed on the movement of arms and legs. Fixed on the turning of heads, the blinking of lids. Fixed on the wriggling of fingers and toes . . .

EDGAR: Gertrude, may I point out in passing that old Panther Man's gaze is presently fixed on nothing!

EDWARD: Panther's Man's gaze is presently fixed on the real you, Gertrude! *(He purrs)*

GERTRUDE: The real me?

EDWARD: Gertrude, you will never be more than you were when you lay sprawled across the Nietzsche Chair, singing your theme.

GERTRUDE: What, exactly, was I?

EDWARD: You were your essential self. *(He purrs)*

GERTRUDE: But you say I was asleep, dreaming . . .

EDWARD: You were your essential self, Gertrude!

GERTRUDE: *(To Edgar)* Is what he's saying true?

EDGAR: Gertrude, Edward's an *idealist;* he cannot deal with anything unless it's not really there!

(Edward roars, his gaze fixed on the Nietzsche Chair)

GERTRUDE: But he's looking at what he calls "the essential me" with such genuine sincerity.

EDGAR: What you call his "genuine sincerity" is a misnomer for his genuine psychosis. Gertrude, believe me, even if he wanted to, there is no way he *could* turn his gaze.

EDWARD: Oh, yes, I could.

EDGAR: Oh, no, you couldn't.

EDWARD: Oh, yes, I could!

EDGAR: Oh, no, you couldn't!

(Edward roars, begins to turn his gaze)

GERTRUDE: Oh, King Edgar, the Panther Man is turning his gaze!

EDGAR: Gertrude, say you'll marry me!

GERTRUDE: In another moment, he'll be looking right at me!

EDGAR: But he still won't be seeing *you,* Gertrude! He'll be seeing *her!*

GERTRUDE: Who?

EDGAR: The you, you were! Gertrude!

(Edward, fixing his gaze on her, purrs)

GERTRUDE: Too late! Oh, Mr. Panther Man!

EDGAR: Damn it, woman, I'm the one who's had congress with you!

EDWARD: *But I'm the one who's going to eat her alive!*

GERTRUDE: Eat me alive?

EDWARD: Be eaten by me, Gertrude, or be eaten by *time!*

GERTRUDE: Be eaten by time?

EDWARD: Tick-tock, tick-tock—*(Turning his gaze back to the Nietzsche Chair)*—tick-tock . . .

GERTRUDE: Oh, God, *Time!*

EDGAR: *(Edgar can sing these lines, softly)* Gertrude, we'll have a family! We'll make the future!

EDWARD: Tick-tock, tick-tock . . .

GERTRUDE: Oh, God, don't stop looking at me! Panther Man!

EDWARD: Tick-tock, tick-tock, tick-tock . . .

EDGAR: *(Singing these lines a bit louder)* A house with a garden! A dog! A pussycat!

(Edward purrs)

GERTRUDE: I'm sorry, your majesty, but I feel driven to him.

EDGAR: Driven? Why driven?

GERTRUDE: I donno. Because he's my essential destiny, I guess.

EDGAR: Oh, Gertrude . . .

GERTRUDE: It's all right. Ever since I was little, I've had a premonition this moment was on its way. *(She lies down across the Nietzsche Chair)* All right, Mr. Panther Man, I'm ready. Devour me.

EDWARD: Sing your theme, Gertrude.

(Gertrude sings her theme. Edward lifts her arm, growls)

GERTRUDE: Could I make one small request before you eat me, Panther Man?

EDWARD: Hurry.

GERTRUDE: If it's all right with you, I'd like to leave my uniform to my husband, Stuart.

(Edward tries to roar but gags)

EDGAR: Your husband, Stuart, Gertrude?

GERTRUDE: We've been married seven years, and I'd like him to have a remembrance.

(Edward gags)

EDGAR: Why didn't you tell us you were married, Gertrude?

GERTRUDE: The subject didn't come up till now.

EDGAR: But you allowed us both to assume you were *free.*

GERTRUDE: Yeah, well . . .

EDGAR: *(Imitates her)* Yeah, well, my colleague and I don't particularly enjoy pissing into the wind, Gertrude! Why did you allow us to make such fools of ourselves?

GERTRUDE: Curiosity . . .

EDGAR: Curiosity?

GERTRUDE: I don't normally spend much time around guys who are so . . . verbal.

EDGAR: Stuart doesn't talk?

GERTRUDE: Stuart talks . . . only he doesn't really say too much.

EDGAR: What does he do for a living, your Stuart?

GERTRUDE: He's in construction.

(Edward gags)

GERTRUDE: Hey, you guys, I wouldn't want you to get the idea I was a tease or anything. *(They look at her)* I'd have left Stuart like that for either of you.

EDGAR: Does that mean we still have a chance?

GERTRUDE: Uh—no.

EDGAR: Why not?

GERTRUDE: I donno. Taken separately, either one of you is a terrific catch. But together, you kind of cancel each other out.

EDGAR: So we do.

GERTRUDE: And then there's my three kids.

EDGAR: You have children, Gertrude?

GERTRUDE: Sandy, Ducky, and Orlando.

EDWARD: Six more and you could start your own softball team.

GERTRUDE: Do you still want to eat me, Panther Man?

(Edward, shaking his head "No," slips back into the other chair)

GERTRUDE: Just as well, I guess. I'm expected home for dinner. I promised the kids my lasagna. I'd invite you guys, but the kids are absolute pigs at the table, and I'm afraid Stuart would find you both a little weird.

(Pause. Gertrude turns her head, sighs. She doesn't move)

EDGAR: Gertrude?

GERTRUDE: Yes?

EDGAR: What seems to be the problem?

GERTRUDE: I donno. All of a sudden, I just don't feel like going home anymore.

EDGAR: Why not?

GERTRUDE: Because the whole scene is all so predictable. *(Signs of life in Edward, who turns his head in her direction)* I can already see just how everything will happen. I'll open the door. Stuart and the kids will all be huddled in the living room round the TV set, watching the ball game. "Hey, Babe," he'll say, lifting the can of Schlitz in his hand. "How'd the Kongs do?" "We lost," I'll say. "What score, Mom?" "Seven to six, honey." "Oh, tough luck," they'll shout. "Well, commere anyway, an' we'll give you a great big loser's hug." And while they're all hugging me, I'll burst into tears. And they'll all think I'm crying because The Queen Kongs lost, but that's not what I'll be crying about. I'll be crying because there's no way in the world I can tell any of them what happened to me at the Philosophers' Club, and make them understand. *(She has risen, a bit weepy)* I mean, "Hey, you guys, this afternoon I had congress with the Fugitive King of the Earth! And then, I was almost eaten alive by a Panther Man! And both of them proposed, and promised to fill me with the secret exaltation, but I chose *you* instead—*(Now she is caught up in her own discovery)*—Instead of the secret exaltation, I chose to come home to *you! (She is talking to them via the house)* Stuart . . . Sandy . . .Ducky . . .Orlando . . .I chose *Death* today for you . . .*What did you choose for me, you selfish, inconsiderate, filthmaking bunch of predictable sons-of-bitches?* . . .And then, they'll all look at me like they've never seen me before. Yeah. And Stuart will drop his Schlitz and fall to his knees and cover his face with his hands and weep! Yeah! And Sandy will scramble for the Electro-lux and vacuum all the popcorn from the shag rug, *yeah!* And Ducky will collect all the empty soda bottles and throw them neatly into the trash, *yeah!* And Orlando will go to the fridge and fix me a gin and tonic strong enough to knock over an elephant, *Yeah!* And then we'll all sit down *together* at the table, and like civilized ladies and gentlemen, we'll eat lasagna, and have some meaningful conversation, YEAH! *(The bat is raised in one hand. Gertrude is almost transfixed)* Hey, you guys?

EDGAR: Is she talking to us?

EDWARD: I hope not.

GERTRUDE: Now I know why I stormed the Philosophers' Club!

BOTH MEN: Tell us, Gertrude.

GERTRUDE: So I could meet your two amazing minds and fill up with it.

BOTH MEN: It?

(Gertrude sings her theme)

BOTH MEN: The Secret Exaltation!

GERTRUDE: Yeah! *(She turns; over to Edgar)* Thank you for the congress, your Majesty. *(She gives him a sweet kiss)*

EDGAR: Gertrude.

GERTRUDE: *(Over to Edward)* And thank you for the beast. *(She gives him a sweet kiss. Edward purrs, a bit despairingly)*

GERTRUDE: *(To audience)* And thank you for—I donno—just being there. *(She blows them a kiss)* I'm going home to my family now! *(She turns, begins singing her theme, exits. Pause)*

EDWARD: Edgar?

EDGAR: Hm?

EDWARD: I think . . .

EDGAR: Therefore . . .

EDWARD: I hate my life.

EDGAR: Yes, well, I hate mine even more.

EDWARD: Edgar?

EDGAR: Hm?

EDWARD: I don't suppose you'd consider . . .

EDGAR: A double suicide?

EDWARD: . . .Switching chairs.

EDGAR: Switching chairs?

EDWARD: It would be a great comfort to feel as though some kind of physical mobility were still possible.

EDGAR: Yes, one could almost imagine a whole new world if some kind of physical mobility were still possible.

EDWARD: Shall we give it the old college try?

EDGAR: I don't see that there's anything left to lose.

EDWARD: *(With great effort)* I rise . . .

EDGAR: Therefore, I also rise . . .*(He does so)*

EDWARD: I take a step! *(He takes a step)*

EDGAR: Therefore, I take a step! *(He takes a step)*

EDWARD: I take a second step!

EDGAR: Therefore, we walk!

EDWARD: We walk towards each other! *(They meet, take each other's hands)*

EDGAR: Panther Man!

EDWARD: Fugitive King of the Earth!

(They sing Gertrude's theme, continue to walk to their respective new chairs, turn, collapse. A great feeling of achievement as each fetches for his pipe and tobacco)

EDWARD: Well, now, that's done, we'll have to speak to the club management about providing us with a new waiter.

EDGAR: Yes. Someone who knows what it means to check his body at the door, hm?

(They look at each other)

BOTH MEN: There we agree!

(They light and smoke their pipes. Edgar hums Gertrude's theme as they puff, puff, puff. Lights dim)

The End

Romulus Linney

WHY THE LORD COME TO SAND MOUNTAIN

Romulus Linney

Romulus Linney makes his fourth appearance in the *Best Short Plays* series with *Why the Lord Come to Sand Mountain,* a Biblical tall tale based on the author's book, *Jesus Tales.* In a review of the play as directed by the author and presented by the Whole Theatre of Montclair, New Jersey, *New York Times* reviewer Mel Gussow describes the tale: " . . . Jesus and Saint Peter, in humanly guise, visit a 'hard-time family' in a lonely shack." As the characters sip brandy and exchange stories, "what might in some hands seem blasphemous—or precious—is comic in Mr. Linney's patented mountain Gothic style." The tall tales "eventually lead to a testament of faith, as late at night, Jesus reveals the true reason that he came to Sand Mountain."

In the 1986 edition of *Best Short Plays* Mr. Linney's *The Love Suicide at Schofield Barracks* presented a riveting and searing drama in the inquiry on a major general and his wife who have carried out a murder-suicide pact. Two earlier plays in this series from Mr. Linney are *F.M.,* published in the 1984 edition, and the Obie winner, *Tennessee,* which appeared in the 1980 edition.

Mr. Linney's most widely produced play, *The Sorrows of Frederick,* is a psychological drama about Frederick the Great. Its many stage productions include the 1967 premiere at the Mark Taper Forum in Los Angeles with Fritz Weaver in the title role. Subsequent productions of the play were presented in New York with Austin Pendleton, in Canada with Donald Davis, in Great Britain with John Wood, and later, Tom Conti. It also was performed at the Dusseldorf Schauspielhaus in Germany and at the Burgtheater in Vienna, where it successfully played in classical repertory through the season of 1969-70 in a production that won two Austrian theatre awards.

Born in Philadelphia, Pennsylvania in 1930, Romulus Linney grew up in Madison, Tennessee, and spent his summers in North Carolina. He was educated at Oberlin College, where he received his B.A. in 1953, and the Yale School of Drama, earning an M.F.A. there in 1958. He has taught playwriting at many schools, including Columbia University, Brooklyn College, the University of Pennsylvania, Connecticut College, Princeton, and currently, the University of Pennsylvania.

Mr. Linney received two fellowships from the National Endowment for the Arts, and from 1976 until 1979 served on its literary panel. In 1980 he was awarded a fellowship from the Guggenheim Foundation, and in 1984 he received the Award in Literature from the American Academy and Institute of Arts and Letters.

He is also the author of two highly regarded novels, *Heathen Valley* and *Slowly, by Thy Hand Unfurled,* and he has recently written a third novel. In addition, he has written numerous other plays, including *Democracy, Holy Ghosts, Old Man Joseph and His Family* and *Laughing Stock,* picked by *Time* magazine as one of the best plays of 1984. Mr. Linney has written extensively for television, has had an opera made from a short play, *The Death of King Philip,* and has published a number of short plays and fiction in numerous literary magazines.

As a director, Mr. Linney recently staged his own plays for the Philadelphia Festival of New Plays, the Actors Studio, the Alley Theatre in Houston, and the Bay Area Playwrights Festival in California.

His most recent plays include *Childe Byron,* produced in New York by the Circle Repertory Company, in Louisville by the Actors Theatre, in Costa Mesa, California by the South Coast Repertory, and in London by the Young Vic; *The Captivity of Pixie Shedman,* at the New York Phoenix Theatre and the Detroit Repertory Theatre; *El Hermano* and *Goodby, Howard* at the Ensemble Studio Theatre in New York; *April Snow* at the South Coast Repertory; *A Woman Without A Name* at the Empire State Theatre in Albany, New York and at the Denver Center Theatre Company; *Sand Mountain* at the Philadelphia Festival for New Plays and the Whole Theatre in Montclair, New Jersey; and *Pops* at the Bay Area Playwrights Festival in California.

Characters:

SANG PICKER
SAINT PETER
THE LORD
JACK
JEAN
FOURTEEN CHILDREN
PROSPER VALLEY FARMER

Time:

Awhile ago.

Place:

Sand Mountain.

Mountain music, which fades into a man whistling.
   *The stage is backed with aged wood, suggesting the Smoky
Mountains. There is a platform at center, representing the
interior of a mountain cabin. In darkness, three figures sit
turned away, before a large battered cupboard. On the wall or
next to the cupboard hang two extra slat chairs.*
   *The lights fade and narrow into one light down center. Into
it steps the Sang Picker, a mountain woman. She wears a long
black coat-like dress, carries a hoe, a barlow knife, and a burlap
sack. She holds up the sack.*

SANG PICKER: Gen Sang. Grows wild on Sand Mountain but
powerful hard to find. Bring ye one whole dollar a dried pound.
And why not? Hit'll keep yore body young. Gen Sang is China
language. Hit means root of life. *(She reaches into the sack and
pulls out a ginseng root. She rubs the dirt off it, slices a piece from
it with her knife, chews it.)* Mmmmm. Good. Make ye tingle.
(She looks up. Sound of wind) Ravens. Sailing the updrafts.
Wings out, like that. Yore raven was the firstest creature Noah let
out of the Ark, to go fly—see if tar was ary thang a-growing after

the flood. And that bodacious bird, hit never come back. Bible says so. But don't say why. I'll tell ye why. Noah and them ravens just didn't get along, that's why. Ever soul on Sand Mountain knows yore raven will jest downright dispute with ye. We are like that too, hereabouts. Can't read no Bible, but love to dispute the thang anyhow. *(She looks about)* Big, these mountains. I never seen the end of them, never will. Lived here all my life. Pleasant baby, purty woman, and what ye see now. Had three men. All died farmers. Firstest one all right, second a mite bettern that, the third God-awful. He was the disgust of the world, he was, half-man, half-buzzard. Worked four wives to death, figured I'd be the fifth. Fooled him. How? Gen Sang and Bible stories, that's how. Roots of life. You understand walnuts? The shell is jest like yore skull. The meat is jest like yore brain. So eat it. Best thang ye kin do, when ye get woobles in the head. Ear ache? Split a trout. Lift out the bones. Tie each half of 'at trout to the soles of yore feet. Walk around. Think I got woobles in the head? Try it. Cure a fever blister, kiss a dog. And chew Gen Sang, ponder Bible tales. Keep yore body alive in spite of debts, doctors and even husbands. *(Pause)* I reckon you've heard Smoky Mountain head benders a-plenty. "How Little Jack Killed the Giant" and "The Ghost of Daniel Boone," all that. And Bible tales a-plenty, too. "Noah in the Ark," "Jonah in the Whale," "Daniel in the Den," "Moses Up the Mountain," all that. Ain't no disputing them. But around here, we fancy 'em all mixed up tegether, something a body ain't heared four hundred times, something a body kin dispute. Like "Why The Lord Come To Sand Mountain." *(Thunder, far off. Wind. Lights change)* Hit was a day powerful gusty, some years back, when the top of Sand Mountain was all a forest. Clouds had black bellies, rain wus in the air, and something up thar downright mean, a-figuring whut to do. *(Enter The Lord and Saint Peter. They wear long dark coats, mountain hats and kerchiefs, and carry small packs on their backs. They move toward the Sang Picker)* Outlanders. I seen them afore they seen me. *(She steps back. The Lord moves forward, and looks around. Saint Peter follows)*

SAINT PETER: Lord, are you sure you know where we are.

LORD: Well, just about. *(He sees the Sang Picker. He takes off his hat)* Hidy.

SANG PICKER: How do.

LORD: That river called Little Scataway?

SANG PICKER: Hit used to be, yes, sir.

(Pause. The Lord smiles)

LORD: Is it still?

SANG PICKER: Is by me. I don't speak for nobody else.

SAINT PETER: Lord, she's not going to tell us anything. Why waste time?

LORD: Hush. *(To Sang Picker)* We're looking for Sand Mountain.

SANG PICKER: From whar?

LORD: We just came down the Shenandoah.

SANG PICKER: Over Roan Ridge? And Little Snowbird?

LORD: *(Enjoying her)* That's right.

SANG PICKER: Through Torn Britches Woods, Stand Around Gap, and Dog Slaughter Creek?

LORD: Yes, m'am.

SANG PICKER: You willing to pass through Odd Bottom Cove, Hell Fer Breakfast, and Prosper Valley?

LORD: I am.

SANG PICKER: Then I suspect you'll come to Sand Mountain jest about dusk.

LORD: You saying it's just down the river?

SANG PICKER: I ain't saying hit's not.

LORD: I thank you kindly.

SANG PICKER: Don't say nothing about it.

(The Lord moves away. Saint Peter, with a doubtful look at the Sang Picker, follows. Thunder again, and wind)

I tell ye plank flat, them men are Saint Peter and the Lord Jesus hisself. Come to the Smokies a-looking fer Sand Mountain. But when they come on Prosper Valley, with a mountain night at their heels, and the sky all a-clabbering up fer a storm, Saint Peter wanted to stay thar.

(The Lord and Saint Peter have walked around the stage. Now Saint Peter breaks away from The Lord and comes to the edge of the stage, looking out over Prosper Valley. The Sang Picker moves to one side of the stage and sits on a crate)

SAINT PETER: Come here, Lord! Look down there! Must be Prosper Valley.

(The Lord comes up beside him. From the valley below, we hear voices singing a hymn: "What a Friend We Have In Jesus." A figure enters from behind the Sang Picker. He is a Prosper Valley Farmer, a large well-fed man. He listens)

Look at that good bottom land, Lord!

FARMER: *(To himself)* Lord?

SAINT PETER: Black dirt crops. Pens, fences and barns. Timber and plaster houses. Good solid folks down there. Listen to them sing your praises, Lord Jesus!

FARMER: His praises? Lord Jesus?

SAINT PETER: I know we'd be welcome. Let's go down there and spend the night.

(The Prosper Valley Farmer, hat in hand, comes to The Lord and Saint Peter)

FARMER: Begging yer pardon, Outlanders, but am I a-visualizing little sort of circle-thangs over yore heads?

SAINT PETER: You might be. Some see them, some don't.

FARMER: Then could you really be the Lord Jesus and . . .

SAINT PETER: Saint Peter, beloved of the Lord. That's right.

(The Prosper Valley Farmer falls to his knees)

FARMER: Well, Hallelujah! Lord! Saint Peter! I'm from Prosper Valley, down yonder! Please come set a-spell, and spend the night, too! A storm's clabbering up, and we'll take good care of ye, and feed and rest yore bodies. We all love ye, Lord, and to worship ye day and night, why, that's what we love a-doing most! Come set a-spell.

(Saint Peter smiles broadly)

SAINT PETER: We certainly thank you kindly. We will. Let's go, Lord! *(He turns to The Lord, who abruptly turns away)* Lord?

LORD: This way.

SAINT PETER: What?

LORD: Follow me.

SAINT PETER: But where?

(The Lord points upstage)

LORD: Up there. Up Sand Mountain.

SAINT PETER: But it's almost dark! And those clouds! I think there's a storm coming.

LORD: There is. And we're going up there.

(The Lord begins to walk around the stage. Saint Peter follows him)

SAINT PETER: All right, Lord. Whatever you say. *(To Prosper Valley Farmer)* Sorry, Mister. So long.

(Thunder, loud. Wind and rain. Lights flash as lightning strikes around them. They move from one side of the stage to the other. The Prosper Valley Farmer, at a distance, follows them)

SANG PICKER: Storm commenced to break on their heads, powerful ornery. They climbed Sand Mountain purt near two mile. Cold and bone-marrow damp, hit was. Raw wind, gusts sweeping the slopes. Hit was plain uncomfortable.

(Saint Peter and The Lord struggle through the storm, followed by the Prosper Valley Farmer)

SAINT PETER: Lord, wait a minute! *(He sneezes)* Where are we going? *(He sneezes again. The Lord points to the center of the stage)*

LORD: There. Right up there.

(In the cabin, a dim figure of a woman lights a candle)

SANG PICKER: Now 'pon my word and deed, through the wind and the rain Saint Peter seen a little tee-ninesy light in what was jest the worst kind of slattery old cabin. Timber all warped, held together it was by sticks and mud. There wasn't even a dog around the place to bark at them.

(The Lord and Saint Peter approach the cabin. They stand before the platform at stage center. The Prosper Valley Farmer hides and watches.)

LORD: Knock. *(Saint Peter knocks upon an imaginary door. Nothing happens)* Again. Harder. *(Saint Peter knocks again, harder)*

SAINT PETER: If I knock any harder, it'll fall down.

(The figure of a man picks up the candle and comes to the door. With him is Fourteen Children, played by one child, a boy about twelve, who is dressed very poorly, dirty and ragged. The man's clothes, hair and beard are all unkempt and his eyes are feverish. He opens the door a crack)

JACK: Whatchu men want here?

SAINT PETER: *(To The Lord)* Lord, this is pitiful.

LORD: Ask.

SAINT PETER: *(Sighs)* All right. *(To Jack)* I am Saint Peter and this is the Lord. Can we come in?

(Pause. Jack and his child stare at them)

JACK: Yer who?

SAINT PETER: Saint Peter and the Lord. We've been walking all the day long. We're tired, hungry, cold and rained on. We'd appreciate a place to spend the night.

(A woman in the cabin turns around. She is much younger than the man, but gaunt and pale. She calls out)

JEAN: Who is it?

JACK: Two men. Allowing as how they're The Lord and Saint Peter. They want in.

JEAN: Well, tell 'em to possess their souls in patience.

(She goes to the door, lurching unsteadily. She is also dressed in rags, unkempt as her husband. She stares out, squinting and weaving. Saint Peter turns away from her)

SAINT PETER: Whew! Lord, this woman's drunk. Smell her breath?

LORD: They both are.

(Thunder crashes down on them. The rain pounds down. Lightning flashes. The wind howls)

JEAN: Why, shore. I kin tell. At thar's The Lord and at thar's Saint Peter. Of a sartin. Ask 'em in.

JACK: Reckon we should?

JEAN: No, but whut difference do hit make? Whoever they be, if they figgur on cutting our throats, all they have to do is kick down the door.

(Thunder, rain, wind and lightning. Jean takes the chairs down from the wall)

SAINT PETER: I'm sorry to trouble you, but we're getting wet. *(He sneezes again)*

JACK: Well, come on in.

JEAN: *(Laughing)* Jest in time fer supper.

(Jack and Jean step back. Lights come up on the interior of the mountain cabin. It is stark and primitive. Outside, the Prosper Valley Farmer has seen The Lord and Saint Peter enter the cabin. With a gesture of disgust, he exits)

SANG PICKER: Hit wasn't much more'n a shack. A stone fireplace, some slat chairs, an old battered cupboard, a split log fer a dinner table, some corn-shuck mattresses and that was all. Saint Peter seen what this was. A hard time family.

JEAN: All right, then. The Lord gets the head of the table, I reckon, and Saint Peter sits the foot of it, or something like that. Shore. At's right.

(They sit around the table. The Lord at right, Saint Peter at left. Jean goes to a pot hanging in the fireplace, over a meager flame)

SANG PICKER: The woman give them what she had. Shaller clay bowls of thin corn soup. A thumb of cornbread apiece. And now, friends, that there was all. There wasn't no more.

(Saint Peter and The Lord look at what they have to eat, and then they look at the child, who gets the same, sits and eats greedily)

An old man and his young wife, the way men do in these mountains, her having babies one a year since she was a little girl herself, fourteen children now, non of 'em too happy mealtimes. They took what they got, sat down and fought over it.

FOURTEEN CHILDREN: *(Fighting)* Gimme that! No, I won't! Yes, you will! No, I won't. Let that be! I'll bust you upside the head! I'll tear out yore gizzard! No, you won't. Yes, I will! Ow! Ow!!

JEAN: Hush, chillun! Eat yore supper!

(Fourteen Children quiets down, grumbling)

SANG PICKER: Hit was jest plain squalid. Saint Peter had a hard time a-choking down 'at soup. This kind of thang got on his nerves. He appreciated one thing at a time, calm at the dinner table and quiet chillun. And 'at soup was hog slop.

(The Lord finishes his soup, with relish)

LORD: Hmmm. Very good.

(He reaches for his switch. He twitches it. There is a sudden glare and blaze of fire in the fireplace. The Lord smiles. Fourteen Children, finished, erupts again)

FOURTEEN CHILDREN: I won't neither! Ow! Give 'at back! I'll bust ye open! I'll funeralize ye! I'll kill ye graveyard dead! Ow! Owww!!!

(The Lord stands up. He goes to Fourteen Children)

LORD: *(Quietly)* Hush. Listen to me.

(He takes his chair, turns it facing away. He holds out his arm. Fourteen Children goes to The Lord, leans against him facing away, and listens to him)

SANG PICKER: The Lord told Fourteen Chillun a story about a sad, worried peacock. Then he turned around and told anothern about a fat mountain lion. Then he told a story about chillun like them, all lost in the dark forest, what couldn't get theirselves home. They smiled at the first two stories, but not at the last un. The Lord waved his stick and the fire blazed up agin and Fourteen Chillun commenced to yawn. Afore a grown man kin spit, they got drowsy and stayed that way.

(The Lord gets up, leaving Fourteen Children settled peacefully in the chair. They all stare at Fourteen Children, then Jack and Jean stare at The Lord as a bright light glows around him)

SAINT PETER: You see? I told you he was the Lord. He can do anything.

LORD: *(Smiling)* He's right. What you're seeing now are halos. *(The light glows brighter, on him and on Saint Peter)* That is Saint Peter. I am the Lord. *(Clumsily, Jack and Jean get to their knees before The Lord)* No, now don't do that. You're not used to it, for one thing, and you're both drunk for another. Just be yourselves.

(The light fades. Jack and Jean stand before The Lord and Saint Peter, hanging their heads.)

SANG PICKER: Hit was a plain embarrassment. Neither soul thar knowed whut to say.

(Pause)

SAINT PETER: *(Sternly)* What are your names?

JACK: Jack, Saint Peter.

JEAN: Jean, Saint Peter.

SAINT PETER: Jack and Jean. Old man, young woman. Whiskey. You two married? *(They look at each other, then shake their heads)* You go to church? At all? *(Same)* Well, no wonder you're in such a mess.

JACK: Lord. Saint Peter. Hit warn't always thisaway. We figgered we wus like everbody else, fer a time. But we can't farm no moren a passle of corn, land here above the waterfalls is powerful sandy, last year our cow died, and whut with the chillun being so puny and poorly, we stopped going places much, and afore we knowed it, we wus living up here alone.

SAINT PETER: Up here by yourselves, with fourteen children and a jug of whiskey, drinking until the world looks little.

JACK: Yes, sir.

JEAN: Not 'at much at first, then the littliest bit more, and then some more and now all the time. We've come to that.

SAINT PETER: And when you drink, do you fight? Get mad, yell and shout, hit each other? The children?

(They nod)

JACK and JEAN: *(Quietly)* Sometimes. Yes, sir.

JACK: *(To The Lord)* Whut happened to us, Lord?

SAINT PETER: I just told you. Old man, young woman, no wedding, no church, and too much corn liquor.

LORD: *(To Saint Peter)* Hush. *(To Jack)* We can't really tell you. Life can be mysterious, sometimes, and sad. *(Pause)* Let me put it this way. I have no sermons on the matter. *(With a look at Saint Peter)* And neither does he.

SANG PICKER: Well, since the Lord ruled that plumb out, Saint Peter didn't know whut else to say, and give up a-wondering why they wus there. Hit was another embarrassment. The onliest question left hanging wus whut sort of tribute 'at miserable shack could pay to the Lord and his Apostle Peter, who'd been good enough to visit. Jack figgered he only had one thang.

(Jack, making a decision, goes to the cupboard and gets a clay jug and some clay mugs. He sets them down before The Lord and Saint Peter)

JACK: Sand Mountain brandy, Lord. Ain't very much and ain't very good, but hit's the best thang we got here, and hit's yours.

SAINT PETER: Man, put that away. That's what's caused all your trouble in the first place.

LORD: Hush. *(To Jack)* That will do. We thank you.

(Jack pours brandy for them and for himself, to Saint Peter's exasperation. When he is finished, we see he has poured out the last drop in the jug and there is nothing left. The Lord lifts his cup)

LORD: To this house.

JACK and JEAN: Thank you, Lord.

SAINT PETER: Whew. To this house. *(They sip the mountain brandy. Saint Peter makes a face, and The Lord glares at him, kicks him under the table. Then he holds out his switch, swishes it slightly. The fire, with a whoosh, flares up again. They drink and watch it burn. Pause)*

SANG PICKER: 'At brandy wus hair raisin'. But, in the least little while, they wus all feeling powerful improved, like that pore corn soup had been nourishment a-plenty, and the awful brandy good fer a body, too. 'At fire, which wus almost burned out, flared up agin, and they found themselves sitting around the place in tollable comfort, drinking and pondering the fire. *(Pause)* Hit was the Lord what commenced it.

LORD: Know what it means when you stumble over a stone?

JACK: No, Lord. Whut?

LORD: *(Slowly)* It means on that spot a fiddle player lies buried. *(Pause. Jack and Jean look at each other. Jack gets a chair, sits at the table)*

JACK: Know whut's the onliest thang kin cure the deadly curdles or leper sickness?

LORD: No. What?

JACK: Ye have to wash yore skin in the blood of a man whose life you saved.

(The Lord nods)

SANG PICKER: The Lord pondered 'at. So did Saint Peter.

SAINT PETER: Now, where did you hear that?

JACK: Here on Sand Mountain, awhile ago. I know a feller around here, too, says he onct taught cats to hold candlesticks.

(Pause)

SAINT PETER: Oh, stop. What for?

JACK: So he could turn a mouse loose, and see whut'd happen.

LORD: What did?

JACK: Them cats dropped them candlesticks and went after 'at mouse. *(Pause)* Ye learn, but ye fergit.

SAINT PETER: What?

LORD: You learn, but you forget.

JACK: I reckon.

(They acknowledge each other's approval)

SANG PICKER: Now you know Saint Peter, 'pon my word and deed, he couldn't comprehend why Jesus had 'at littliest piece of a smile on his face, or why Jack and Jean did too. Hit wus like the three of them wus taking a few throws and tosses afore some kind of a ball game.

(Pause)

JEAN: A humpback and blind man down, around Hazel Creek, robbed a traveling salesman. They set down to divy up the goods. And fell out. "You damn scoundrel," said the blind man, "you're a-cheating me." "You miserable lint-head," said the humpback, "you ain't blind at tall." "Yes, I am," said the blind man and "No, you ain't," said the humpback, and then they both said, "You son of a bitch." The humpback rubbed dirt in the blind man's eyes, and that gave him back his sight. The blind man hit the humpback with a stick, and that broke his hump. The blind man seen the humpback standing thar tall and handsome-bodied, and the humpback seen the blind man a-looking at him with two big shiny-smart eyes, and they fancied each other so much, they lived together happy and pleasant all their lives.

(Pause)

SANG PICKER: This time Saint Peter jest looked out the one winder of the cabin, at the rain a-coming down. He did his best to put it together some way, the blind man and the humpback, and make some sense out of 'em, but he couldn't and gave up.

(The Lord holds out his cup)

LORD: Could I have a drop more of this good brandy?

JACK: We're sorry, Lord.

JEAN: There ain't no more. That wus all we had.

LORD: Take a look.

(Jack picks up what he is sure is an empty jug, and finds it heavy and full)

SANG PICKER: Shore enough, the jug was full, so Jack poured them all a big fat dollop. And hit didn't taste like no sulfur this time, no, sir, hit tasted like the bestest gum tree mountain brandy a body ever had. I mean, hit wus smooth as cedar and warm as a cat. *(Thunder, wind, rain, and a surge of flames in the fireplace)* And while 'at storm broke open above 'em, big logs, thick and fat, jest plain grew in the fireplace, a-sizzlin and a-poppin. Outside 'at pore miserable shack, goobers and gusts of rain passed right over the roof, and never touched it nowhere.

(Saint Peter makes a show of stretching and yawning)

SAINT PETER: I sure am sleepy. That brandy. This fire. All the rain. Lord, isn't it about time we turned in?

LORD: Not yet. *(He smiles, sips his brandy and waits)*

JACK: One day, near Hangman's Gap, a deef man went to see his sick neighbor. *(Saint Peter sits back, groaning)* He set down by his neighbor's bed and said, "How are ye?" Sick man said, "Dying." Deef man said, "Thank God fer that! Who's yer doctor?" Sick man said, "Doctor Death! Now git out and leave me alone!" Deef man said, "At's wonderful! Whut medicine is he a-giving ye?" Sick man said, "Poison! Now will ye plain damn go away and let me die?" Deef man said, "Why, shorely, and I'll come see ye tomorrow, too."

(Pause. Jack, Jean and The Lord relish the story. As before, Saint Peter shakes his head)

SANG PICKER: Right about here Saint Peter plain decided Jack had woobles in the head. He looked over at the Lord to sort of shrug, but there the Lord was, a-smiling agin. And then, whut floored Saint Peter, The Lord was a-telling one!

(The Lord leans forward in his chair, and tells a story, inaudible to us, to Jack and Jean. Saint Peter stares at him, open-mouthed)

Some story about folks he'd heared of near the Cumberland Gap, where the men were so contrary, if ye throwed them in a river, they'd float upstream. Where the women wus so ugly they had to blindfold babies to get 'em to suck.

(Jack and Jean nod their approval, without smiling more than they need to, and The Lord turns to Saint Peter, nodding. Thunder. Lightning)

Logs burned. 'At jar stayed full of brandy. Rain and wind flew past the shack, leaving it dry. Jack told . . .

JACK: The Moon Frog.

SANG PICKER: Jean told . . .

JEAN: The Water Man.

SANG PICKER: The Lord told . . .

LORD: The Child Who Could Not Shudder.

(Thunder, lightning, rain and wind)

SANG PICKER: Then Jack told . . .

JACK: The Breaking of the Stone of Patience.

SANG PICKER: Jean told . . .

JEAN: Sheriff Unexpected and the Bony Bandit.

SANG PICKER: And The Lord told . . .

LORD: Flowering Cholera, Phantom Funerals, and Sleeping Kings.

(Pause. Saint Peter smacks a fist into the palm of one hand, decisively)

SANG PICKER: Saint Peter figgered this'd gone fur enough. Crazy wild stories, well, he'd fight fire with fire, and give 'em something strong, human, and down-to-earth sensible. With a meaning to it!

SAINT PETER: Once upon a time, there was a Sailor and a Parrot. The Sailor sold his Parrot to the Queen, who was beautiful and proud. She kept him in a golden cage in her castle bedroom. One day the Queen stepped naked out of her bath. The Parrot whistled and said, "Whew-o! I see your ass!" This made the Queen furious. She opened the golden cage, pulled out that Parrot by the throat, choked him, banged him on the floor, and threw him out the window. He landed on a pile of garbage outside the kitchen. He was lying there when a scrawny Chicken came sailing out of the kitchen window, neck wrung, too, and landed on the garbage pile next to the Parrot. The Parrot thought a minute, and then said, "Whew-o! Whose ass did you see?"

(Saint Peter laughs at his own story, slapping his knees with jovial mirth, then sees they are all politely waiting for him to finish)

SANG PICKER: Jack, Jean and the Lord were real polite about it.
JEAN: That us plain interesting.
JACK: Hit wus, of a sartin.
SANG PICKER: Then Jean told . . .
JEAN: The Lady Who Gave Birth To A Rat!
(There is a terrific burst of thunder, wind, and lightning. Saint Peter shrinks back in his chair)
SANG PICKER: Saint Peter's skin plain crawled. In the rain outside, 'at Sand Mountain wind howled like bobcats. Then Jack and Jean together told . . .
JACK: Goforth Baines . . .
JEAN: And his devil son, Stamper.
SAINT PETER: Oh, really.
JACK: . . . And how he died. You want to hear it, Lord?
LORD: We do.
(A low rumble of thunder)
JACK: First you must know Stamper Baines got a Sand Mountain girl named Sally Newell pregnant.
JEAN: Sally loved him fer that. She come a-running with shining eyes, to tell him about the baby. When did he want to marry her?
JACK: Stamper jest laughed. Whut kind of a fool did she take him fer? 'At baby's got as many daddys as a pickle's got warts.
JEAN: Sally hated him fer that. When Stamper went off from her still a-laughing, hit were a mistake.
JACK: She got her three brothers, Jack, Zack and Mack Newell. They waited fer Stamper Baines behind a chincapin tree, fell upon him graveyard deadly with barlow knives, cut him all apart, throwed the pieces in a totesack, and give it to Sally Newell. From his bones . . .
JEAN: She made a chair.
JACK: From his skin . . .
JEAN: She made her a mattress.
JACK: From his skull . . .
JEAN: She made her a goblet.
JACK: Wine from his blood.
JEAN: Candles from his fat.
JACK: Candlewicks from his hair.
JEAN: Stew from his fingers.
JACK: And soup from his balls.
JEAN: Then she invited his father, Goforth Baines, to supper.

(Saint Peter chokes and coughs)

JACK: But Goforth Baines had his doubts. He come to Sally Newell's cabin, but with eyes in the back of his head. When she laid out the big meal afore him, he asked her what she'd been a-doing lately. Sally smiled at that.

JEAN: She answered him with a riddle, and a song. *(She sings)* I BEEN A-SITTING WITH MY LOVE-O . . .

JACK: *(Speaking)* The chair . . .

JEAN: *(Singing)* I BEEN A-DRINKING WITH MY LOVE-O . . .

JACK: The goblet . . .

JEAN: *(Singing)* I BEEN A-SLEEPING WITH MY LOVE-O . . .

JACK: The mattress . . .

JEAN: *(Singing)* I BEEN A-READING WITH MY LOVE-O . . .

JACK: The candles . . .

JEAN: *(Singing)* I BEEN A-EATING WITH MY LOVE-O . . .

JACK: The soup and the stew . . .

JEAN: *(Singing)* I'LL GIVE YOU SOME WINE-O . . .

JACK: The blood . . .

JEAN: *(Singing)* IF YOU GUESS ME A-RIGHT-O!

JACK: But all fer naught, cause Goforth Baines guessed her hateful riddle, unsheathed his own great barlow knife, and called her she-devil. In rushed Jack, Zack and Mack Newell, to cut Goforth apart too, but mighty Goforth Baines, in a tantrum, killed them all, afore he cut off Sally Newell's head.

(Jack and Jean sing lustily, with mountain harmony, stamping their feet)

JACK and JEAN: *(Singing)*
HE SWUNG AROUND HIS BARLOW KNIFE,
THEM BAD MEN THEY DID FALL;
HE CUT SALLY'S HEAD FROM HER SHOULDERS,
AND HE THROWED IT AGIN THE WALL.

JACK: Then Goforth Baines, he stood thar in mortal dread at the dinner table. Stamper Baines, his evil boy. He wept his bitter tears, a-touching the bone chair, a-lifting the burning candles, and a-smelling the simmering soup.

(Saint Peter, watching, shakes his head)

SAINT PETER: Really.

SANG PICKER: Now you know Saint Peter didn't begrudge nobody no story, but he did figger hit ought to have some mortal point to it. I say, be about life as hit really is. He did mislike jimcracky tales about people eating other people, rats born in place of babies, and wooble-headed heroes with names like Stamper and Goforth. So he stopped listening. Fer awhile.

JEAN: Lord, you strike a body dead, they tell a Jesus Tale?

SAINT PETER: Tell a what?

LORD: *(Smiling)* No. Which ones you know?

JEAN: All of 'em, purt near.

LORD: Tell some.

JEAN: You plain positive?

LORD: I'm plain positive.

SAINT PETER: Lord, what's this now? Jesus Tales?

LORD: That's right. Hush.

JEAN: *(To Jack)* Whut'll we tell?

JACK: Well, thar's Saint Peter's Divorce.

SAINT PETER: Saint Peter's what?

JEAN: That's whar Saint Peter is womberjawled miserable cause his wife talks too much, and he asks the Lord to git him a divorce, and the Lord says well, all right, but only if Saint Peter will marry the next woman coming down the road.

SAINT PETER: Now, Lord. Wait a minute.

LORD: Hush. *(To Jack and Jean)* Tell it.

JACK: And the next woman down the road is decent looking and nods, yes, she'll marry Saint Peter, and be grabbies hit turns out she can't talk at all, so Saint Peter gets right happy until the Lord takes a nail pulled out of a coffin, sets it agin her back tooth, knocks the tooth out . . .

JEAN: And 'at woman commences to talk and talk and she can't stop, so Saint Peter gives up and goes back to his good decent wife and forgets about divorce.

SANG PICKER: And Saint Peter got up then, right stiffly, stood thar resenting all 'at. But the Lord was smiling, so whut could he do?

(The Lord leans forward and starts telling Jack and Jean another story. Fourteen Children wakes up and listens, too)

Then the Lord told Jesus, Saint Peter, the Goose and the Bean, which they hadn't never heard.

(Saint Peter turns away, offended)

And Saint Peter, he wondered then, jest a mite bitter about it, why it wus he wus forever the dummy in these doings.

(Saint Peter looks at The Lord, rubs his head)

Why does the Lord treat me thisaway? When I love him and always have and always will. Why are we a-setting here in this miserable shack with these crazy people got woobles in their heads? Why ain't we down thar in 'at Prosper Valley we seen, with them good healthy Christian farmers, singing hymns. None of this makes no sense.

(Scratching his head, Saint Peter sits again. The Lord finishes his story, which goes over big. Jack and Jean laugh and applaud. And Fourteen Children likes it, too. Smiling, The Lord fills their cups again with brandy)

LORD: Well, one more.

JACK: What'll hit be, Lord?

JEAN: You pick it out this time.

(Pause. The Lord is suddenly serious. He speaks very softly)

LORD: Tell Joseph the Carpenter.

JEAN: Old Man Joseph?

LORD: And his family. You know it?

JACK and JEAN: *(Together)* We all do. *(They look at Fourteen Children, who nods)*

LORD: Good. Tell it.

JACK: All right.

JACK and JEAN: We will.

SANG PICKER: And they did. Before the Lord and Saint Peter, this man and his young wife told the old story the Lord needed to hear, and to hear it, from them, is Why The Lord Come to Sand Mountain.

(Change of light, spilling out over the stage, expanding it. After consulting each other, Jack, Jean and Fourteen Children sing)

JACK, JEAN and FOURTEEN CHILDREN: *(Singing)*

OH, JOSEPH WAS AN OLD MAN,
AN OLD MAN WAS HE,
HE MARRIED VIRGIN MARY,
THE QUEEN OF GALILEE.

JACK: Joseph was an old man when he met Mary.

JEAN: He wus eighty-nine, and she wus fourteen.

JACK: And she wus fourteen. His wife of sixty years'd jest died. He wus about ready to pass on, too. Then he met Mary, this young girl, who didn't want no young man.

(They move downstage, out of the shack. Fourteen Children stays in his chair. Their scenes will be played around the tree stump at right, the clump of logs at left and in front of the cabin)
JEAN and JACK: *(Singing)*
OH, JOSEPH WAS AN OLD MAN,
AN OLD MAN WAS HE,
HE MARRIED VIRGIN MARY,
THE QUEEN OF GALILEE.
(Jean, as Mary, turns to Jack)
JEAN/MARY: If you want me, Joseph, take me.
JACK/JOSEPH: At my age?
JEAN/MARY: Yes.
JACK/JOSEPH: Honey, whut would I do with ye? Be sensible.
JEAN/MARY: All right. *(Pause)* You were the perfect man.
JACK/JOSEPH: Sorry.
JEAN/MARY: 'At's all right. *(She sighs, looks away bleakly. Jack/Joseph watches her)*
JACK/JOSEPH: Now whutchu thinking about?
JEAN/MARY: Hot boys. Goodbye, Joseph.
JACK/JOSEPH: Now, wait a minute. *(Jean/Mary weeps)* Stop a-crying! *(She weeps)*
JEAN/MARY: I ain't crying!
JACK/JOSEPH: I might could use me a housekeeper.
JEAN/MARY: You could?
JACK/JOSEPH: Fer awhile. I'll be gone soon. So we'll have no talk of marriage.
JEAN/MARY: Why not? I'll marry you. I want to!
JACK/JOSEPH: Well, iffen ye still don't want no hot boys a year off, and I'm still here, maybe then. How's 'at?
JEAN/MARY: 'At's jest fine.
JACK/JOSEPH: Now, Mary, I'm a plain country man, 'at's all.
JEAN/MARY: Yes, sir. I'm glad.
(Pause)
JACK/JOSEPH: My children, my grandchildren, my great grandchildren, when they see you, they will piss green. I beg yore pardon. I swear sometimes. That bother you?
JEAN/MARY: When other men swear, I see darkness. When Joseph swears, I see light.
(Joseph holds out his arm. Mary takes it and they walk together across the stage)

JACK/JOSEPH: You'll think agin, about hot boys. I won't keep 'em away.

JEAN/MARY: You won't have to.

JACK/JOSEPH: Oh, yes, I will. Whut'll ye do, in a year?

JEAN/MARY: Marry you.

JACK/JOSEPH: On my ninetieth birthday? Hush.

JEAN/MARY: I will, though. *(Pause)* Joseph?

JACK/JOSEPH: Whut?

JEAN/MARY: Hit ain't the ending what's important. Hit's the beginning.

(They move to the clump of logs. Joseph gives her his coat, and she shakes and brushes it)

SANG PICKER: And two year later, Joseph wus ninety-one, married to Mary, and looking thirty years younger.

JEAN: *(Singing)*
OH, MARY AND JOSEPH
WALKED THROUGH A GARDEN GREEN,
THERE WERE APPLES AND CHERRIES,
A-PLENTY TO BE SEEN.

(Mary helps Joseph put on his coat, happily)

SANG PICKER: She kept his house, give him hot meals, washed his clothes and cut his hair. He told her all them thangs he'd seen in his long life, and whut life wus all about and she felt safe.

JACK and JEAN: *(Singing)*
OH, MARY AND JOSEPH
WALKED THROUGH A GARDEN GREEN,
THERE WERE APPLES AND CHERRIES,
PLENTY TO BE SEEN.

SANG PICKER: He even commenced working agin, as a master carpenter, and acause of his great long age and experience, he wus in demand, too. One day, he wus a-going on a trip.

JEAN/MARY: Joseph.

JACK/JOSEPH: *(With a little jig)* They want four cabins and a general store. How about that?

JEAN/MARY: Joseph.

JACK/JOSEPH: *(Dancing)* This is going to be some junket, I tell ye.

JEAN/MARY: Joseph.

JACK/JOSEPH: *(Dancing)* Honey, whut is it?

JEAN/MARY: I'm pregnant.

JACK/JOSEPH: You're whut?

JEAN/MARY: I'm fixing to have a baby. You care about how it happened?

JACK/JOSEPH: I reckon I kin figure that out by myself.

JEAN/MARY: No, you can't.

JACK/JOSEPH: Didn't I give ye a whole year. Say, git ye a hot boy when ye want one.

JEAN/MARY: I never wanted one.

JACK/JOSEPH: Ye want one now.

JEAN/MARY: No, I don't *(Pause)* Joseph, I am still a virgin. *(Pause)*

JACK/JOSEPH: Honey, I have reached the age of ninety-one year. Jest don't talk like that.

JEAN/MARY: It's the truth! Three months ago, you went off fer four days. The first afternoon, I got sleepy. I took a nap, and I dreamed a young man was standing outside my winder. He opened the winder. He clumb in the winder. Sunshine come in and mountain air. He stood by my bed. He told me something wonderful was fixing to happen to me.

JACK/JOSEPH: Yes, by grabbies, I reckon he did.

JEAN/MARY: He had big wings on his back. Dark-green and copper-colored they were, Joseph, and they wus moving up and down like big fans. Ever so gentle, he blew in my ear. He told me I would have a holy child. Then he flew out my winder, into sunshine. I felt so peaceful. I slept awhile. I dreamed a star fell into my mouth. Then I woke up. Now I'm pregnant. *(Pause)* What do hit mean?

JACK/JOSEPH: Hit means ye git pregnant through yer ear!

JEAN/MARY: Joseph, Almighty God kin do anythang!

JACK/JOSEPH: Maybe He kin, but He don't! He made the rules! He sticks to 'em! Virgins don't have no babies! *(Pause)*

JEAN/MARY: Whut do ye want me to do? Go way?

JACK/JOSEPH: Be best. *(Pause)* But if ye did, child, I'd die.

JEAN/MARY: Then I won't. Go on yore trip, Joseph. But I have to ask ye this.

JACK/JOSEPH: No, you don't. What kin I say? 'At child ain't mine, hit's a green-winged angel's?

JACK: Will you allow hit's yore'n?

JACK/JOSEPH: I won't say hit ain't.

JEAN/MARY: All right, then. Bye. Be careful.

JACK/JOSEPH: Yeah. You, too. *(He moves away from her, taking a file from his pocket and sitting on the tree stump, begins to work a piece of wood)*

SANG PICKER: When the baby wus born, Joseph never believed them wise men or shepherds or that star wus ary thang but accidents. He'd get fired up whenever Mary allowed as how Jesus was ary sort of special child at tall.

(Jack/Joseph turns to Fourteen Children, who comes to sit beside him, watching him quietly)

JACK/JOSEPH: Hit'll be up to yore Daddy, Least One, to tell ye. Yer nothing special. Git 'at through yer head. Be the worstest thang I could do to ye, son, to say ye are. Puff ye up like a fool, send ye out into the world a Momma's boy, a-thinking ye hung the moon. No, sir. Ye gonna be like my Daddy and his. Yer gonna know straight plumblines and honest buildings. Yer gonna know square scored-off beams set so flush an ant can't get between, the fireplace drawing strong and the home whut's built to last. Hit's my duty, Jesus, to teach you all 'at. Take ye to town, show ye good men up and doing, a-building and a-sweating, opening the stores, swinging hammers, banging horse shoes, and working like men! I'll set you straight in this life, my boy. Yes, by God, I will! *(Joseph finishes his work. He holds a wooden toy out to Jesus. When one part of it is rubbed, another part spins)* Here. This is fer you. Rub hit right thar. *(Jesus does. The primitive toy spins)* Hit's a whimmy-diddle. Play whilst ye kin, son.

(Fourteen Children goes back to his chair)

SANG PICKER: Now because Mary believed the boy was a holy child and old Joseph didn't, Jesus had passles of trouble as a boy. He acted up. Wouldn't mind nobody. Talked back. Got into this fix and that with other chillun.

(Joseph and Mary meet at center)

JACK/JOSEPH: Where is he? Whut's happened?

JEAN/MARY: They were all on the river bank, making animals out of clay. One little boy was making a sparrow. They say Jesus took it away from him, blew on it, and it flew away!

JACK/JOSEPH: More crazy talk. Hit's all them stories told about him. Holy child. Wise men and stars and all that. See what happens? People commence gitting outlandish ideas about somebody and hit won't never stop.

JEAN/MARY: When I got thar, he had all them chillun setting at his feet. He wus telling them all stories.

JACK/JOSEPH: Where is he now?

JEAN/MARY: I don't know. When he saw me, he ran off.

(F.C./Jesus, stands before them. Joseph gets up, stares at him coldly)

JACK/JOSEPH: Well. Come home fer supper, did ye? Hm.

(F.C./Jesus turns away from Jack/Joseph. Jean/Mary sits by him)

JEAN/MARY: I should have stopped him a long time ago. Making you a man too soon. He's wrong. You're not a man yet, you're still a boy. He shouldn't be so hard on you. All that work. Hit's no way to treat a little boy. No wonder you run away and tell stories. I won't have it. My son will never be a ditch-digger. Or some lackey. Or some carpenter. We don't make too much of ourselves, you and me. You are better than all this. There is more to life than what we know. You will find it.

(Jack/Joseph stands before them. Jean/Mary turns away)

JACK/JOSEPH: I should have stopped her a long time ago. She's kept you a child too long. You ain't the sun and the moon. We're dust, Jesus. You, me, yore Momma, yore little friends, all the world. Don't stir it up. *(Pause)* I dreamed about all 'at, when I was a boy. My kingdom. But I had to go to work, like a man, with a hammer and saw. I did the best I could. Try to do more, is crazy. So git hit straight. Please me, ye'll cross her. Please her, ye'll cross me. Take yore pick, and never mind kingdoms. You ain't a baby no more.

(Jack/Joseph turns away. Pause. F.C./Jesus lets out a cry of frustration and rage and runs away)

SANG PICKER: That little boy become a little demon that night. Run through the town, breaking winders, turning thangs upside down. Folks yelled at him, called him a child terror, and the whole town chased after him. They caught him, cornered him. Joseph and Mary had to come git their boy, and when they did, there was a plain squalid, pore-ways family fight, right there for everbody to see.

(Jack/Joseph and Jean/Mary face F.C./Jesus)

JACK/JOSEPH: Tell these people yer sorry and come on home.

F.C./JESUS: I won't.

JACK/JOSEPH: Oh, yes, you will.

F.C./JESUS: You go to hell.

JEAN/MARY: What did you say?

F.C./JESUS: *(Shouting)* You, too!!

JACK/JOSEPH: Ah! *(Jack/Joseph strikes F.C./Jesus)*

F.C./JESUS: Ah! *(F.C./Jesus grabs Joseph's staff and hits him with it, knocking him down. In the cabin, The Lord suddenly stands and moves forward. Frightened, F.C./Jesus drops the staff and runs to his mother. They go to Joseph, who holds up one hand, warding them off)*

SANG PICKER: He wouldn't go to bed. He hobbled to his workshop, sat there in the dark and wouldn't talk to nobody.

(Jack/Joseph sits by himself, on the edge of the cabin, The Lord standing just behind him)

JEAN/MARY: Joseph. *(No answer)* Joseph.

JACK/JOSEPH: Burning up. Burning up.

JEAN/MARY: Come to bed, Joseph.

JACK/JOSEPH: On fire, like wood.

JEAN/MARY: Jesus is here. He's sorry for what he done.

JACK/JOSEPH: And the wind a-blowing. I'm burning up. *(Pause. He looks at a wall)* Ah! I see him! There he be! *(He points at the wall)* He's come!

JEAN/MARY: Who's come, Joseph?

JACK/JOSEPH: Angel of Death, that's who! I see him, all in black, with 'at shining sword! With a littlest drop of gall on hit's tip I got to drink, afore he cuts my soul from my body, and throws me away. Jesus!

F.C./JESUS: Yes, sir.

JACK/JOSEPH: You look. Tell me what ye see.

SANG PICKER: Jesus looked outside. There wasn't nothing thar. Not one blessed thang.

(F.C./Jesus stares out the window)

'At young boy's hands, what struck his father, ached. His tongue, what cursed his mother, ached. He wus powerful scared but he knowed what he wus a-going to do.

(F.C./Jesus sits by Jack/Joseph, takes his hand and holds it. The Lord speaks for him)

LORD: Yer right, Daddy. 'At angel is thar, and on the tip of his sword hangs the gall you got to drink. He's fixing to cut yore body from your soul and throw hit away.

JACK/JOSEPH: Jest like I said?

LORD: Jest like ye said. But I'm here, too. Yore boy. I tell ye, magic is mine, powers whut stretch beyond this earth. Kin ye hear me? Ain't nothing stronger than my love fer ye. Kin ye hear me?

(F.C./Jesus gets up, looks out the window)

LORD: I'm a-telling 'at black-dress angel, put up ye great sword, and step aside. Angel of Death, ye going to wait. I got to talk to my Daddy. I got to tell him goodbye. You wait.

(F.C./Jesus sits again, holds Jack/Joseph's hand)

LORD: The rivers of fire are cool water. The mountains of hell are sweet bottom land. Nary thang burns ye. Nary thang kin hurt ye. Everythang is all right. Go in peace, Daddy.

(Jack/Joseph dies. F.C./Jesus lets go of his hand, bows his head)

SANG PICKER: When Joseph died, Jesus wept.

JEAN: *(Singing softly)*
OH, JOSEPH WAS AN OLD MAN,
AN OLD MAN WAS HE,
HE MARRIED VIRGIN MARY,
THE QUEEN OF GALILEE.

SANG PICKER: When 'at story got told, the fire was a-going out, and the Lord didn't make it burn no more. He'd come to Sand Mountain to hear tell about his Daddy, and Mary and hisself as a child, and he had.

(Pause. Saint Peter, who some time before fell asleep, now wakes up)

SAINT PETER: Ah. Well. Some story. But now, Lord, none of that really happened, did it?

SANG PICKER: And the Lord loved Saint Peter, the fisherman he knowed as a man, who reminded him of the carpenter he'd knowed as a boy.

SAINT PETER: I mean, what's the use of a story about things that never happened? What's the point of it?

(The Lord looks at Jean. Jean looks at Jack)

JACK: Hit ain't the ending whut's important. Hit's the beginning.

SAINT PETER: What?

LORD: Never mind. *(Smiling)* Let's turn in.

(They all sit in their chairs and go to sleep. Short pause. They wake up, and stir themselves)

SANG PICKER: In the morning, when the Lord and Saint Peter were fixing to move along, Jean was about to wash the family rags in a beat-up old tub.

(Jean sets a battered wooden washtub on the table)

SAINT PETER: Wash day, Jean?

JEAN: Yes, sir, shore is. We'uns are pore but clean.

SAINT PETER: Well, we appreciate your hospitality.

JACK: Don't say nothing about it.

(The Lord faces them. He holds up his hands)

LORD: Now's the time for your knees, if you like.

(The family kneels before The Lord) What this morning, you first begin, will not stop until tonight.

(They look at each other, puzzled. The Lord makes the sign of the cross over them. They get up and all shake hands)

JACK, JEAN and FOURTEEN CHILDREN: Goodbye! Goodbye, Lord! Goodbye, Saint Peter!

SAINT PETER and THE LORD: Goodbye! Goodbye!

(Saint Peter and The Lord leave the cabin, turning their backs and walking in place. Jean goes back to washing clothes)

SANG PICKER: Hit didn't take long.

JACK: Oh. Oh!! Ohhhh!!!! *(She begins pulling clothes out of the tub. Beautiful, magical music)*

FOURTEEN CHILDREN: Momma! Momma!

JEAN: Looky here! Looky here!

SANG PICKER: Work clothes, Sunday clothes, hunting clothes, sleeping clothes, lace kerchiefs and colored bandanas, purty dresses, sheep-wool coats, big thick socks, everthang like that!

(Jack, Jean and Fourteen Children hold the clothes. The Prosper Valley Farmer watches)

JACK, JEAN and FOURTEEN CHILDREN: Thank you, Lord!

(They put the clothes back in the tub and set it aside, turning their backs. The Prosper Valley Farmer runs around to the other side of the stage, waiting for The Lord and Saint Peter.)

SANG PICKER: Now 'pon my word and deed, when 'at fat Prosper Valley Farmer seen 'at, he skittered after the Lord and Saint Peter and jest plain faced them down.

(The Prosper Valley Farmer stops The Lord and Saint Peter)

FARMER: Hold on! Both! Come see us, we'd a-give ye real comfort. Bean-bacon soup, goat barbecue, corn, black-eyed peas, feather beds, holiness hymn-singing and powerful preaching in yore sacred name. Ye didn't care fer it. All right! But at least do fer us the same ye done fer them shiftless no-good cornsqueezers ye spent yore time with. All we ask, if you are really the Lord and Saint Peter, is jest be fair!!

SAINT PETER: He's right, Lord. You have to.

LORD: Have to what?

SAINT PETER: You know. What you did for Jack and Jean and their children.

LORD: I won't do it. *(He turns away. Saint Peter gets mad)*

SAINT PETER: Well, why not?

LORD: Never mind. I just won't.

SAINT PETER: Now listen! I stayed up half the night listening to lunatics tell crazy stories, when we could have been down in Prosper Valley with the faithful and the devoted. I tolerated your kind of folks, now you tolerate mine!

LORD: You sure about that? The faithful and the devoted?

SAINT PETER: Yes!!

LORD: All right.

(He turns to the Prosper Valley Farmer, who quickly falls on his knees before The Lord)

LORD: What-this-morning-you-first-begin-will-not-stop-until-tonight.

(The Prosper Valley Farmer jumps up)

FARMER: Thank you, Lord.

SAINT PETER: Thank you, Lord.

LORD: Follow me.

(Saint Peter follows The Lord, and they exit. The Sang Picker moves down to the edge of one side of the stage)

SANG PICKER: Well, 'at farmer lit out fer Prosper Valley like a scaulded dog, and got everybody tergether.

FARMER: "What this morning you first begin, will not stop until tonight." So! Everbody git yer purse. Open 'em up! We'll commence now, a-counting silver dollars! We'll not a body stop all day long, and like them clothes, them silver dollars'll keep on a-coming till hits dark! Let's go! *(He turns away, stops, turns back)* No, hold it! Everbody best light into the woods thar and relieve yeselves. 'At way we won't never have to stop all day long!

(He runs off. The Sang Picker moves to the center of the stage, and looks at the audience)

SANG PICKER: Yep. Like the preachers say, "The Lord he moves in mysterious ways."

(We hear a whistle, offhand, the tune of the Joseph and Mary ballad. In the cabin, Jack and Jean hang up the two extra chairs on the wall again, and sit with Fourteen Children in their mountain home, amid the colors of the clothes, and the lights go down on them)

The top of Sand Mountain is a bald now, in timothy grass. Hits peak is a sunshiney meadow, with wildflowers pleasant as a scenery of children. Some say the wind keeps clear, some say ghosts of run-off Indians tend. But some on Sand Mountain say hits a-bald because the Lord hisself won't let nothing overgrow it. That thar was onct an old mountain shack up thar he set a spell in one night, laughing and telling tall tales, and he liked the way he wus treated. *(The light focuses on the Sang Picker's smiling face. The whistling ends)* Course, a body kin deny it. Say the Lord never did laugh or tell no tall tales. Well, I never heared him laugh, but everbody knows he liked a story, and I'll dispute that anywhar. 'At's whut I think. *(Pause)* Now. *(She leans forward, smiling)* What do you think?

Blackout

The End

Stephen Metcalfe

SPITTIN' IMAGE

Stephen Metcalfe

One of the hits of the 1985 SHORTS Festival presented by Actors Theatre of Louisville (A.T.L.), Stephen Metcalfe's *Spittin' Image* (then entitled *Megs*) won plaudits from reviewer William Mootz in the Louisville *Courier-Journal:* "*Megs* reveals Metcalfe as a playwright of considerable skill. He writes vividly, and he has a sure sense of theater. His play is sleekly constructed and, under his own direction, its A.T.L. production purrs along beautifully." In March of 1986 the play was teamed with two companion pieces, *Sorrows and Sons* and *Pilgrims,* composing a trilogy of one-acters focused on the common theme of the grief that came to families who lost relatives in the Vietnam War. In *Spittin' Image,* the second of the trio, Megs, a strung-out truck driver, invades the dormitory room of Bucky, a student at a small Pennsylvania college, to recount his wild adventures on the road. During the course of the narrative, however, Megs's fears about life surface as he recounts the death of Bucky's brother in Vietnam. Commenting on the three plays, D. J. R. Bruckner, reviewer for the *New York Times,* writes, ". . . these little plays are deeply moving; the laughter and sorrow in each of them come together naturally as our understanding of the fragile characters grows. They are compact, complex and intelligent, and they convey a vision of life that is humane and compassionate." The trilogy of one-acts has recently been published in an acting edition under the collective title, *Sorrows and Sons.*

Earlier one-act plays by Mr. Metcalfe, *Jacknife* (the first version of *Spittin' Image*) and *Baseball Play* were staged by New York's Quaigh Theatre in 1980. Other plays, *Vikings, Strange Snow,* and *Half a Lifetime,* premiered at the Manhattan Theatre Club with subsequent productions at regional theatres around the country. *Vikings* was also produced at the 1981 Edinburgh Festival, while *Strange Snow* was published in the anthology *Coming to Terms,* a collection of plays dealing with the Vietnam War. *Half a Lifetime* has also been presented on Home Box Office, and *The Incredibly Famous Willie Rivers,* a rock-and-roll drama with music by Denny McCormick, was directed by Stephen Zuckerman in 1984 at the W.P.A. Theatre in New York and printed in *American Theatre* (January, 1986), the magazine published by the Theatre Communications Group. *White Linen* was produced by the Michigan Public Theatre, and *Loves and Hours* by the Cincinnati Playhouse in the Park. A recent play, *Emily,* premiered at the Old Globe Theatre in San Diego, California in July of 1986.

Mr. Metcalfe was born in New Haven, Connecticut, in 1953 and is a graduate of Westminister College in Pennsylvania. He has received a Creative Artists Public Service Program (CAPS) grant for his work and was awarded a playwriting fellowship from the National Endowment for the Arts.

Characters:

BUCKY
MEGS

Time:

November of 1974.

Scene:

The dorm room is dim, lit only by a desk lamp. Bucky is asleep at his desk, his arms folded across a pile of books and papers, his head resting on his arms. He is in a T-shirt and underwear. He snores softly. There is a knock on the door: soft, then louder, more insistent. Bucky stirs. The knocking stops. Bucky rubs at his eyes, still half-asleep. He starts. He looks at his wristwatch. He sags in his chair.

BUCKY: Aw, shit . . .
(The person outside has heard him. The knocking starts again, loud enough to wake the dead. "Hah!? Hah!?" is heard. The knocking continues until Bucky opens the door. Bucky jumps up from the desk, grabs some jeans and struggles into them as he heads towards the door)
I'm coming. Wait a second. Just a—hey! I said I'm coming! Stop the knocking! I'm coming! Yeah, what?
(It is Megs. He is about ten years older than Bucky. He wears blue jeans, pointy-toed cowboy boots, a cowboy hat, aviator shades, a down vest and leather gloves. He barges into the room, immediately throwing slaps and playful punches)
MEGS: Hah!? Hah!? How you doin' there, Bucky boy?
BUCKY: Megs.
MEGS: Hah! *(Slap)* Hah!? *(Punch)* How you doin', you big whore?
(He sees the light switch. He hits it)
MEGS: Surprise! What 'a ya got to say for yourself!?
BUCKY: *(Zipping his pants)* I fell asleep.

MEGS: Rack time, huh? Or maybe you was floggin' that ol' dolphin, huh, stud? I catch you in the middle of spankin' that monkey?

BUCKY: No! No. I was working at my desk and I fell asleep. *(Looking at his watch again)* Aw, man, two hours ago. What are you doing here, Megs?

MEGS: Listen there, Big Daddy, can you spare your old buddy Megs a job? I ran out of gas outside and I need a few bucks for petro. Hah!? Hah!? Just kiddin', stud, just kiddin'! Hey, look at you! Big number 88 in the flesh. It's so good to see you! Been too damn long! How you keepin' that ass?

BUCKY: Hey, uh . . . not so good right now, man. I wish you'd called. You caught me right in the middle of cramming for exams.

MEGS: Yeah? You always do your studyin' in your sleep, stud? Hey, I'm just kiddin'! You got exams, I won't stay long. See, I was just passin' by. I was in the area and I thought to myself— damn, my man, Buck, is right around here! I better stop by and check out his digs. So! These them, huh?

BUCKY: Yeah.

MEGS: Well. Fuck a duck. Ain't much, are they.

BUCKY: They're O.K. Listen, Megs, I appreciate you stoppin' by. I appreciate the thought behind it. And what I think we should do is make plans to get together the next time I'm home. Right here and now, jeez, Megs, bad timing. So much I have to do, y'know? You understand what I'm saying?

MEGS: *(Grinning)* Hah!? *(Slap)* Hah!? *(Punch)* Hah!?

BUCKY: What!?

MEGS: How long's it been, stud?

BUCKY: *(Confused)* What?

MEGS: Since you and I seen each other. How long's it been?

BUCKY: Uh . . . it's been long.

MEGS: Too long. It's been too long! But I been thinkin' of ya. I been keepin' tabs. You! Are doin' great! I know. *(Pause)* So how you doin' anyway?

BUCKY: Megs . . .

MEGS: Great, huh? I been keepin' tabs! Hey! You been keepin' tabs on me?

BUCKY: I've been cramming for exams.

MEGS: You remember the last time? We watched the tube at your folks' house. We ate chips and we drank brews. I had

Ruffles and you had Doritos. A good time, huh? Hey! A great time. We coulda gone all night except for that headache you got.

BUCKY: It was a bad headache, Megs.

MEGS: Hey! They can be! You big swingin' dick! Look at this place!

BUCKY: Megs, what about the holidays. We'll get together for something. Megs?

MEGS: Big Buckaroo, you should maybe hire someone to clean this place now and again.

BUCKY: You're not listening to me. I've been working very hard lately for exams. No breaks. I haven't had time to clean.

MEGS: Well, I guess not. This place is a sty, stud.

BUCKY: I've been busy. I *am* busy.

MEGS: Yeah . . . well, I'm just passin' through. Wanted to see how you're looking. Real fine! Spittin' image. So. You're busy, huh?

BUCKY: Yeah. I'm sorry, Megs.

MEGS: Well . . . it's a bad time for all a' us. Damn! A college boy! I can't get over it. Posters on the wall and shit all over the place! More books than a five and dime! Hey, you gettin' smart? I bet you are. You ain't too busy to bullshit a spell, are ya?

BUCKY: Jesus. You're not going to be happy until you sit down for awhile.

MEGS: I'll stand, you don't mind. I been drivin' a long time and I need to stretch my legs.

BUCKY: Yeah, O.K., fine. But Megs, listen. Only a few minutes. Please. I'm going to be going all night as it is.

MEGS: Hey, I hear you! You do your work and I'll stretch my legs. How's that sound? I mean, I'm not stoppin' by any legit reason or nothin'. Just wanted to say hello and jerk off a little bit of your time. Knew you'd be angry if I didn't.

BUCKY: *(Sitting at his desk)* I jerk off my time well enough for both of us. *(A moment)* What are you doing out this way, Megs?

MEGS: Workin'!

BUCKY: You in your truck?

MEGS: Hell, yeah! Got that pig parked outside. Comin' through from Saint Lou—Mo. Steel humpin' bleachers. They been rattlin' and rollin' all the way here, drivin' me crazy. I made a new land speed record gettin' here. Stud, I drive so fast, nobody can keep track of me. You been tryin' to keep track of me?

BUCKY: *(Studying)* No.

MEGS: And no wonder. I been busy. You oughta see the terminal, Buck. Back ordered and beyond up to our assholes. Everything's sittin' around and we're losin' our shirts. But hey! You're sure lookin' good, you big swingin' dick!

BUCKY: Looks are deceiving, Megs.

(Megs pulls a book off Bucky's desk, disrupting him)

MEGS: What's this manure you're chompin' on? Psychology!? You gonna psychologize me, stud? Go for it, boy, go for it! You can analyze my problems! *(He throws himself on a bed, reclines like a patient)* Heater on Bertha's screwed. Bertha's my truck. Colder than a eighty year old woman. I keep tellin' the people in the dispatcher's office to fix her or they're gonna find me stuck 'tween somewhere and somehow one a' these days. They never listen. Fuckers never do. Never. Bertha's not a bad truck. For a fuckin' truck. Actually she's a mudhumpin' dinosaur! That's why they give her to me all the time. *(He jumps up)* Stud, I drive trucks like I'm goin' off a divin' board. Two weeks ago I jackknifed one outside a' Hartford. This VW cut me off and there was ice all over the place. Didn't help that it was midnight and I was still wearin' my shades. That jackknife coulda turned into a swan dive into the hereafter, stud. That close! An' the trouble it caused? You jack a truck an' you wind up in trouble as high as the eyeballs; cops, union, company; all of'm tellin' you that you fucked up. It's wearin'. *(He throws an affectionate punch)* Know what? You're good at this. Psychology.

BUCKY: Megs, I couldn't psychoanalyze a stone.

MEGS: No. You got a knack. You're easy to talk to.

BUCKY: Sure. *(Pause)* Like my brother, right?

MEGS: Well . . . yeah. Kinda.

BUCKY: Wrong. Knack. You want to know what kind of knack I have? I'm failing this stuff. I'm failing just about everything. Flags everywhere. I'm about as good a student as you are a driver.

MEGS: Hey, Bucky . . . I am a stud driver, man.

BUCKY: Except for the jackknifes.

MEGS: Well, y'know, hey! So I'm a lousy driver. I get there; that's about it. Hey, but that's all that really counts, right?

BUCKY: No. Getting there doesn't count at all. Getting back again, that's what counts.

MEGS: Yeah. Wow. You're right. Hey! You want to know a driver? Flanagan.

BUCKY: *Flanagan* Flanagan?

MEGS: None other. That son-of-a-bitch! He drives.

BUCKY: I haven't seen him since . . . I understand he drops by to say hello to the folks all the time. He'll shovel the front walk in the winter time, rake some leaves if the yard needs it.

MEGS: Flanagan does that?

BUCKY: The folks say.

MEGS: Oh . . . hey, like, y'know, I also sometimes stop by to say hello to your folks, too.

BUCKY: They appreciate it.

MEGS: I figured they would. I mean, we just sit there. I never know what to say or nothin'. Hey, you think next time they'd maybe let me mow the lawn?

BUCKY: Why not? They need things to appreciate.

MEGS: *(Messing Bucky's hair)* They got you, don't they? One mudhumpin' beautiful guy! Spittin' image! Flanagan, I love that stupid fuck. We argue all the time, me and him but, hey, you know, like that! *(He holds up two entwined fingers)* Flanagan, he makes the run, Apple to Detroit Motor City three times a week. Guns it across Eight-O in Pee-A which is only the worst section of concrete in the entire world. Does it like he was shot out of a howitzer! Shakes the balls and socks off a rig, Flanagan. And he don't touch pills, Bucky, not one. Hardly. Crazy son-of-a-bitch . . .

BUCKY: Megs.

MEGS: Huh?

BUCKY: What's going on? I've told you I'm not doing well in school. I've told you that I need to work. You don't listen. How come? Megs, I'll tell you again. I need to work.

MEGS: I'm buggin' you, huh? Yeah, I am. See, you're by yourself when you drive. You don't talk much. You get with a good buddy and you make up for lost time. Conversation, you know? Talk—listen. Talk—listen. You do your work, stud. Me? I'm quiet. *(Megs sits in a chair. His hand plays with something in his pocket. Bucky yawns)* You tired?

BUCKY: Yeah.

MEGS: You want something to keep you awake?

BUCKY: I want to be left alone!

MEGS: Sorry. *(Pause. Silence. Megs suddenly begins to giggle silently to himself. He springs up and begins pacing)* Flanagan and me, see, we used to pop whites so much we were higher than sunshine. Flanagan, you're with him an' he's seein' unicorns and trolls alongside the road. I was . . . he was strained thinner than a sheet. Insane!! It was V. that did it. Good ol' Southeast Asia! We got ourselves over to V., took one look around, and shot ourselves directly into the ozone. Stayed there on whatever we could get our hands on. Flanagan, he comes back from Nam a first class head, but now sometimes he don't touch a thing.

BUCKY: What about you, Megs, are you touching?

(Pause)

MEGS: Tough stuff to drive on, man. *(Pause)* Flanagan's something, stud. A friend. A mudhumping, true-blue friend. My best friend in the whole world. The mudfucker. *(Long silence. It's as if Megs is suddenly frightened, surrounded by invisible dangers. He struggles to control his fears)* Talk to me some, won't you, Bobby?

(Bucky starts as if hit with an electric shock)

Oh, fuck me, fuck, would ya listen to me callin' you . . . I must be fried or something . . . thirty hours a drivin' . . . *(Tenderly)* Talk to me some, Bucky, won't ya, please?

BUCKY: *(A moment)* Flanagan once told me that the worst road he's ever been on is Interstate 49 through West Virginia.

MEGS: *(Delighted)* Four-nine through the smokies worse than Eight-O through Pee-A!? He *musta* been on pills.

BUCKY: That's what he said.

MEGS: That's crazy!

BUCKY: It's what he said!

MEGS: He said! He was probably seein' leprechauns pissin' in the pine trees!!

BUCKY: Who knows. Who cares . . .

MEGS: You ever been on a rig, studhoss?

BUCKY: *(Exploding, furious)* Now what the fuck would I be doing on a rig, Megs!?

MEGS: *(Happily)* Psychology is all very well and good, stud, but it is neither here nor there concerning trucks. I take these rigs out. I know.

BUCKY: I know. *(He sighs)* I know you know.

MEGS: When the man from the big team comes around, I better know.

BUCKY: What's the team, Megs?

MEGS: The big team! The fuckin'-A big team! The what-the-fuck-happened-to-Jimmy-fuckin'-Hoffa big team. You either put out or shit or lock the doors on Fort Pitt.

BUCKY: You put out?

MEGS: Hey, man, they crumple you like a piece of paper, you don't! *(He crumples sheets of paper on Bucky's desk)* Aw, Jesus ... I'm sorry. I'm sorry. Notes for your test? *(He tries to smooth them out)* I'll fix'm. You pissed? You pissed, Buck?

BUCKY: Megs, I think you should get going.

MEGS: O.K. O.K. Uh ... but what I was sayin' was this. The team, see, they say jump, you say how high. They say shit, you say where.

BUCKY: I said I think you should ...

MEGS: But Flanagan don't!! No way, big steer! You say shit to Flanagan, he'll ask you if you're ready to eat it. What a monster. His rig ever broke down, he'd carry the load on his back. Know what his handle is? Frankenstein!! Know what mine is? Road-runner! 'Cause I fly! *(Bucky doesn't respond. Then Megs, desperately)* No, that's not it, not really. They call me "Jacknife." From jackin' all the trucks. You, uh ... Bucky? You really think I'm that bad a driver, stud?

BUCKY: What do you want me to say, Megs? What do you want to hear? Megs ... you fly!

MEGS: You great, big, swingin' dick! And you're a good student! Smart!!

BUCKY: Yeah, I'm a great student.

MEGS: Smart!

BUCKY: I'm failing.

MEGS: That don't mean nothin'.

BUCKY: To some people it does.

MEGS: Well, yeah ... some people. But not to me. Me, I fly! All I need is a place to come from an' a place to go to! Hey! You do your work. You do it good. Me, I fly an' I'm cool.

(Bucky sits at his desk. Megs sits in the other chair again. Silence. There is a yearning in Megs, a need for something. He moves his chair closer to Bucky. Bucky looks up. Megs signifies that he is "cool." Silence. Megs stares at Bucky. His fingers find the edge of a newspaper he's sitting on. He slowly tears off strips. He tears the strips into strips. Finally:)

BUCKY: What are you doing?!

MEGS: Talk to me some more, will ya?

BUCKY: Jesus, Megs, I . . .

MEGS: Anything.

(A moment)

BUCKY: *(Throwing it away)* A lot of people think there must be a certain romance to driving.

MEGS: *(Delighted)* Hey, you know you're right!? There is!

BUCKY: *(Wistful)* No books, no exams, no hassles. Just a port and a horizon. A beginning and an end. A womb and a grave.

MEGS: You tryin' to gross me out or something?

BUCKY: What?

MEGS: A womb?

BUCKY: It's just a word.

MEGS: A fucking womb?

BUCKY: It's not a dirty word.

MEGS: Stud! There are just certain words that drivers don't use! Maybe I'm a fuckin' puritan or something, but, like, that's one of 'm. What's the matter?

BUCKY: I have a headache.

MEGS: Hey, me too. Maybe we should go out for a beer or something.

BUCKY: Goddammit, I can't! Everything I've said to you has gone in one ear and right out the other!

MEGS: I'll be quiet.

BUCKY: No, you won't! Not for more than a minute at a time! What do you want from me, Megs? What's the matter with you?

MEGS: I'm edgy is all. I'm sorry. You want I should go?

BUCKY: YES!!

MEGS: I'm just a little edgy! I'll sit tight! I'm cool! You're gettin' psychology done, ain't ya?

BUCKY: Are you kidding me!?

MEGS: I bet ya are.

BUCKY: Listen to me. I'm failing. I'm on probation.

MEGS: No, you're not.

BUCKY: I am!

MEGS: Nah.

BUCKY: Yes! The only thing I'm passing is a cake course on children's literature. A kid's course, and it's the only thing I like.

MEGS: Ya like psychology, don't ya?

BUCKY: I hate it! I hate it! *(He suddenly sweeps books and papers to the floor)* I hate all this shit. Psychology. People are unhappy. History. People fight wars. Biology. People are going to die. What else you want to know? I've been going over this shit for days and it's still alphabet soup to me! If it weren't for the folks . . . *(He starts picking things up)* How am I supposed to explain it to them . . .

(Silence)

MEGS: Hey! You want to hear something funny? It'll make you laugh! They got me carrying air conditioners in November. Who orders 'm? You think they woulda ordered mink coats or something. Oh, well. I carry what they tell me. That's what they pay me for. They want ski boots in Death Valley, I'll take 'm. Fuck their brains, they're callin' the shots. They always do. Always. *(Pause)* You look very tired, Bucky. Are we takin' a break?

BUCKY: *(With resignation)* No. You look hungry, Megs. Why don't you go out and get yourself something to eat.

MEGS: That's very kind of you, but I had a sausage sub very recently. Listen, you work. I'll make myself comfortable. Maybe I'll read something. Something educational. *(He looks at the bookcase)* Maybe I won't read. Save my eyes for drivin'. Which bed's yours?

BUCKY: That one.

MEGS: You mind if I lie on it?

BUCKY: *(Not looking up)* Throw the stuff on it anywhere.

MEGS: You read a lot? *(A moment)* Huh?

BUCKY: Always the wrong stuff at the wrong time.

MEGS: Ohhhhh . . . nice bed. I usually sleep in the truck. When I sleep at all. Real nice bed. I hardly ever sleep at night. Maybe that's why I'm edgy. I could sleep in this bed. Easy. Yeah. You studyin'? Sorry. *(There is still a football on the bed. He picks it up, plays with it)* You play this year?

BUCKY: Huh? No. I mean, I got tossed halfway through. My grades.

MEGS: Too bad.

BUCKY: Just about killed the folks. Especially Dad.

MEGS: Football on Monday nights. Huh? Amazing. On the West Coast the games start at six, on the East Coast at nine, yet everybody sees them at the same time. This is unbelievable. Crazy. Nights.

BUCKY: And Bobby being all-league, too. God.

MEGS: Nights are such a bitch. I drive at night as much as possible. Sometimes.

BUCKY: And captain of the team. Every team . . .

MEGS: Flanagan he also drives at nights. What do you do at night, Big Buckaroo?

BUCKY: Huh?

MEGS: Whatcha do in the p.m., studhoss? You go out with the ladies?

BUCKY: Sometimes.

MEGS: You sleep?

BUCKY: With the ladies?

MEGS: No. Just you.

BUCKY: Yeah. I sleep.

MEGS: Yeah? That's great. Me, I drive. The road, stud, she's a hog. She's a big snake with her teeth set deep in your ass but all in all, she's good. She keeps you occupied. You're not occupied, you're like an empty house. Useless. *(Megs's eyes close. It looks for a moment as if he will sleep. He comes suddenly awake with a quiet jolt. It's as if a nightmare was coming and he willed himself awake to prevent that. He looks around in panic. He tries to laugh)* Some people would be lonely, I guess. Shows what they know. Me, I know every burger, beer, and bus stop on every route goin'. I know them, they know me. That's lonely? *(A moment)* Hey, Bucky, is that lonely?

BUCKY: *(Quietly)* Not if they know you, it's not.

(Megs jumps up, grabs the chair and moves it close to Bucky and the desk. Megs sits)

MEGS: Damn straight! You gotta hear this one. I was in Pittsburgh this one time, see, and this babe starts buyin' me drinks. A knockout! An' she's buyin'! Not only is she buyin', she's sittin' on my lap, lickin' my ears and buyin'. That's lonely!? Hah!? *(A moment)* You gonna ask me or what.

BUCKY: What?

MEGS: What? What 'a you mean, what!? You gonna ask me if I scored? You gonna ask me if I layed some pipe?

BUCKY: Did you?

MEGS: Come on!!

BUCKY: You come on.

MEGS: Listen, the kind of babe she was, you wouldn'ta wanted to score.

BUCKY: You said she was good.

MEGS: Good!! She was great!! But halfway through the evening I hit the head to bleed the monster, and this guy comes and tells me the babe just finished making it with the entire kickoff team of the Pittsburgh Steelers.

BUCKY: That stopped you?

MEGS: Come on, stud!

BUCKY: Wouldn't have stopped Flanagan.

MEGS: Listen, Bobby used to say leprosy wouldn't stop Flanagan.

BUCKY: Yeah. I bet he did. I want you to leave, man.

MEGS: But ain't you gonna ask me what happened? *(Pause)* Ain't you gonna ask me what happened?

BUCKY: *(Sighing)* What happened.

MEGS: You won't believe what happened! I get out a' the head and the babe wants a ride home in my rig. A ride *on* my rig is what she wanted! I figure I'll dump her off an' go.

BUCKY: Why would you dump her off?

MEGS: I told you, man, she was a slut!

BUCKY: She was buying you drinks.

MEGS: Hey, you wanna hear this story or what?

BUCKY: I want you to leave!

MEGS: BUT SHE LIVED WITH HER PARENTS!!! *(He giggles, beside himself)* She did, stud, I swear. We're sittin' in her folks driveway, my rig is aimed at her front door and I say, hey!, now you can tell all your friends that you been in an eighteen-wheeler. She was very impressed. Hah!? Hah!? So what does she do? She gets out, takes off her panties, climbs under the rear wheels a' the truck and says she won't move till I pork her!

BUCKY: *(Wanting him to leave so desperately)* Aw, come on, Megs!

MEGS: The slut!

BUCKY: Give me a break!

MEGS: The slut! Under the wheels! The rear wheels! I shoulda run her over. An' I was gonna. 'Cept all of a sudden her old man came out a' the house. He musta noticed something. I mean, an eighteen-wheeler ain't a taxicab. So, it's a mess. There I am, there he is, and there's his daughter under the wheels with her panties in her hands. The old guy walked. He went back in the house shakin' his head ... He musta been used to it or something! Hah!? Hah!? You gonna ask me? Did I take her to the hoop? Did I go the whole nine yards? I surely did not! I put that stick in first gear, jammed the wheel, swung right through the tulips and LEFT HER LYIN' THERE IN THE DRIVEWAY WITH HER

PANTIES IN HER HAND!!! *(Pause. He waits for Bucky to laugh. Bucky doesn't)* See, I don't kid around, stud. *(A moment)* Uh . . . course, ol' Flanagan woulda porked her probably. Ol' Flanagan'd pork a donut if it was flesh and blood. Bobby always said so.

(Bucky closes his eyes as if in pain)

Ol' Bobby . . . I sure miss ol' Bobby . . . Know what I mean? And your folks, they must miss him too.

BUCKY: Parents never get over something like that.

MEGS: You were . . . you were how old?

BUCKY: Fifteen.

MEGS: Yeah. And now you look just like him. Spittin' image. Put out or shit or lock the doors on Fort Pitt.

BUCKY: Yeah. Put out or shit or lock the doors on Fort Pitt. *(Pause)* I'm not dumb, Megs. I'm not a genius but I'm not dumb. I should be doing well, but somehow I get sidetracked. I get jack-knifed. And the folks want so much. They need so much. Bobby was going to be a lawyer. He was going to be president of a company, of a university, of the whole country maybe. What am I going to be? What do I tell them? I try to study, and I end up looking at the same sentence for a half hour.

MEGS: *(Not understanding)* You tryin' to memorize it or some-thin', you look at it for so long?

BUCKY: *(Laughing but on the verge of crying)* Yeah.

MEGS: Well, that's great. You're really something, studhoss. Me, I got no memory at all. If a babe didn't grab me by the ears and pull me down, I'd get lost along the way. College!! You don't kid me. You learn interesting things of note, I bet. Hey, you get laid a lot? You hang around cafes drinkin' coffee? Truck drivin', you drink a lot of coffee. Maybe that's why I don't sleep at night . . . well, hey! Look at you! You should be studying! Pay me no mind. I'm gonna lie on your bed. Nice bed.

BUCKY: Captain of every team. Straight A's. Drive. Ambition. Bobby set his mind to do something, he'd do it whether he liked it or not. How come I'm not like that? I try.

(A silence)

MEGS: Hey, Bucky? Buck-Buck-Buck? Read the letter. *(Pause)* Would ya? I just want to hear it once. I was there, ya know? He wrote it down, and he read it to me. I like hearin' it. Ya sound so much like him. Will ya?

BUCKY: I don't have a copy. Sorry.

MEGS: *(Scrounging in his wallet)* I do. He let me copy it, so I did. I thought maybe I'd send it to somebody sometime. I never did. If ya want to read it, ya can. You sound so much like him.

(Megs holds out the dog-eared copy. A moment. Bucky goes to his drawer and takes out an envelope. He removes a carefully folded letter)

BUCKY: *(Reading)* "Dear Bucky, just a note to let you know I think of you often. What a place this is. You know what nobody ever tells you about? The sunsets. The sky turns a brilliant orange and red in the evening. I always try to take a moment from whatever is going on to watch for awhile."

MEGS: That's how they were. I never noticed them but they were.

BUCKY: "There is violence here and death but it will pass. The sun sets in the evening. It rises in the morning. Life goes on. *(He is no longer reading but reciting from memory)* Do you remember the fights we used to have when we were small? We'd be swinging, going for the face and head and suddenly we'd realize what we were doing. We'd stop. We'd hug each other. We would cry. The things you think about over here. Take care of the folks, little brother. I think of you always. Love, Bobby."

MEGS: I wouldn't ever send anybody the second part. That's yours. You don't mind, do ya, that he read it to me 'fore he sent it?

BUCKY: *(Far away)* No.

MEGS: He was always doin' stuff like that, readin' ya stuff, keepin' morale up. We was scared so shitless, but Bobby never showed it so he made it easy for us to, like, act brave. He'd make us laugh. His beer would get warm, his cards'd get cold. He didn't care. He'd listen to your troubles. You're just like him, stud. You take the time to listen. I want to thank you for it. I know you're only pretendin' to study that shit so I won't feel bad and think you got important things to do.

BUCKY: I'm not doing that, Megs.

MEGS: God love you for a liar, kid. You're a college student! You got movies to see, frisbees to fuck around with, basketball games to play. I know.

BUCKY: You know, huh?

MEGS: I know. I play a little B-ball myself. Got a stop in the windy city, Chicago. Got a hoop set up in the lot near the fuel pumps. Always a little game goin'. The guys, most of 'm, all they do is drive and drink, so most of 'm are out of shape. Some got guts that bounce as much as the ball does. Hey! Hey, man! Double dribble! The ball and your gut!! *(A moment)* It's from the sittin'. And the drinkin'. Drivin's tough on your body. Hey, but look at you, you lovely, sweet whore! All muscle and bone! Spittin' image! Yeah . . . drivin's tough . . .

BUCKY: *(With an edge)* You have any friends, Megs?

MEGS: What do you mean?

BUCKY: People you can talk to?

MEGS: What do you mean, talk?

BUCKY: You bone-dumb fuck! What do you mean, what do I mean? Talk! The economy, the 55 mile per hour speed limit, anything!

MEGS: I could sure talk about that limit. Trucks are the backbone a' this country and they are trying to cut our balls off! How do they think products get anyplace? They must think elves bring 'm by spaceship.

BUCKY: Megs! Do you have anyone you can go to besides me?

MEGS: Flanagan. We get together for cheeseburgers. He's like me. Most he sees a' people is glimpses as they pass by in cars. And there was Bobby.

BUCKY: Man, I am not Bobby!

MEGS: You're his brother.

BUCKY: Exactly! You don't even know me.

MEGS: Sure, I do.

BUCKY: You don't.

MEGS: Sure, I do. You're Bobby's brother.

BUCKY: What is that? I get that from everybody! My mom, my dad, Bobby's old girl friends, Bobby's old buddies. They all look to me for something Bobby gave 'm. I am not Bobby, man. I can't be solving everybody's problems.

MEGS: Problems, yeah, everybody's got problems, Big Buck, and me, like me, I keep like, I dunno, havin' this flash lately, huh?

BUCKY: No!

MEGS: You listen! *(A moment)* I can be sittin', I can be standin', anytime, man, like and like, fuck, it's uh, V. again. I'm back. And I'm hit. It was when I was hit. It's not like I feel the pain or nothin' but I'm hit. Bobby's with me. I look at him. I laugh. I say to him, I say . . . well? Well? What's that mean, ya think? Huh? Like, he doesn't answer. He doesn't say a word. He smiles. He shakes his head, sadlike. I mean, it didn't happen like that, but that's how I seem to remember it sometimes. You think he blames me, Bucky? You think he does? And do, like, your folks blame me? Me and Flanagan? What a' you think, stud?

BUCKY: I think it's time to forget all that.

MEGS: Yeah. But I flash. And I remember. And you, you look just like him.

BUCKY: Aw, Megs, aw. You think he'd be failing? He'd be mowing through this stuff like it was short grass.

MEGS: Oh, he sure would. He could do anything! He was a superstar! *(Picking up a basketball)* He was twenty points a game, swoosh! *(Picking up a tennis racquet)* And tennis! Huh!? I didn't know a tennis racquet from a fuckin' banjo but during basic Bobby taught me to play. Was it fun? It's been such a long time . . . since I played.

BUCKY: You want to?

MEGS: You'd play with me?

BUCKY: Next time I'm home.

MEGS: Or I could stop by here again!

BUCKY: Or in the mean time you could teach somebody else. For practice. Teach Flanagan.

MEGS: He'd want to learn?

BUCKY: Sure he would.

MEGS: I'd like that. Hey, I'm gonna get that big whore playin'!

BUCKY: Great!

MEGS: I was pretty good. Not as good as Bobby but good enough!

BUCKY: And you and I will play when I get home.

(Bucky is backing Megs towards the door)

MEGS: Or when I stop by! I'm gonna buy some stuff tomorrow. One a' them metal racquets. Bet you feel like an astronaut, you got one a' those in your hands. You're on, stud!

BUCKY: Terrific.

MEGS: Hey, and I'm buyin' the beer after!

BUCKY: I'll let you.

MEGS: You ain't buyin' a thing!

BUCKY: Fine with me.

MEGS: Hey, you need some bucks now? I'm loaded.

BUCKY: I'm set.

MEGS: You gotta put out or shit . . .

MEGS and BUCKY: Or lock the doors on Fort Pitt.

MEGS: Yeah! Slap me five! And we'll go cruisin' for college girls after, huh? Beer and college girls! Man, I bet college girls are special. Listen, I might be kinda weird and I drive a piss-toilet of a truck, but my heart's in the right place and that counts for something.

BUCKY: It's a date, Megs, you got it. *(He opens the door)* So, listen, you take it easy.

MEGS: Oh. I'm leaving?

BUCKY: Yeah.

MEGS: You're a beautiful kid. I love you. Well, you study now. You do good. Like Bobby. Well . . . this dude is hittin' the pike. Unless you're going to be finished soon? *(Before Bucky can reject him)* Hey, but no, thanks anyway. I gotta be makin' up for lost time. Well . . .

BUCKY: *(Leaving him at the door)* It's been good seeing you, Megs.

MEGS: Adios, Buster. *(He pauses in the doorway. He turns to leave. He freezes. Long pause)*

BUCKY: What's the matter? *(Pause)* What's the matter!?

(Megs closes the door and moves back into the room, wild-eyed)

MEGS: When you close your eyes after drivin' a long time, the road still comes at you. It's like a roller coaster. No scenery. The lines come at you like . . . the sound of the engine could be . . . LEMME STAY, MAN!! I'll be quiet. I swear to Holy Christ, I will. Bucky? I'm begging. There's this feeling in my guts and if I drive I just know I'm gonna be seein' him walkin' at the side of the road with his thumb out.

BUCKY: Who?

MEGS: Oh! You fuckin' fuckhead! What the fuck's wrong with you, huh? I been fuckin' talkin' all night and you ain't fuckin' heard me!

BUCKY: You and your problems, everybody's problems, make me want to die! Get out of here! Leave me alone to do what I have to do!

MEGS: Study your books. Take your tests. I wish you'd seen it. Packed in a helicopter to who-the-fuck knows where. Put down, start throwin' us out and hell breaks loose. Firin'. Explosions! The copter takes off and they ditch the last of us from twenty feet! Lousy copter jockeys! Thinking a' nothin' but their own asses! What were we? Tomatoes? Flanagan falls wrong and breaks his ankles. Bobby and me are carrying him when I get hit. Shithead!! Why'd he come back for me!?

BUCKY: Every time you tell me this! How many times do I have to hear this!?

MEGS: Hear it again, fuckass. Your brother came back for me, and he opened up like a rose in front a' my eyes. His guts came out to greet me. Aw, Christ . . . nobody cares. *(He starts to exit)*

BUCKY: My Dad sits at the breakfast table and mutters into his coffee? I go home for Christmas and my mom sobs in front of the tree? He was my favorite, man. When we were kids I'd wake up at night, scared, and I'd go down the hall to his room and I'd tap him on the shoulder and I'd say, wake up, Bobby, I don't want to sleep alone. He'd pull back the covers and let me in. He'd tell me stories till I fell asleep. You tell me nobody cares? You gotta put out or shit or lock the doors, man! Nobody gets shit from looking over their shoulder. Things would of changed by now if people did. I can't help you.

MEGS: But ya see . . He was . . . He talked to me like I wasn't a dip. He talked to me. Sports, cars, girls. Aw, girls. Bobby said, certain girls, they glowed. When they touched you, you weren't scared or tired. When they stood next to ya, you weren't weird and confused. Bobby woulda found a woman like that, And they woulda invited me over to dinner sometimes and it woulda given me such a charge to be with 'm. I woulda felt that someone, somewheres, was *keeping tabs*. A truck driver, travelin', people don't know if I've come or gone. An' my women, they all got bleached hair and black gook around the eyes an' the only moonlight they've ever seen is over the humpin' shoulder a' whoever's on top of them. I ain't feelin' sorry for myself or nothin', Bucky. You are what you are. Hey, I buy their spaghetti, their cheeseburgers, their fries. I put quarters in the jukebox so they can dance. Blow whole paychecks gettin 'm beers and sloe gin fizzes. I just can't love 'm. That's too much to ask. I just wish Bobby had lived so he coulda invited me over to dinner.

(Silence)

Well, hey there, you big swingin' dick! Look at me, wastin' your time! I gotta get a move on. Been awful good seein' you, stud. You keep that big swingin' dick from draggin'!

BUCKY: I will.

MEGS: And we are gonna play tennis! Don't forget!

BUCKY: I won't.

MEGS: And I'll be buyin' the beer after. Remember!

BUCKY: Yeah!

MEGS: Thanks for your time, Big Buckaroo.

BUCKY: Sure.

MEGS: You study now. You get an A.

BUCKY: Yeah.

(And suddenly Megs embraces Bucky; grabs him in his arms and hugs, his head on Bucky's shoulder. Bucky's hands stay at his side. He looks towards the ceiling)

MEGS: Oh, dear Lord, you look so much like him! Spittin' image! *(He releases him)* I'll say hello to Flanagan for ya.

BUCKY: Thanks.

MEGS: I hardly ever speak to that son-of-a-bitch, but I will.

BUCKY: Thanks, Megs.

MEGS: Well . . . Adios.

(Megs exits. Bucky closes the door. Leans against it. It seems that at any moment he will break into sobs. He fights them, forces them down. Silence. And suddenly Bucky turns and pulls open the door)

BUCKY: Megs!! Hey, Megs!! Wait a second!! Megs!! *(Megs enters at a fast run. Bucky almost laughs)* Uh . . . Oh, Jesus . . . Like I was thinking.

MEGS: Yeah?

BUCKY: It's late.

MEGS: Yeah.

BUCKY: Maybe you oughta spend the night. You'll get a good rest and make time tomorrow. I mean, what's the rush on air conditioners in November, right? What's the rush on steel humpin' bleachers? *(And Bucky laughs, giddy)* So. You want to.

MEGS: You want me to stay here?

BUCKY: You can take my bed. I have a down bag in the closet. I use it all the time.

MEGS: What about your test?

BUCKY: The hell with it. Piss on it. I could pass it with my eyes closed. You want to stay?

MEGS: You really want me to.

BUCKY: Very much.

MEGS: You big, beautiful whore!

BUCKY: We could go buy some beer.

MEGS: You great big, beautiful whore!!

BUCKY: You want to?

MEGS: Fuckin-A, studhoss!!

BUCKY: We could go in your rig. I've never been on a rig.

MEGS: Bucky, you never been in an eighteen-wheeler?

BUCKY: Not mother-humpin' once!

(Megs takes off his hat and jams it on Bucky's head)

MEGS: Oh, Big Buck, you are gonna be very impressed. Bertha's a beautiful woman. She just rides and rides. I'll go warm her up.

(Megs exits. Bucky stands motionless for a long time. He suddenly laughs as clean and clear as a bell. He pulls the hat down tight on his head)

BUCKY: Whoo!! *(He exits. Lights to black)*

The End

Doug Wright

THE STONEWATER RAPTURE

Doug Wright

One of the joys of compiling this anthology each year is that of providing a talented, new playwright with a first publishing opportunity. Doug Wright makes his debut in print with the humorous and poignant *The Stonewater Rapture,* a play which drew this rave from the reviewer for *Yale Daily News:* "Wright has constructed an excellent play about the paradoxes of pleasure and pain, peer pressure and popularity, and religion and the 'real world.' He understands his subject, adolescence, extremely well, and there are many telling as well as hilarious lines about growing into sexual awareness." When the play was presented by the American Stage Directions company of San Francisco for the 1984 Edinburgh Festival Fringe in a production directed by Steven Ullman, it received the Fringe First Award for Enterprising New Work. An earlier draft of *The Stonewater Rapture* was premiered by the Yale University Dramatic Association in 1983 and directed by the author. Subsequently, the play has had staged readings at Playwrights Horizons in Manhattan, New York University, and the Williamstown Theatre Festival Workshop in Massachusetts.

Callbacks, another short play by Mr. Wright, was paired with *The Stonewater Rapture* in productions at Yale, the Edinburgh Festival Fringe, and Playwrights Horizons—with an additional production at the Thirteenth Street Theatre in New York City, featuring Tony Spiridakis and Michael Knight, and directed by Richard Brooks, all of ABC television's *All My Children.*

The locale for *The Stonewater Rapture* is Mr. Wright's home state of Texas, where he was born and raised in Dallas. Leaving the South, Mr. Wright attended college at Yale University in New Haven, Connecticut, where he received a B.A. in Theatre and Art History in 1985. After completing his work at Yale, he enrolled in the Graduate Program in Dramatic Writing at New York University, receiving an M.F.A. in the spring of 1987.

A number of distinguished writing instructors have nurtured his work including: John Hersey, Michael Earley, Oscar Brownstein, Norma Rosen, Terrence McNally, Franklin Reeve, and Janet Neipris (whose play *The Agreement* appeared in the 1986 edition of *Best Short Plays*).

An actor also, Mr. Wright has appeared in plays at Yale University, Theatre Three in Dallas, and the Williamstown Theatre Festival in Massachusetts. He has studied acting with Bart Teush, Lynn Singer, and Nikos Psacharopoulos.

His current writing projects include a full-length play based on the life of the artist Marcel Duchamp, a screenplay entitled *Window Dressing,* and a collection of short stories. The promise of his writing talent was recognized in 1984 with the James Ashmun Veech Prize for Fiction, and we look forward to seeing many stimulating future works from this young writer.

Characters:
   CARLYLE, *eighteen and pretty*
   WHITNEY, *the same age and rather pensive*

Setting:
   *Part of the living room and the entire porch of a small, white
   frame house in a West Texas town. The area of the porch is
   surrounded by trees and shrubbery. It is well kept and even
   charming with a few potted plants and possibly a porch swing.
   A pair of plaster kittens play on a nearby tree. Indoors, the
   house is simply and cleanly furnished. The slipcovers and
   handsewn, covering faded upholstery and there are a few
   needlepoint pillows on the couch and on the chairs, and a few
   small pettipoint pictures of flowers and cocker spaniels hanging
   on the walls. There is a magazine rack containing such
   publications as* Family Circle, Better Homes and Gardens,
   Parents Magazine *and a wide variety of religious material. The
   familiar bearded portrait of Christ hangs over the mantel, and a
   sumptuous leather-bound Bible sits on its own stand.*
       *It is dusk and the sky is awash with streaks of stormy blue
   and orange. Stars are barely visible. There is the buzz of
   insects and in the distance the soothing sound of wind. The
   porch light is on, and Whitney enters, followed by Carlyle. As
   they talk, they enter the house, flip on the lights and settle
   themselves on the couch.*

Scene One:

CARLYLE: Whitney, Ted Pewter was the only other boy who
had a chance and he's guilty of the sin of pride. Look at the way he
blow dries his hair.

WHITNEY: I don't want to be president.

CARLYLE: How do you think that makes me feel?

WHITNEY: I'm glad you got secretary. Carlyle, I'm not going to
be a preacher.

CARLYLE: Getting president doesn't mean you have to be a
preacher.

WHITNEY: You want to see something?

(Whitney crosses to the desk and pulls out a thin stack of papers. He hands it to Carlyle)

CARLYLE: You didn't tell me you were applying to seminary school! Whitney, I think that's wonderful. Look. You typed all the answers.

WHITNEY: My Dad filled it out for me. He wrote all the essays to make sure I wouldn't tell them I was Hindu or something. Now all it needs is my signature, then it goes in the mail, and WHAM! I'm behind a pulpit.

CARLYLE: They might not accept you.

WHITNEY: I was just voted president of the Youth Ministry. It's the kiss of death.

CARLYLE: It doesn't mean you'll get in. It takes a lot more to be a good preacher. You have to be blessed with strength and faith and love for your fellow man . . .

WHITNEY: There's something more.

CARLYLE: What?

WHITNEY: You have to be a good public speaker. I suck.

CARLYLE: You're not so awful.

WHITNEY: You saw me this afternoon.

CARLYLE: You knew if you won, you'd have to make a speech. You should've had one ready.

WHITNEY: I did. My father gave me this whole five-page speech on the positive power of prayer in adolescence. It was right in my back pocket. But you saw. I practically fainted, all because of the word "puberty." I couldn't stand up there and say "puberty" in front of all those ladies. They would've choked on their egg salad. I suck.

CARLYLE: Then they probably won't take you.

WHITNEY: They'll take me. I make all *A's* and my uncle is on the board.

CARLYLE: Mama says you have the calling.

WHITNEY: Dad says there are only two honorable professions in the world: carpentry and preaching. I made him a tie rack for his birthday and the wood split. That's my calling.

CARLYLE: Where are your folks?

WHITNEY: Cleaning up after the picnic. Then they're teaching that singles seminar on "Finding a Mate Through God." Dad says a lot of nice bachelors show up. He thinks your mom should give it a try.

CARLYLE: Can we go out on the porch?

WHITNEY: It's hotter than hell and there are mosquitoes.

CARLYLE: You shouldn't have me over if your parents aren't here.

(She leads him out onto the porch)

WHITNEY: We've been seeing each other for two months now and I'm still afraid I'll get a face full of tear gas if I brush up against your knee.

CARLYLE: Whitney, I've made a list of the things we should start doing. *(Whitney groans)* First, we're going to start making those Wednesday night sing-a-longs at the nursing home mandatory attendance for the whole group. I feel stupid singing all by myself. It keeps the old people from joining in. They think it's a solo. Miss Willoughby, she tries to help out, but whenever she sings it's always the wrong song. I could be singing the Doxology, and she still thinks it's "Indian Love Call." It embarrasses everybody, but she refuses to wear her hearing aid. Second, I'm sick and tired of the way some people come to the Fellowship parties for the food and not the faith. It makes us look bad. Part of that is your responsibility. If you'd try harder to attract people at school . . .

WHITNEY: I was going to go out for the football team, but that's shot to hell now. I can't be at practice and Bible Study at the same time.

CARLYLE: Your legs are too skinny. You'd get bulldozed.

WHITNEY: They are not.

CARLYLE: You could soak your feet in a Coke bottle.

WHITNEY: Cut it out. I've been eating more.

CARLYLE: Let me see.

WHITNEY: No.

CARLYLE: Come on. Please.

WHITNEY: Uh-uh.

CARLYLE: You told me you hated football. I don't know why you want to play now.

WHITNEY: Everybody plays.

CARLYLE: Who?

WHITNEY: Arthur Horrishill and Michael MaCaffey.

CARLYLE: But they're mean to you.

WHITNEY: No, they're not.

CARLYLE: Yesterday they put vaseline all over your steering wheel.

WHITNEY: It was a joke.

CARLYLE: You zig-zagged all the way home.

WHITNEY: It was funny. Anyway, if I was on the team, do you think they'd do that?

CARLYLE: But you're better than they are. Mama says you're the only decent boy for miles. She'd rather talk to you than most people her own age. She says boys like Arthur and Michael have one-track minds that lead straight to hell, and knives where their flesh should be, but not you.

WHITNEY: Thanks.

CARLYLE: Which brings us to the third thing on my list.

WHITNEY: What?

CARLYLE: Thelma Peeler.

WHITNEY: What about her?

CARLYLE: You mean you don't know?

WHITNEY: How would I?

CARLYLE: Your friend Michael MaCaffey took advantage of her.

WHITNEY: Michael wouldn't be seen with Thelma. He's captain of the team.

CARLYLE: What's worse, he did it on a dare. Arthur Horrishill took a pool, and the whole team bet he couldn't do it. They ended up paying him fifty dollars.

WHITNEY: Somebody started a rumor, and you believed it.

CARLYLE: It's true. He got her so drunk she didn't know her own name. I know she has pimples and those orthopedic shoes. But he did it just the same.

WHITNEY: Did what? Kiss her through her mustache?

CARLYLE: Made her pregnant. Michael wouldn't even offer to make it right. His family just gave her family money for one of those operations. Well, she wasn't about to let them kill it, so she ran away and now there are patrol cars looking all over the state for her. Can't you just see her clomping along the roadside in those big black shoes? They'll catch her in a minute and then her parents'll send her back to that detention home, after they cut the baby out. And it wasn't even her fault. It was his. Mama says he's damned without a chance. Anyway, I think the Youth Ministry should take up a collection to pay for the birth of that baby.

WHITNEY: If the kid looks anything like his mother, the first thing it'll need is a clean shave.

CARLYLE: Stop. Don't be ugly. And don't go thinking Michael MaCaffey is any great shakes just because he's captain of the team.

WHITNEY: Is that the list?

CARLYLE: We have to choose the verses for next Sunday's meeting.

WHITNEY: You can.

CARLYLE: You have to help. You're president.

WHITNEY: My Dad probably rigged the election. Ted should've gotten it.

CARLYLE: You don't want it because you're lazy.

WHITNEY: I don't want it because the guys'll think I'm a fairy. Ted should've gotten it because he is one.

CARLYLE: He's always at Sunday School and he always wins the Old Testament Crossword Puzzle Contest.

WHITNEY: He hangs around the grammar school and feels up the fifth grade boys.

CARLYLE: He'd never do that. Not in Stonewater. He'd be in jail.

WHITNEY: He gives them dollars. They buy cigarettes.

CARLYLE: Let he who is without sin cast the first stone.

WHITNEY: I don't feel up fifth grade boys.

CARLYLE: You're talking about it. That's pretty bad.

WHITNEY: You're welcome to change the subject.

CARLYLE: If Ted were a homosexual, he wouldn't be Christian. It says so in the Book of Leviticus. He'd be struck dead, and his blood would be upon him. Do lots of people know about him?

WHITNEY: All the guys at school suspect. I don't think his parents know.

CARLYLE: If I were his mother, I'd do whatever I could to keep from finding out.

WHITNEY: He always stops and talks to me in the hall. People think he's my friend just because I'm not mean to him. He asked if he could borrow my World History notes right when Arthur Horrishill walked by, and I said yes. Suicide.

CARLYLE: Can't you be just a little mean?

WHITNEY: What am I supposed to do?

CARLYLE: If he's really homosexual, don't talk to him.

WHITNEY: I'm supposed to just stand there after he's said "Hello" and is looking all expectant? One time he really got me in trouble. We had lockers right next to each other in gym and we were getting undressed and he bumped into me. I felt him. Part of him was touching me.

CARLYLE: Which part?

WHITNEY: I couldn't move. I just stood there. I froze. Then he started . . .

CARLYLE: What?

WHITNEY: Horrishill saw, I know he did, because later the coach had to assign me to a team. No one would take me. No one would talk to me. All because of that fucking fairy.

(Silence. Whitney slaps a mosquito)

CARLYLE: Have you been reading that book for English?

WHITNEY: On and off. It's boring.

CARLYLE: My Mama threw it out. Is it really obscene?

WHITNEY: If it was, it'd go faster.

CARLYLE: It doesn't tell the details, does it?

WHITNEY: About what?

CARLYLE: It just tells she's pregnant, right? And that she has to wear the "A". It doesn't tell how she got pregnant . . .

WHITNEY: I don't think she did it some new or unusual way.

CARLYLE: Marcia Stunt says no one even kisses in the book.

WHITNEY: Are you still failing?

CARLYLE: Of course, if I can't read any of the books! Stories about unwed mothers. Naked boys on islands who slice up pigs. Plays where men sleep with their mothers. If I didn't know Mrs. Ratchet on the textbook committee, I'd swear it was a dirty book club. Mama says they might as well hand out copies of *Hustler* magazine. Have you ever seen one of those magazines? *(Whitney picks at his shoe)* Oh, Whitney, you have.

WHITNEY: Everybody has. Except you.

CARLYLE: You're the new president.

WHITNEY: I didn't look by choice.

CARLYLE: I'm so disappointed.

WHITNEY: It wasn't my fault. Arthur Horrishill cut out a bunch of pictures and taped them on the inside of my gym locker while I was in the shower.

CARLYLE: Why'd he do that?

WHITNEY: So when I came back and saw the pictures they could rip off my towel.

CARLYLE: Why?

WHITNEY: It was a test.

CARLYLE: For what?

WHITNEY: Never mind, but it worked. *(Silence)* It was a joke. I laughed.

CARLYLE: What were the pictures like?

WHITNEY: Pictures.

CARLYLE: Ladies?

WHITNEY: No, sports cars.

CARLYLE: Men, too?

WHITNEY: No.

CARLYLE: Just ladies?

WHITNEY: One. One had men.

CARLYLE: That's so disgusting. They were just lying there?

WHITNEY: The pictures?

CARLYLE: The men.

WHITNEY: Yeah. Or standing by pools. Or bending over to pick up footballs. One of them was riding a motorcycle. I don't want to talk about it.

CARLYLE: I couldn't live with myself if I saw one of those pictures. I'd want to stab myself.

WHITNEY: They're just paper.

CARLYLE: Looking at them must feel so lonely.

WHITNEY: When I was looking at them, I felt a hell of a lot more like they were all looking at me.

CARLYLE: It must be like looking at the Shriner's posters with the burn victims on them. You've never bought one of those magazines, have you? You don't have one lying under your bed or sitting somewhere in your house?

WHITNEY: I don't have the courage.

CARLYLE: Those men must've had something on.

WHITNEY: Some did.

CARLYLE: Like what?

WHITNEY: Hats mostly. One had a motorcycle helmet.

CARLYLE: Mama said most of the people who would pose for that trash are ugly anyway. I bet they all looked half-deformed.

WHITNEY: They seemed pretty healthy.

CARLYLE: They weren't just standing there, facing the camera?

WHITNEY: Yes.

CARLYLE: But you couldn't see . . . you know . . .

WHITNEY: That's the whole point.

CARLYLE: You could? All of it?

WHITNEY: Stop asking questions.

CARLYLE: That's so sad. People can be so gross. It's what makes us so imperfect and unworthy. People looking at those pictures when they're lonely or bored when there are so many beautiful and inspiring things to see. I saw this huge book on Michelangelo in the library, with color plates. Now he was a genius. I could look at that book all day. There's this one statue of Christ, right after they tore him from the cross. He's all stretched out on Mary's knees, and he's naked except for a little cloth, looking so beautiful, twisting on the folds of his mother's dress. He's smooth and angled at the same time. But he's bleeding from all these horrible wounds. You look at those wounds, not at the angles. And he just lies there while you stare away. Or the slaves Michelangelo carved. They're naked, too, and tied up with ropes, and their muscles are rippling and snapping like rubber bands, but if you look real close you can almost see tears on their stone faces. I look at them, and my heart beats, hard. They're beautiful.

WHITNEY: My mosquito bites need stitches. Can't we go inside?

CARLYLE: Only if you keep the front door open.

WHITNEY: Why? I promise. I won't rape you.

CARLYLE: It's appearances, smarty.

WHITNEY: So if I do rape you, we should close it?

CARLYLE: Whitney!

(They go inside)

CARLYLE: How long are your folks going to be gone?

WHITNEY: Eleven.

CARLYLE: That class lasts four hours?

WHITNEY: They have chips and dip and everybody mingles.

CARLYLE: We're losing all the air conditioning. Close the door.

WHITNEY: I thought . . .

CARLYLE: It's a sin to waste. *(Whitney closes the door)* Look at this. You left the hall light on and the porch light on. *(Whitney turns out all but one small living room lamp)* That's nicer.

WHITNEY: I can't even see you.

CARLYLE: Course not. You're way over there.

(Whitney sits by Carlyle on the couch)

WHITNEY: Hello, Carlyle.

CARLYLE: Hi, Whitney. Do you think I'm pretty?

WHITNEY: Oh yes.

CARLYLE: Damn. Mama says the ugly girls are the lucky ones because they don't have to worry. I was at the nursing home visiting Miss Willoughby and she showed me a picture of herself when she was my age. She was perfect—like an old-fashioned china doll. And she never got married, her whole life through. She was never together with a man. Now, as sweet as she is, her face looks like a road map and her teeth are all pushed out and yellow. And all I thought was, boy, is her chance over now. If I were as gorgeous as Miss Willoughby was, I'd always be worried that time was running out. I wouldn't want to waste being pretty by being good. So I don't want to be all that pretty.

WHITNEY: Are we going out together or what?

CARLYLE: What do you mean?

WHITNEY: You're here every night, or I'm at your house, we study together, now we're on the Youth Ministry, and we've never even kissed.

CARLYLE: Whitney . . .

WHITNEY: That makes us abnormal by most standards.

CARLYLE: But I . . .

WHITNEY: Sort of reverse perverted.

CARLYLE: You can kiss me. *(She offers her cheek)*

WHITNEY: You're not my grandmother.

CARLYLE: You can kiss me on the lips if you'll sit on your hands.

WHITNEY: What?

CARLYLE: Or go hungry.

(Whitney sits on his hands and kisses Carlyle. She submits for a moment, then pulls back suddenly)

Mrs. Maxwell found out I made all *A's* in art, so she put me in charge of all the decorations for the pep rallies and football parties. Arthur Horrishill's having a party at his father's barn tomorrow night but it's not school sponsored and there may not be chaperones. He wants me to do the decorations, and it sure would be good practice. But I'm not sure I should go if there aren't going to be chaperones. What do you think?

WHITNEY: Can I kiss you again?

CARLYLE: Yes.

(They do)

CARLYLE: You moved your hand.

WHITNEY: I know.

CARLYLE: Take it off.

WHITNEY: Move it.

CARLYLE: Please.

WHITNEY: If you really like me, you'll do me a big favor.

CARLYLE: I said take it off, not move it up.

WHITNEY: I think it has a mind of its own!

CARLYLE: NO!

WHITNEY: It's no different than when someone brushes up against you in the grocery store. That's not sinful. Pretend I'm reaching for the canned peaches only I miss. Excuse me. In which aisle will I find the canned peaches? Seven? Ooh, thank you. Canned apples, canned pears, canned cherries—ah, here we are—peaches!

CARLYLE: *(Laughing)* Stop it. No more.

WHITNEY: I want to make a whole fruit salad.

CARLYLE: Order out.

WHITNEY: Please, Carlyle. I need this.

CARLYLE: Nobody needs it, Whitney.

WHITNEY: Oh yeah? It's all I've been thinking about. For weeks. Years. Ever since sixth grade. I've lost sleep some nights because there isn't any blood to go to my brain. I can't concentrate on anything. I look at cars, and I think of backseats. I look at people crossing the street, and they're all naked. I look at this couch, and I know it folds out. It's driving me crazy.

CARLYLE: Mama lets me see you because she knows I'll be safe. You're not like Arthur Horrishill and Michael MaCaffey.

WHITNEY: I'm just like them, only not as brave.

CARLYLE: If Mama knew I let you kiss me, she'd kill me.

WHITNEY: We don't have to do anything. Just let me put my hand there. Just once. For five seconds. You can time it.

CARLYLE: I don't have a watch.

WHITNEY: You're not twelve years old! We're both eighteen and we've never done a thing. Don't you think that's a bit weird?

CARLYLE: "It is good for a man not to touch a woman." First Corinthians, chapter seven, verse one.

WHITNEY: Don't be such a prude! I'm dead serious. This is hard for me. Unless I make a move soon, it's all gonna dry up and my chance will be over.

CARLYLE: Whitney . . .

WHITNEY: People make fun of me for it. Please. You're the only girl who even likes me. The others are all so eerie. When I'm around them, my whole mouth turns into Jell-O. I can talk to you. Sometimes I think you're my only friend.

CARLYLE: Well, you don't make it very easy. Sometimes they give me a pretty hard time about you.

WHITNEY: Who does?

CARLYLE: The girls. Saying all you do is make wisecracks and that sometimes you try too hard because you're nervous.

WHITNEY: They talk about me like that?

CARLYLE: So it's pretty nice of me to even be here. *(Silence)* Aw, Whitney. I don't care what they say. They're silly. But don't do this to me.

WHITNEY: You're the only person I've ever gone out with. You know that. And I always pay for everything. We've never dutched. I think of how old I am and I get scared.

CARLYLE: Five seconds. No more. *(Whitney places his hand on Carlyle's breast)* One. Two. Three. Four . . . *(She jerks away)* I said you could put it there, I didn't say you could flex it!

WHITNEY: My palm itched.

CARLYLE: Try again. *(Whitney replaces his hand)* One thousand. Two thousand. Three thousand. Four thousand. Five thousand. *(Whitney removes his hand)* Was I counting fast?

WHITNEY: I'm not sure.

CARLYLE: You count.

(Whitney replaces his hand)

WHITNEY: One, one thousand . . . two, one thousand . . . three, one thousand . . . four, one thousand . . . five, one thousand . . . six, one thousand . . . seven, one thousand . . . eight, one thousand . . . nine, one thousand . . . ten, one thousand . . . eleven, one thousand . . . *(Whitney has pushed her down on the couch and with his free hand he has opened his fly and is guiding her hand to his crotch. She runs her hand in and out across his thigh. Suddenly, she pulls back fiercely)*

CARLYLE: DON'T! DON'T YOU DARE! *(Carlyle bolts off the couch)* GOD IS NOT READY FOR ME TO FORNICATE!

WHITNEY: . . . What?

CARLYLE: I'd never say that unless I was very serious.

WHITNEY: Who said anything about . . . What's wrong with just groping?

CARLYLE: I can't go to bed with you or anybody else. No matter how much I'd like to, which may be very, very much. So please don't think it's you. You're very cute and sweet.

WHITNEY: Even in the Bible sometimes people made it when they weren't supposed to and God forgave them.

CARLYLE: Don't torture me. You don't understand.

WHITNEY: No, I don't.

CARLYLE: I had a celestial vision.

WHITNEY: Huh?

CARLYLE: A revelation. I was sleeping one night, and I heard this soft chorus of bells from upstairs. Only my room is on the top floor.

WHITNEY: Look, Carlyle, you don't have to . . .

CARLYLE: I have to tell you. I trust you. The bells got louder and louder and I woke up. The ceiling of my room was glowing. We just had the room painted cream and now it was white with heat. I thought I was dreaming so I went to the kitchen to get a Tab 'cause I thought the caffeine would wake me up more and I'd stop hearing the bells and seeing the fire . . .

WHITNEY: Carlyle . . .

CARLYLE: Listen to me! When I got back, it was all still there. I crawled up on my bed, and my sheets turned into clouds and I looked down at the carpet and it was whirling like water. For some reason, I wasn't scared, even though my whole bedroom was a vortex. My closet doors turned golden and all these angels flew out and landed on my cloud. And they were all boy angels and they were all naked. Not like Christmas display angels, more like Sistine ceiling angels. I was really embarrassed 'cause I'd never seen a naked man before, and they didn't look at all like Mama said men's bodies should look. They were beautiful and majestic and clean. And they were smooth. Like plastic baby dolls are smooth. There was nothing there. And I knew I was safe, because they were angels and it wasn't dirty. Only naked mortal men are dirty. Only mortal men slice you open and leave you a baby and then run away. And then the angels told me that I was being preserved for the heavenly host. Then I saw that I was naked, too. And beautiful. And they all crawled closer together and I was really nervous but they said they'd give me strength. So we sat together naked and abstained and read Bible verses. We read the Rites of Purification from the Book of Leviticus and sacrificed a lamb right over my pillow. And two turtle doves. When I woke the next morning, everything was normal. So you see, Whitney, there's a real reason.

WHITNEY: All you had to say was "no."

CARLYLE: I'm not lying! Lying would be sacrilegious! I remember right before junior high school, Mama said to me, "Whenever you start thinking nasty sinful thoughts about boys' bodies, just think of your Heavenly Father and your obligation to love and be true to Him."

WHITNEY: Please say you're joking.

CARLYLE: Not about this.

WHITNEY: We can't do anything because I'm not from heaven?

CARLYLE: I'm sorry.

WHITNEY: When do you think all this happened?

CARLYLE: Late July the night after the Youth Ministry Swimming Party—Michael MaCaffey's bathing suit came off in the water and somebody hid it in the bushes. You remember.

WHITNEY: What was all that stuff about being beautiful and not wanting to waste it?

CARLYLE: You don't know how hard it is for me. It drives me crazy sometimes, all right. I want to so bad and I can't. I think about Miss Willoughby and how it might get too late for me, too, and I panic. But I can't. If I could, you'd be the person I'd choose. I love you, Whitney. But I'm being saved. Look at it this way. If God and I went to the same college, and he were in a fraternity, I'd be wearing his pin. That's a stupid way of putting it, but that's how serious it is.

WHITNEY: You had a sex dream.

CARLYLE: I'm going to pretend I didn't hear that.

WHITNEY: Maybe you should read some of those books for English. You might loosen up. Or learn something. Or you should go out and buy one of those magazines you're so curious about.

CARLYLE: You're being mean.

WHITNEY: That's about the dumbest story I've ever heard. I'm desperate, and you're telling me about all these naked Holy Rollers. And I'm sorry, but I think your mother is just a little fried!

CARLYLE: You don't know a thing about my mother.

WHITNEY: And you are so fucking holier-than-thou! Do you want to know something? Katey Whitmore, vice president of the Student Council, screws Arthur Horrishill. And Barbara Mercy gives head to the entire defensive line . . .

CARLYLE: And Thelma Peeler slept with Michael MaCaffey! Look what happened to her!

WHITNEY: Arthur, Michael, all the guys at school, they're all making fun of me. They know I've never done anything with a girl. They even told the coach and he moved me to an empty locker bank. And somebody took a black marker and wrote "FAG" on every page in my calculus textbook. Even the index. I went to lunch, and I opened my lunch bag, and instead of a banana, there was a dildo. I just can't take it anymore.

CARLYLE: Girls who sin wind up all alone.

WHITNEY: What about Miss Willoughby? She's all alone. *(Short silence)* Carlyle, you have to help me. They don't let virgins on the team.
(Carlyle slaps Whitney, hard)
CARLYLE: You'll wind up going to hell.
WHITNEY: I'm already there.
CARLYLE: Whitney, you're way ahead of those boys. You don't need the same things they do. You're chosen.
(Whitney picks up the seminary application)
What are you doing?
(Whitney starts shredding the papers)
You can't do that.
WHITNEY: I'm not such a great person, Carlyle. All I want right now are two things. To get on the team, and to get laid.
CARLYLE: Your father's going to kill you.
WHITNEY: Fuck him.
CARLYLE: Whitney, you're turning your back on God.
WHITNEY: Fuck Him, too. *(Carlyle gasps and her eyes fill with tears)* And you are one hell of a prick tease.
CARLYLE: Please, Whitney, I'm not! Every night I pray for strength to get through the next day without thinking about it. Pray with me. You can take back what you said. It's frustrated people like us who fall from His Grace and become rapists and prostitutes. Our God is a jealous God.
WHITNEY: You're not being lusted after by God. God doesn't lust! *(Carlyle starts to leave)* If you were normal, you'd want it, too.
CARLYLE: I am not a pervert!
WHITNEY: Fooling around doesn't make you a pervert. It makes you a part of the Animal Kingdom.
CARLYLE: Blasphemer. *(She stares at him)* Poor Whitney. I'm going to pray so hard for you tonight.
(Carlyle exits onto the porch. Whitney looks after her. She turns and re-enters the living room. She sits beside him on the couch and tries to kiss him on the cheek. He resists, and she grabs his face and plants an urgent kiss on his lips. He begins to pull her down onto the couch. She wrests herself away and storms out again. She stops for a moment and wipes her lips)
CARLYLE: I'm going to pray real hard for both of us.
(Night overwhelms them both)

Scene Two:

(A cool night three weeks later. The far-off moaning of wind. Whitney is alone in the house. Carlyle comes to the door)

CARLYLE: Anybody home?

WHITNEY: Hi. Haven't seen you in a while.

CARLYLE: Well, I'm here now. Can I come in?

WHITNEY: Sure.

CARLYLE: Are your parents home?

WHITNEY: The singles seminar was losing money so they started a new one. "God's Role in Divorce." We can sit outside again.

CARLYLE: That's all right. Tonight it's better if they aren't home.

WHITNEY: Why are you so dressed up?

CARLYLE: I just came from Miss Willoughby's funeral. There were three people there. Me, her first cousin once removed, and this old man who didn't know he was at the wrong funeral until it was over. He thought Miss Willoughby was someone else. It was very depressing.

WHITNEY: I'm sorry.

CARLYLE: Oh, it was time for God to take her. I liked visiting her and taking her magazines and her dental floss, but she knew I was only a church volunteer. I think she was lonely for a real relative. Half the time she called me Carmine instead of Carlyle. How are you?

WHITNEY: Fine.

CARLYLE: I just came for a quick visit. How are you feeling?

WHITNEY: You just asked me that.

CARLYLE: Sometimes people say "fine" when they're really not. Miss Willoughby told the doctors "fine" and she had cancer. *(Short silence)* I heard about the team. I'm sorry.

WHITNEY: I wasn't good enough, that's all.

CARLYLE: I heard Arthur Horrishill told the coach things about you that weren't true and kept you off the team.

WHITNEY: You heard wrong.

CARLYLE: I'm glad. Because the stories were awful.

WHITNEY: What were they?

CARLYLE: They were horrible. All about you and Ted Pewter staying after school in the locker room. Alone.

WHITNEY: That's bullshit, Carlyle. Bullshit.

CARLYLE: I know. It's just what I heard.

WHITNEY: From who?

CARLYLE: Marcia Stunt.

WHITNEY: Who told her?

CARLYLE: Barbara Mercy. Or somebody. I don't know.

WHITNEY: Arthur wouldn't do that to me. He and Michael MaCaffey both told me I had a great tryout. They said I was faster and better than half the other guys. I'm underweight, that's all. Arthur just said I should eat more. Then he and Michael invited me out for a few beers, to start fattening me up, but I had to go. I promised them another time.

CARLYLE: They only talk to you to call you names.

WHITNEY: You're wrong. You're so wrong. They're great guys.

CARLYLE: Did you get the car repainted?

WHITNEY: What?

CARLYLE: I saw what they did to the car. *(Whitney is silent)* They smashed the windshield with rocks and wrote "Queer" in black spray-paint on the hood. I saw it, Whitney. The whole school saw it. It was in the middle of the football field. That's your father's car.

WHITNEY: It wasn't them. I don't know who it was, but it wasn't them.

CARLYLE: Was your father mad?

WHITNEY: He and I aren't talking much. It wasn't those guys.

CARLYLE: Then who?

WHITNEY: Probably the little faggot, that's who. He's jealous because I've got friends, and he doesn't. You should've seen him in the locker room. All spindly and naked, flopping around beside me, never leaving me alone, making people think things. Whiny shit. He did it.

CARLYLE: Whoever did it had no right.

WHITNEY: What do you expect? He tries to pick up grammar school kids . . . It wasn't Arthur and it wasn't Michael. You should be ashamed of being so suspicious. That's not Christian. It's small-minded and mean.

CARLYLE: They've done things to you before.

WHITNEY: Jokes. Never slander. Sounds to me like your girl friends are the guilty ones. Be careful how you accuse other people. "Thou shalt not bear false witness."

CARLYLE: Just remember. Michael MaCaffey ruined Thelma Peeler's life.

WHITNEY: How do you know it was his fault? How do you know she didn't beg him for it? She was an ugly girl. Probably horny as hell. She probably slept with a lot of guys, then just blamed him because he's captain of the team. She just wanted a good catch. But he was too smart for that. That's the trouble with you. You're so judgmental. You're the one who's so quick to call names. You sling your Bible around like it was a machete.

CARLYLE: I wish you'd told me you were going to quit the Youth Ministry. I just started coming to the meetings and you weren't there. I felt pretty stupid, making up stories about why the president didn't show.

WHITNEY: I've been busy.

CARLYLE: You could've called if you weren't coming. We would've elected a new president, instead of just sitting there like dumb bunnies, waiting. *(Short silence)* You've been skipping a lot of school. Marcia said you were too ashamed. I don't think you should be ashamed of lies other people tell, or damage other people do.

WHITNEY: Carlyle, will you get off my fucking back?

CARLYLE: You're so much sweeter than all those boys, I don't know why you try so hard to be like them. There are a lot of big-time football players. I don't think there're so many sincere preachers. Your father must be so disappointed.

WHITNEY: Why did you come over here?

CARLYLE: To see you.

WHITNEY: Well, I wish to God you'd stop picking on me.

CARLYLE: I came to ask your help.

WHITNEY: You're doing a pretty piss-poor job.

CARLYLE: I just wanted to see how you were, first, before I asked.

WHITNEY: What do you want?

CARLYLE: Remember the last time I was here and after you kissed me I told you about the party Arthur Horrishill was having at his father's barn? The one without chaperones? And he asked me to do the decorations?

WHITNEY: I missed it.

CARLYLE: Well, I did the decorations. A lot happened at that party.

WHITNEY: Like what?

CARLYLE: Oh, they loved the decorations. I know it's a sin to brag, but I outdid myself. I made goal posts out of wrapping paper tubes and I spray-painted them all gold. And I had this purply tissue left over from the Hallelujah Alliance, so I used it for African violets. The whole barn was goal posts and African violets. I guess it sounds kinda peculiar, but it looked real good.

WHITNEY: They must've lost my invitation.

CARLYLE: Arthur set up the refreshments. An old aquarium filled with punch. I guess it was all he had. And there wasn't any food, which I thought was rude. And then Michael MaCaffey came and Tony Feldman came and Monk Harris and Howard Ritchie and Dude Hawthorne and Fred Stovall and Martin McBride and Runt Adams and pretty soon the whole football team was there.

WHITNEY: Was Marcia there? Or Barbara?

CARLYLE: I was the only girl.

WHITNEY: Huh?

CARLYLE: Oh, Arthur explained it. All the girls were invited for later, and I was early 'cause I'd done all the decorating. And they said how pretty the decorations were, and they toasted me with this grape punch. I couldn't be rude.

WHITNEY: Was it spiked?

CARLYLE: It was tangy.

WHITNEY: But was it spiked . . .

CARLYLE: What?

WHITNEY: Go on.

CARLYLE: They toasted each other. And then they toasted me. And then they toasted Jesus because I asked them to. They just kept filling my glass and thinking up toasts. And there still weren't any girls, so I got nervous. And Arthur kept talking to me in this low voice, telling me how beautiful I was. Everybody was watching. And then Arthur said the only thing that kept me from being the most popular girl in school was that I was too religious. Then, all of a sudden, Michael MaCaffey got real angry and tried to slug Arthur for no reason, calling him all kinds of names and saying he was pulling out and wanted his money back. The other guys all ganged up and threw Michael out. Then Arthur moved in closer and said I had soft eyes. You'd probably enjoy the seminary, Whitney, if you gave it a chance. You don't have to run around some stony field and get all black and blue.

WHITNEY: Tell me what happened.

CARLYLE: We were at that old barn. You know how far away it is from anywhere. And I wished I had a Daddy I could call, who would drive over and get me. But even if I had, there wasn't a phone. And Arthur wouldn't take me home. And I was so dizzy.

WHITNEY: They didn't try to make you do anything you didn't want to do, did they?

CARLYLE: No! Only you've done that, they never once ... Yes! I don't know. They were breathing all over me.

WHITNEY: Did they touch you at all ...

CARLYLE: They asked me to ... they ripped ... they lifted my ... I don't remember. It was too hot.

WHITNEY: They lifted what?

CARLYLE: Me. My legs. Whitney, I have to go.

WHITNEY: You have to tell me.

CARLYLE: I know what you're thinking. How can you think that about me?

WHITNEY: It's not about you, it's about them. Those guys ... they ... they don't know what they do sometimes. Was it just Arthur? Who else?

CARLYLE: It was nobody!

WHITNEY: I'm calling the police. They should be locked up. Fucking sons-of-bitches.

CARLYLE: Nobody did anything to me!

(Whitney lifts the phone)

WHITNEY: Tell me the truth.

CARLYLE: Whitney, I screamed. I screamed so loud. But no one heard me. Everybody has to know that I screamed. *(Whitney dials)* No! *(Carlyle grabs the phone away from Whitney)* I didn't scream! There wasn't anything to scream about.

WHITNEY: You're making things harder. You're going to be O.K., I promise. Give that to me. What you can't tell me you'll have to tell the officer. You shouldn't have waited to tell me. Now give it here ...

CARLYLE: You weren't there. You don't know. Who are you trying to hurt?

WHITNEY: They hurt you.

CARLYLE: You said it was my fault. They're good people.

WHITNEY: They're not. I lied. They trashed Dad's car. I sat in the bushes and watched them do it. And Arthur told the coach not to let me on the team because they didn't think I should be allowed in the locker room. They said I was abnormal. And I haven't been going to school because I can't face them. They call me names in class, and they leave dead things in my locker and one day after gym they made me drink from the urinal. And I haven't been going to church because I couldn't face you. Those guys are shitheads and I hate them and they hurt you, so they're going to pay.

CARLYLE: It wasn't the football team.

WHITNEY: Carlyle, please.

CARLYLE: It was the heavenly host in disguise.

WHITNEY: Give me the phone.

CARLYLE: It was wonderful. Really. They ladled more and more of the punch and they poured it right into my mouth, fresh.

WHITNEY: They forced you to drink it.

CARLYLE: I asked them to. And it wasn't grape juice like they serve at Communion. It was the blood. I was drinking that life's blood. It was running down my throat and down my back and down my chest. It made me cry, but I kept drinking.

WHITNEY: It was a bunch of drunken assholes . . .

CARLYLE: But I didn't know for sure it was the heavenly host, and this is where it gets kind of embarrassing, until their jeans and their rugby shirts just kind of melted away. They were all big and majestic and naked, and I remembered where I'd seen their bodies before. In the Michelangelo book, the chapter on the Sistine ceiling. Not some grubby athletic field. And I didn't feel ashamed because it wasn't like they were just naked boys in magazines or anything. They were huge and beautiful, more like horses than boys.

WHITNEY: Didn't you say they ripped something? What did they rip? Do you still have it?

CARLYLE: They tore my clothes off me because I wanted them to. I mean, God created Adam and Eve naked and that wasn't dirty. Michelangelo's naked sculptures aren't dirty either. It made me feel as glorious as one of them. They were preparing me. They lay me gently on the table and with their belts they bound my limbs just as Christ was positioned on the cross . . .

WHITNEY: Carlyle, stop . . .

CARLYLE: I felt the splinters sticking into my back! And then . . . Oh, Whitney . . . God touched me with his divine light while his angels held me down.

WHITNEY: Who? Was it Arthur?

CARLYLE: It was my vision come true!

WHITNEY: I want a list of everyone at the party. Can you do that for me?

CARLYLE: They were all angels! The angel who looked like Arthur Horrishill had been standing on a barrel, higher up, away from everybody else, casting the reflection of his skin all over the room, like marble. He had the most beautiful smile I'd ever seen. And I knew who He really was. And, as the angels pressed their hands down hard on my limbs, He alone came into me. And He pushed Himself all through me. And I'd never felt the same special way before. All hot, and my skin was shooting electricity so bright I could see it. I haven't felt so good since I was a baby and Mama gave me backrubs on her knee. I was the sun. And I never screamed. Oh, no. I didn't make a single sound except to say "Yes."

WHITNEY: Fucking bastards.

CARLYLE: I'm telling you I was chosen, and it was the most spiritual night of my life.

WHITNEY: How can people do this to people?

CARLYLE: That's blaspheming God, Whitney! Beg forgiveness.

WHITNEY: Wait. Wait a minute. Was this like your first vision? In your bedroom?

CARLYLE: Exactly.

WHITNEY: Oh, thank God. You woke up the next morning, and you were safe and everything was normal.

CARLYLE: Except my head was aching and I was sore.

WHITNEY: But you were in your own bed.

CARLYLE: No. After God came to me I fell into a deep sleep. When I woke up I was lying on my own front lawn, as if I'd fallen from a cloud in the sky. And when I saw the sun rise, I knew it was carrying a little lost piece of me. I went inside, crawled into bed, and nobody knew it had all happened but me. *(Whitney embraces her)* You believe in the infallible truth of our Lord, don't you, Whitney? He'd never play a joke or anything. Say he saw the Russians making bombs and the Americans making bombs and overcrowded cities and forest fires and unmarried people fornicating and homosexuals and He got real mad at the world. Or even just bored. Would He ever play a joke and take it all out on one person?

WHITNEY: God wouldn't.

CARLYLE: Because I'm pregnant.

WHITNEY: What?

CARLYLE: I haven't bled for five weeks.

WHITNEY: Oh, hell. Oh, Jesus. Have you seen a doctor?

CARLYLE: I've never been late.

WHITNEY: Does Arthur know?

CARLYLE: It was not Arthur! If it was, I never would've stayed at the party. I would've walked home even. If it was just Arthur, what would that make me?

WHITNEY: Nothing. Anything that happened isn't your fault.

CARLYLE: A football whore. A Thelma Peeler with normal feet. Somebody someone took a pool and won money over. Is that what you think of me?

WHITNEY: No.

CARLYLE: That's how you're treating me.

WHITNEY: I want to help you in the best way. But you can't make up stories and believe them . . .

CARLYLE: I don't have a choice! I'm not the kind of girl who gets knocked up at a football party. But I'm also not the type who grows ugly and dies lonely. If you want to help me, you'll believe it with me and you won't call anybody.

WHITNEY: Have you told your mother?

CARLYLE: I can't.

WHITNEY: Someone should.

CARLYLE: No. Mary had a Joseph so her mother didn't mind. And God let them all in on the secret. Well, God's only talked to me. Not Mama. I don't have a Joseph. Mama would never question the Lord, but she might question me.

WHITNEY: But it's not your fault.

CARLYLE: Don't keep saying that.

WHITNEY: You don't have to have a baby.

CARLYLE: I'M NOT GOING TO MURDER GOD'S BABY!

WHITNEY: You're not going to have . . .

CARLYLE: Shut up! I'm not listening to you. Please, Whitney. I'm all alone. You have to be on my side.

WHITNEY: I am.

CARLYLE: You see, Whitney, you're the only one who can be my Joseph. You're sensitive and you can make me laugh. And your Dad's a minister and he'd understand. God would talk to him. And that night three weeks ago you touched me like maybe you'd like it if we were married. We'd never have to count to five thousand.

WHITNEY: We have to get you some help.

CARLYLE: Please marry me.

WHITNEY: I can't.

CARLYLE: Why not? You said you wanted to help.

WHITNEY: I do.

CARLYLE: You think I'm a bad person.

WHITNEY: No, I love you.

CARLYLE: So save me.

WHITNEY: I'm the wrong person to ask.

CARLYLE: You won't marry me because you think I'm a football whore. I thought you'd stick by me. Please, Whitney. I haven't done evil.

WHITNEY: I'm not good enough for you.

CARLYLE: No, you're too good. You got elected president of the Youth Ministry and your best buddies are on the football team and your Daddy's a minister and he's sending you to seminary school, so you don't want to speak to me or touch me or anything ever again.

WHITNEY: Carlyle, I'm the one that's bad.

CARLYLE: I can take a lot, Whitney, but I can't take your hating me.

WHITNEY: It's me, Carlyle. Sometimes I have to be with people even more than I have to be with God. Any person. I think that's the reason I didn't move when Ted brushed up against me in gym class, even though I knew people were looking.

CARLYLE: What?

WHITNEY: Oh, I ran home straight after class and took another shower just to get rid of the locker room stink. Then I put on two pairs of Jockey shorts and walked around the house hating myself because this lonely kid touched me. I lay awake some nights worrying, thinking God must hate me and something horrible is wrong with me. Maybe Arthur's right. Maybe I'm abnormal. But I do know one thing. It's normal to want to be held. And sometimes, skin is just skin no matter who's wearing it. It feels good next to itself for a reason.

CARLYLE: Just tell me. Will you marry me or won't you? I need to know.

WHITNEY: I won't go to hell for just standing there and not moving. And you won't go to hell for not screaming.

(Carlyle starts to leave. Whitney follows her outside)

Don't go. I never told anyone those things before.

CARLYLE: I can't stay here. It's not good for me.

WHITNEY: Don't. I want to help you.

CARLYLE: I don't see how you can.

WHITNEY: I'm going to call the police and tell them about Horrishill.

CARLYLE: I'll deny anything you tell them.

WHITNEY: Don't do this.

CARLYLE: All the time I thought they were being cruel to you. Now I find out they were just telling the truth. I don't blame the team. Even God hates fags.

WHITNEY: I didn't do anything wrong.

CARLYLE: No, you just stood there. Did he touch you more than once?

WHITNEY: Stop it.

CARLYLE: Were you hoping for more? Most people do it with girls, Whitney. Maybe you can't. Maybe it's impossible for you to do it, now that you're polluted. Faggot.

WHITNEY: I'd say fuck you, but somebody already did.

(Carlyle lunges at Whitney's chest and begins to pound him with her fists. He doesn't resist. Her arms grow weaker and she begins to sob. Whitney holds her)

It's not fair. It's just not fair. He has no right to be this hard on us. Just us. Other people don't have these problems.

CARLYLE: Other people don't have His grace and His love either. We couldn't know pleasure if we didn't know pain.

WHITNEY: Which is which?

CARLYLE: I don't know.

WHITNEY: I don't want to be a bad person. But I just don't know what else to do.

CARLYLE: God will forgive us.

WHITNEY: How?

CARLYLE: If you said you'd be my Joseph.

WHITNEY: But why would you want . . .

CARLYLE: Who else would I want?

WHITNEY: You're sure you're pregnant?

CARLYLE: I think so.

WHITNEY: All your visions were just very exciting dreams.

CARLYLE: You don't get pregnant by dreaming. I'm a girl, Whitney. If you were my Joseph, you could do it with me.

WHITNEY: I won't be able to stand myself. I'd be like one of them.

CARLYLE: You should prove to yourself that you can do it. Here.

(She takes his hand and places it on her breast)

WHITNEY: No.

CARLYLE: Shhh . . .

WHITNEY: I can't marry you.

CARLYLE: Shhh . . .

WHITNEY: I can't. What would you tell your Mama?

CARLYLE: She loves you.

WHITNEY: What would I tell my parents?

CARLYLE: I don't know. I guess I haven't been promised a star or wise men.

WHITNEY: Carlyle, if we do this, we'd have to tell people I made you pregnant, so we're getting married.

CARLYLE: Whitney, I hoped you'd say that.

WHITNEY: Then it will have to be my baby. It will have to be my baby and not God's. Do you hear me?

CARLYLE: It would sure show the guys at school. You'll be a husband. A father, while they'll still be a sad group of guys who have to place bets and get a girl drunk before . . .

WHITNEY: Don't.

CARLYLE: We'll have the most extraordinary life together.

WHITNEY: We can't.

CARLYLE: You need to know. *(She places his other hand on her second breast)* Now don't talk so much. This is how you'll become my Joseph.

WHITNEY: Jesus. My parents'll be home in an hour.

CARLYLE: A whole hour?

WHITNEY: Can't we at least go inside? It's freezing.

CARLYLE: We're safe. There are trees. And the stars are so pretty. We can pretend we're on one of those clouds, way up there.

WHITNEY: Can I kiss you? *(They do)* This is so wrong.

CARLYLE: You need to know if you can.

WHITNEY: I need to know.

CARLYLE: You can kiss me again. *(She strokes his thigh. They slowly sink to the ground)* Oh, look, Whitney! It's so beautiful. And calm. Look at your hair. In the moonlight it shines. *(She unbuttons his shirt and slips it off his shoulders. She kisses his chest)* Your skin is glowing like marble. It's radiating light. You look like something Michelangelo might paint somewhere high on a ceiling. *(She runs her hands down his sides and kisses him on the forehead)* You look like an angel. Just like an angel.

(Tableau)

The End

RAMON DELGADO, EDITOR

This publication is the seventh edition of *The Best Short Plays* edited by Ramon Delgado, who continues the series made famous by the late Stanley Richards and established earlier by Margaret Mayorga.

An experienced literary advisor, Dr. Delgado has served as chairman for new plays at the Dallas Theater Center, as a literary advisor to The Whole Theatre Company in Montclair, New Jersey, and as theatre consultant to Scholastic Magazine's *Literary Cavalcade*. Dr. Delgado has also been script judge for the Playwrights' Program of the American Theatre Association, the International Biennial Play Competition sponsored by Southern Illinois University at Carbondale, the Illinois Arts Council, and an adjudicator for the American College Theatre Festival.

Born in Tampa, Florida, and raised in nearby Winter Haven, Ramon Delgado started writing plays for marionette shows when he was eleven years old. By the time he had finished high school he had written two full-length plays and several one-act plays. Recognition as a playwright has been received with honors in five regional and twelve national playwriting competitions, including those sponsored by Theta Alpha Phi, the University of Missouri, EARPLAY, and Samuel French. Three of his full-length plays, *Listen, My Children, A Little Holy Water,* and *The Fabulous Jeromes,* received honors in the David Library American Freedom division of the American College Theatre Festival. Seven of his short plays have been published, notably "Waiting for the Bus" in *Ten Great One Act Plays* and *Themes in the One Act Play,* and "Once Below A Lighthouse" in *The Best Short Plays 1972.* His full-length play *A Little Holy Water,* a Cuban-American romantic comedy, was published in 1983.

In 1978 Dr. Delgado's one-act play "The Jerusalem Thorn" was chosen for the Dale Wasserman Midwest Professional Playwrights Workshop, and after expansion into a full-length script, the play was produced Off Off Broadway by the Acting Wing, Inc., at the Shandol Theatre. Two of his short plays have had Equity showcase productions at the No Smoking Playhouse and at The Glines. The New York Hispanic theatre INTAR selected him as a Playwright-in-

Residence in 1980. Three of his short television plays have been aired over PBS, Channel WSIU, Carbondale, Illinois.

Dr. Delgado began his education at Stetson University in Deland, Florida, then studied with Paul Baker and Eugene McKinney at the Dallas Theatre Center. He received an M.F.A. in 1967 from Yale School of Drama, studying playwriting there with the late John Gassner, and later with Christian H. Moe at Southern Illinois University at Carbondale, where he received his Ph.D. in 1976.

Cited twice by *Outstanding Educators of America,* Dr. Delgado has taught acting, directing, playwriting, and dramatic literature at Kentucky Wesleyan College; Hardin-Simmons University in Abilene, Texas; St. Cloud State College, Minnesota; and Montclair State College, New Jersey, where he is presently Associate Professor of Theatre.

Dr. Delgado's latest full-length play, *Stones,* produced at Montclair State College in December of 1983, stimulated discussion on the toxic waste problems of the environment. His acting textbook, *Acting with Both Sides of Your Brain,* was published last year, and he is working now on an acting styles book, an introductory text for theatre appreciation, and is compiling the 1988 edition of *The Best Short Plays.*

DATE DUE